FALSE STARTS

FALSE STARTS

The Segregated Lives of Preschoolers

CASEY STOCKSTILL

NEW YORK UNIVERSITY PRESS

New York

NEW YORK UNIVERSITY PRESS
New York
www.nyupress.org

Library of Congress Cataloging-in-Publication Data
Names: Stockstill, Casey, author.
Title: False starts : the segregated lives of preschoolers / Casey Stockstill.
Description: New York, New York : New York University Press, [2023]
Series: Critical perspectives on youth | Includes bibliographical references and index.
Identifiers: LCCN 2023011449 | ISBN 9781479815005 (hardback) |
ISBN 9781479815043 (paperback) | ISBN 9781479815036 (ebook) |
ISBN 9781479814992 (ebook other)
Subjects: LCSH: Children with social disabilities—Education (Preschool) | Segregation in
education. | Poor children—Education (Preschool) | Preschool children—Social conditions.
| Minorities—Education (Preschool) | Inclusive education.
Classification: LCC LC4069.2 .S76 2023 | DDC 371.826/94—dc23/eng/20230526
LC record available at https://lccn.loc.gov/2023011449

This book is printed on acid-free paper, and its binding materials are chosen for strength
and durability. We strive to use environmentally responsible suppliers and materials to the
greatest extent possible in publishing our books.

Manufactured in the United States of America

10 9 8 7 6 5 4 3 2 1

Also available as an ebook

CONTENTS

Preface: Carriage Rides in Central Park   vii

Introduction: False Starts   1

1 "Is That How We Behave?": Routine Disruptions   29

2 Play Time: The Privileges of Pretend Play   61

3 Toys in Cubbies: The Power of Objects   87

4 Don't Talk about Disneyworld: The Surveillance of Families   110

5 Burned Out: Teaching amid Trauma   136

Conclusion: Looking Forward   157

Acknowledgments   171

Appendix: Research Methods   175

Notes   185

References   193

Index   201

About the Author   213

PREFACE

Carriage Rides in Central Park

I was raised by my mom and my grandma. Neither had graduated college. I went to college at Columbia University in New York City. One of my earliest college jobs was working at a Head Start preschool in Morningside Heights. It paid twelve dollars an hour, which was good money to me in 2008. My job was basically serving as a teacher aide. I helped prepare materials, supervise kids on the playground, and plan events for families. There were about fifteen children in the class, and they had two lead teachers. The kids were clever, honest, and fun. They had real insights about society and inequality, saying things like, "We don't take taxis; we ride the subway." All the children's families were living in poverty, and almost all of them were children of color— mostly African American and Dominican. A typical day at the Head Start preschool was spent doing classroom activities and playing at the fenced-in playground attached to the center. The playground was shaded and pleasant, and in typical New York City fashion, it was right next to the street, so that the people, sounds, and smells of city life were part of the backdrop on the playground. The preschool was a few blocks from the top corner of Central Park, where the teachers and kids could walk to enjoy a different playground and a change of scenery.

My role in the preschool evolved from generally supporting the class to the teachers pairing me with a boy named Leandro. Leandro had a round face with dimples. He was being raised by a single mom who was overwhelmed by his behavior. Leandro was a sweet kid who was bursting with energy. Left on his own, he would jog around the classroom during nap time and pull toys off the shelves. So the teachers asked me to play with him, occupy him, and comfort him at nap time. He seemed to thrive with this tailored attention, and the teachers said it made the classroom calmer when I could spend time with him. I only worked there twenty hours a week, though, and I wondered what the classroom was like at other times. Overall, I loved working there and being part of kids' stories. But I needed more money to pay for my expenses, so I sought out a second, occasional side job.

A friend told me about an opportunity to babysit through an agency that catered to affluent families. My friend had been hired because she was an opera singer and was an attractive babysitter to families that valued music. This agency screened heavily, and said that because I spoke some Spanish, had worked with preschoolers, and, most importantly, was an Ivy League college student, I could join the agency.

My first and only job with the agency was babysitting for a family on the Upper East Side. I still remember being on the crosstown bus, bleary-eyed at 6:00 a.m. as I headed to work. Exiting the bus, I sprinted up Fifth Avenue, worried I would be late. At that hour, Fifth Avenue was empty except for a few slim, white women jogging and then people of color like me, speed-walking to work somewhere.

The doorman sent me up in an elevator. I was shocked when it opened directly into a penthouse apartment. I learned a lot of things very quickly. I had been sent up the service elevator; it is what the family's driver used to load groceries into the house. The family had a four-year-old and two-year-old twins. The kids' mom explained that I was the second "back-up babysitter" they wanted to try out. The kids had a day nanny and a night nanny, who I later learned were both older women from the Caribbean. They also had a regular, daytime babysitter who was a white woman in her midtwenties. I was hired to fill in for that babysitter, in case she was ever sick or on vacation. During the day, these three children always had two adults paid to care for them. The dad was a lawyer, and the mom sort of came in and out during the day—on the days I was there, she went to the gym, to lunch, and then was getting ready for a gala. The nanny changed diapers and made the kids' food; my job was to "enrich" the children by teaching them Spanish, playing with them, and watching over their development. For this work, I was paid twenty-five dollars an hour.

The most jarring experience I had was the time we took the kids to Central Park. The kids kept talking about wanting to see "the ponies." I thought they wanted to look at one of the many horse statues in the park. But the nanny informed me that they meant the horse-drawn carriage rides that tourists take along Fifty-Ninth Street. I had lived in New York City for three years at that point. Riding in a horse-drawn carriage was a luxury I figured I would be able to afford sometime in my forties. The nanny pulled out a roll of petty cash and paid a hundred dollars for us to take the carriage ride. She said they took these rides two or three times a week.

Juxtaposing the inequalities that I experienced via these two part-time jobs was shocking. Both groups of kids had a sense of what was normal. For the Morningside Heights children, it was normal to walk or take the subway to a preschool with a large group of other children. They were used to waiting for teacher attention during the day, including kids like Leandro who seemed to need more tailored adult support. For the Upper East Side children, it was normal to have nearly one-to-one child care attention, to have your driver take you to birthday parties, and to simply walk across the street to the Central Park Zoo and "ride the ponies."

The class inequalities at play were obvious, but the racial inequalities did not elude me. For some reason, I did not last as the second babysitter for that white, Upper East Side family. Though I had temporarily traversed these two spaces, for the white kids whom I babysat, the people of color they saw were mostly people who worked for them. For the kids of color that I worked with, the people of color they saw were their family, friends, neighbors, and teachers.

I had taken some sociology courses at this point, and I decided that I wanted to get a job that would enable me to get to the bottom of the inequalities underneath people's daily challenges. This decision was a big change from my original goal of becoming a social worker who would, in one sense, be bandaging the repeated wounds of an unequal society.

I kept coming back to sociology to help me understand the world and how I fit into it. These initial questions motivated me: What does it mean for young children to grow up in contexts so segregated by race and class? How do children understand their daily lives and the institutions within which they are raised? I had only planned to do a three-month project. But there was always more to understand, and I ended up doing two years of observations and making preschool my main research topic.

My college work experiences were one starting point for my fascination with early childhood. The second starting point was my own biography. My grandma, a hard-working mother of five, sent my mom to a Project Head Start summer program in 1972. I knew the basics of my mother's childhood, but I did not learn that she was a Head Start child until I told my grandma about my developing research on social class and preschool.

My mom's early childhood was one of poverty but hard-won stability. Her father battled alcoholism and ran off. My grandma worked tirelessly to keep the family housed, clothed, and fed. Like my mom's, my own early childhood was also shaped by poverty. But my childhood was unpredictable and unstable. We lived in the Mojave Desert of California, two hours east of Los Angeles. We were evicted several times. I did not attend preschool. I attended seven elementary schools before the age of seven, when Child Protective Services removed me from my mom and placed me with my grandma. My mom battled drug addiction and tackled raising us as a day-to-day jigsaw puzzle. Today I know that these would be called "traumas" or "adverse childhood experiences." But as a little kid, I registered many of these family challenges as mundane, and a few as horrific.

I had a sense of the inequalities of my upbringing even at age four. I remember that a white, middle-class family lived down the street from us, and they would sometimes let us eat at their home. My mom once sent us there to eat Thanksgiving dinner; she wanted us fed but was too embarrassed to come with us. Compared to my house, their house felt blindingly bright with lamps, and I remember thinking that they had a lot of plates in their cabinets and art on their walls. They ate at a big wooden table instead of on the couch. Experiences like these helped me understand that we had less food, clothes, and lights than other people did. I bore witness, coped, and played through all the shifts in my family life. These memories motivated my work. For all that kids have to say, they are often overlooked by adults or are the recipients of adult projections.

I started my preschool research intending to listen to children and observe their experiences of preschool with an open mind. I did not take it as a given that preschool was a positive part of their lives. This book is an account of two segregated preschools in one city in the United States. I focus on the daily problems, possibilities, and joys that preschool children experienced alongside their teachers. My own identity as an upwardly mobile Black woman, as a mother of young children, and, perhaps most prominently, as a trained sociologist flavors both my account of what happened and my analysis of it.

INTRODUCTION

False Starts

Julian,[1] a brown-skinned boy with close-cropped curls, attended Sunshine Head Start, a preschool in Madison, Wisconsin. He was the middle child and only boy in his family; his older sister attended second grade at a nearby public school, and his younger sister was in the toddler room at Sunshine Head Start. Over the two years I knew him, Julian bonded more and more with Adrian, his mom's boyfriend. Some of his teachers frowned when he talked with relish about video games he had played with Adrian over the weekend. For a few months when he was four, his mom was in jail. During that time, Adrian cared for Julian and his sisters. Adrian also bought Julian a giant action figure that Julian talked about excitedly. His mom was out of jail by June, in time for Julian's graduation from Head Start. Adrian came too, and by that point, Julian called him dad.

Julian's mom going to jail was just one of many family challenges that the four-year-old children at Sunshine Head Start confronted. Parents and grandparents went to jail or prison. Families were kicked out of their housing and had to move. Parents met new partners, combining two groups of siblings. For parents and caregivers, these major changes happened amid the ongoing stressors of working and living in poverty. Sunshine Head Start teachers saw their classroom as a haven that would be stable and predictable for children dealing with shifting situations at home.

But classroom life at Sunshine Head Start had its challenges and unpredictability too. When conflicts arose—sometimes initiated by Julian, and sometimes by other children—they riled Julian up. Isaac, who was also four years old, was Julian's best friend. He was sometimes the only person who could calm Julian down.

One morning, Julian and his classmate Bryce got into a fight in the House Area. Ms. Megan went over and asked what happened.

"He hit me!" Julian shouted.

Ms. Megan said, "Well, he's upset too. I'm sure he didn't hit you for no reason. I wanna talk to you boys. Well, what can we do to make you two feel better?"

Bryce hugged Julian, who was crying loudly and allowed the hug but did not hug back. Then Bryce toddled off. Isaac approached and said, "Julian." He waited, but Julian didn't answer.

He repeated "Julian" four times, in a gentle, imploring tone.

But Julian was still sobbing and not answering.

"Are you checking on him?" Ms. Megan asked Isaac.

Isaac nodded.

Later, after Julian had calmed down, Isaac approached Julian in the back corner of the House Area, by the stove.

Isaac asked, "Are you mad?"

"Yeah."

"Why, what happened?"

"He hitted me and I didn't even hit him."

Between classroom conflicts and changes in his family, Julian was moody at preschool. On some days he sang with his friends at Circle Time and played happily with blocks. On other days he was despondent and played alone with small trinkets he had snuck into school. Julian's mom going to jail was awful but not unique within his classroom. This is a testament to race and class segregation. He and his classmates experienced many of the family stressors that are much more likely for families dealing with racism and economic exclusion. All the families in his classroom were poor, and most were families of color.

Across town, at a private preschool called Great Beginnings, none of the students had parents in jail. In fact, all the children had two, married parents—except for Charlie. His parents were divorced. Charlie had pale skin and straight brown hair. When I visited, Charlie often played by himself in the mornings and seemed to enjoy it. One day I joined him in the Math and Puzzles area. I worked on a letter puzzle while Charlie did his own puzzle. Eventually he scooted over to me, and without speaking, started matching the pieces on my puzzle.

Finally Charlie said, "Hey, I went skating on the ice."

"You did?"

"Yeah."

"Who'd you go with?" I asked.

"My dad."

"You play hockey?"

"Yeah," he said. "I have to go tomorrow. I have to go every Saturday when it's winter. But not when it's Thanksgiving. Because then hockey is canceled."

I asked him who took him to hockey.

"My dad," he replied. "It's our thing."

The Great Beginnings teachers were concerned that Charlie might feel judged or different for his family structure. They sought to normalize it by talking openly about how some families lived in two houses. Charlie's uniqueness within his class was a small testament to the segregation that shaped his classroom experience. All the families in his classroom were middle-income or higher, and most of them were white.

Two Excellent, Segregated Preschools in the Same City

When Julian and Charlie got to preschool each day, they encountered classrooms with a lot in common—enriching routines, abundant toys, and experienced teachers. Sunshine Head Start and Great Beginnings were both high-quality preschools. They were given a five-star rating by the state rating system, which placed them among the top 10 percent of preschools in Wisconsin.[2] Both had low student-teacher ratios, with one teacher per six students, an improvement even over the ratio of one teacher per ten students, which is what industry groups recommend for maximum classroom quality.[3]

Sunshine Head Start was in a large community building that had been converted into a preschool. To enter, you had to use a code or be buzzed in. The entrance chamber had bulletin boards listing resources for families. Sometimes there were donated toys or clothing set out on the tables in this chamber. Ms. Ashley usually sat at an oval-shaped desk just inside the inner doors. She often had sunglasses perched on her forehead, atop her long red hair. She was undoubtedly the friendliest person in the building and knew everyone by name.

Just left of Ms. Ashley's desk was Ms. Roxanne's class, where I spent two years observing. Ms. Roxanne, a dedicated preschool teacher who had worked at Sunshine Head Start for eight years, was the lead teacher. As a Head Start teacher, she had to manage paperwork for multiple assessments, the school's curriculum, and interventions for things like mindfulness. Ms. Roxanne was a white woman in her thirties. She worked with two assistant teachers: Ms. Lisa, a white woman in her twenties, and Ms. Julie, a white woman in her fifties.

On paper, Ms. Roxanne's class had seventeen children enrolled. But in reality, there was often a child or two absent, as well as a spot in the class that was unfilled because a family had transitioned out and a new family had yet to transition in. The rest of the center was divided into classrooms by age, with separate classrooms for infants, toddlers, and then for preschoolers aged three and four. Each classroom had large floor-to-ceiling windows in at least one area. This allowed the children to see out onto the playground. Isaac and Julian both had younger siblings in the toddler class and loved to wave to them through the large glass windows.

The center had a private, enclosed playground with a climbing structure, a large sandbox, a small hill, and a bike path. When the weather was too harsh for the playground, the children instead played in a multipurpose room they called "the Big Room." The Big Room had containers holding scooters, bouncy balls, collapsible play tunnels, and gymnastics mats for children to use.

Sometimes the class took walking field trips to one of three places: a nearby city park, a nearby grocery store, or a nearby pedestrian bridge. The children took one big field trip via school bus per year, to the free local zoo.

Because Sunshine Head Start was a Head Start program, families could enroll if they earned near the poverty line, which was about twenty-four thousand dollars per year for a family of four at the time of my research. The center also offered family support: a family social worker who did home visits and helped families with housing and food issues if they arose. The center ensured that children visited the doctor, dentist, and optometrist. The teachers mostly communicated with families when they dropped off and picked up their children.

Great Beginnings was built in the 1990s as a child care center. It was located near several private companies that regularly donated to the preschool. It was a building at the top of a small hill. Upon being buzzed in, you entered a ground level that had many rectangular tables for eight. The kitchen was nearby, and I often caught a pleasant whiff of what the cooks were making for breakfast. One wall of this room had bulletin boards for school advertisements about upcoming field trips and fundraisers. The whole school ate breakfast and lunch in this multipurpose room, sitting at tables with their classmates and teachers. To the right of the meal room were classrooms for infants and toddlers. To the left, and up a small ramp, were the preschool classrooms.

Four-year-olds at Great Beginnings were split across two connected classrooms that shared an entrance. If you headed right after entering, you were in Ms. Kim and Ms. Erica's classroom, where I spent one month observing. This classroom was for younger four-year-olds, most of whom would be eligible for public kindergarten the following year. To the left was Ms. Jessica and Ms. Paula's classroom. This room was for older four-year-olds, some of whom had fall birthdays and had just missed the public kindergarten cutoff, and some of whom had summer birthdays and could have gone to kindergarten, but their parents decided to keep them at Great Beginnings for another year.[4]

Great Beginnings had an expansive, impressive playground. There was a garden, a large sandbox, and a big jungle gym. There were several rolling hills that the children sledded down in the winter and rolled down in the summer. When the weather was bad, the children played in an indoor play space. This space had a colorful, permanent indoor jungle gym, as well as balls, tunnels, and mats tucked away into bins.

Ms. Kim, who had been at Great Beginnings for thirteen years, was the lead teacher. Because her program did not use Head Start funding, she had far less paperwork to complete than Ms. Roxanne at Sunshine Head Start. Ms. Kim did not adhere to one specific curriculum, but instead used the play-based lesson plans she had developed over the years.

The teachers spent a little time each week working on the children's portfolios, which showed children's increasing development. Both Ms. Kim and Ms. Erica were white women.

Great Beginnings offered families some "extras." For example, Great Beginnings children took frequent trips, mostly walks to a local library or nearby businesses. The school also hosted either a field trip or an exciting in-school experience each month. For example, they had a magician visit, a science show, and a trip to the pumpkin patch. Parents paid one-time fees, usually around ten dollars, for their children to attend these trips. The center also hosted "Parents Night Out" a few times a year, when families could pay for their children to have a movie night at school. Some of the families also hired the teachers as private babysitters on mornings, nights, or weekends. The Great Beginnings teachers communicated often with families. In addition to chatting at drop-off and pick-up times, the teachers wrote daily messages on a whiteboard describing what the class had done that day and indicating whether each child had slept during nap time. The teachers also emailed a weekly newsletter with photos of the children.

Madison, Wisconsin, is a segregated city, much like other medium-sized cities in the United States. White, affluent residents are concentrated in the west side and downtown neighborhoods, while Black and Hispanic residents, who together comprise 15 percent of the population, are concentrated in the south, the east, and the outer suburbs. Both the city and many of the schools within it are racially segregated, and this segregation is visible within the preschools I observed. Racially, if these schools had represented the city population, their students would be 85 percent white and 15 percent children of color. Instead, both preschools were segregated. Sunshine Head Start had 95 percent students of color, while Great Beginnings had 95 percent white students.[5]

These patterns reflect the racialization of poverty. Nationally, Black, Hispanic, and Indigenous children have nearly 2.5 times the poverty rate of white children.[6] The Black-white poverty gap is particularly egregious in Dane County, where Madison is located. Seventy-four percent of Black children live in poverty, while 5.5 percent of white children live in poverty.[7]

In the United States, two-thirds of preschool children are in classrooms of one of two types: either classrooms with mostly poor children of color, or in classrooms with mostly white, affluent children. Nationwide, preschools are more segregated than elementary schools, middle schools, or high schools.[8] In this book, I argue that segregating preschool children by race and class exacerbates inequality. This happens through differences in class sizes and teacher-student ratios, and, most importantly, in extreme differences in the number of children per class acting out due to family traumas that trace to poverty and racism.

Rather than seeing preschool as an individualized intervention that is simply delivered through classrooms, I contend that classroom, neighborhood, and societal contexts matter. Preschool researchers often talk about a bundle of classroom-level "quality measures," on the one hand, and then about children's individual academic and social outcomes on the other. Based on my experience observing preschoolers on a near-daily basis for two years, my findings suggest that segregated classrooms hold important consequences for children's relationships with teachers, for daily routines, for personal property experiences, and for family engagement. These consequences are complex and not neatly captured in the observational checkboxes used to rate the classroom quality of preschools.

A Brief History of Segregated Child Care

The segregated conditions of Sunshine Head Start and Great Beginnings trace as far back as the 1800s. Early group child care in the United States has gone by several different names,[9] including "day nursery," "nursery school," and "kindergarten." Group child care has always been segregated by race and class, and it has often had higher aspirations for children who were affluent and white. In the different aims of day nurseries—designed for poor children—and nursery schools and kindergartens—made accessible mostly to affluent children— the discourses of preschool are apparent. Child care for poor children emphasized preschool as compensatory for family shortcomings, while child care for affluent children emphasized preschool as a supplement to presumed positive parenting at home.

Group child care for the poor did not flourish until the early 1900s, but the first formal institutional child care space in the United States was the Boston Infant School, which opened in 1828. The school provided extended hours of care for poor children from age eighteen months to four years. Its founders justified the school by noting that it would allow children's mothers to work, while keeping children from "the unhappy association of want and vice" that they might experience at home. These philanthropists then started the Infant School Society and began opening more schools for the children of "indecent and uneducated parents."[10]

Affluent parents soon began to establish infant schools for their children, inspired by the infant schools for the poor. A *Ladies Magazine* column described the children at infant schools, saying they would "be the richest scholars. And why should a plan which promises so many advantages, independent of simply relieving the mother from her charge, be confined to the children of the indigent?"[11] In cities such as Cincinnati, Boston, and Detroit, a few affluent parents began sending their young children to infant schools to give their children an educational boost.[12]

But affluent parents' interest in infant schools was short-lived. The opening of public schools, which accelerated between 1832 and 1838, and which sometimes accepted children as young as age four, dampened some affluent parents' initial enthusiasm for the infant schools. These early forms of group care were also supplanted by a cultural shift in the 1830s emphasizing separate spheres for men and women. Under this "domestic revolution," some education scholars of the day underlined the belief that mothers—rather than an institution like an infant school—should provide care and education for their children at home. Most of the infant schools, for rich and poor children alike, closed. The Boston Infant School Society had dissolved by 1835.[13]

After the fizzling of the infant school movement, formal group child care did not return until the late 1800s, when philanthropists started day nurseries. Day nurseries were designed to solve what philanthropists viewed as a pressing social problem: the very fact that some mothers had to do paid work. In its 1903 annual report, the Franklin Day Nursery in Philadelphia claimed that the children in their care "have no mothers. They are dead or working ten and twelve hours a day in shops and mills." Working motherhood was likened to death in this report. The fact that mothers had to work was seen as less than ideal—it meant that fathers had failed in their bread-winning duties. Day nursery advocates saw the institution as patching a hole in family life, helping children to stay with their families.[14] One nursery shared this poem about its admissions process:

> D.D.D. was the key to the code
> Desperate, deserted and destitute.
> The louder the wails, the shorter the road,
> That led to this child care institute.[15]

With the term "deserted," the poem refers to fathers having abandoned their families, either literally by leaving or financially through drunkenness or inability to work.

The construction of working mothers as a problem was racialized. Historian Elizabeth Rose contends that seeing European immigrant women work in factories was particularly jarring to some: "It was the presence of white mothers in factories, not of African-American mothers in domestic work, that seemed to threaten the social fabric." The native-born white women who typically ran these day nurseries viewed the immigrant children they served as capable of assimilation. Though safety and cleanliness demanded much of their time, native-born white day nursery matrons incorporated moral lessons when they could, with an aim toward "assimilating" the immigrant children in their care.[16]

The day nursery founders had wanted to assimilate and "improve the morals" of European immigrant children. Poor Black families, in contrast, were seen as broken and incapable of assimilation. Having been enslaved mothers and then working mothers for decades, Black mothers were defined by white day nursery reformers of the Progressive Era as workers who could support white middle-class mothers, rather than as mothers in their own right.[17]

In addition to progressive day nurseries being part of a racial project of assimilating immigrant children, racism affected the day nursery movement in the form of segregation. Black mothers with young children worked at higher rates than white mothers at the turn of the twentieth century. Half of Black mothers worked, compared to 25 percent of white mothers. Black women who worked tended to work as domestics. Yet when northern and Rust Belt cities began opening day nurseries, they largely did not serve Black children. In the North, most day nurseries either refused to enroll Black children or would enroll only a few

Black children at a time. In Philadelphia, for example, only four day nurseries enrolled Black children. One of these, Women's Union Day Nursery, was founded and operated by Black women. In other cities, elite Black women who worked together in churches and clubs created day nurseries. In 1902, Black women in Harlem founded Hope Day Nursery for Black Children to provide care for Black children with working mothers.[18]

Accounts of day nurseries suggest dire conditions. The adult-to-child ratios were reported as being one adult to twenty or thirty children. The facilities were bare. Observers reported crowded spaces, lack of toys and play space, and babies sharing cribs. With so many children to care for, much of the day consisted of feeding, washing, and getting children to sleep. Occasionally the children went out for playtime. An observer described playtime in one nursery: "The nursemaid sits at one end with the two or three 2-year-olds who are fretful and crying, while some twelve or fifteen children under four years old wander disconsolately about the enclosure."[19] The experience that day nurseries provided to children was largely custodial. It could be hard to deliver even nutritious food and clean conditions, given the many children and low funding. Ethel Beer visited dozens of day nurseries in the early 1900s, and observing one day nursery, she remarked, "The building was gloomy . . . and row after row of ugly iron cribs with plaques advertising their donors left little space to play . . . The personnel was untrained and some were mentally dull."[20] Though the experience might be lacking, day nursery matrons prided themselves on keeping the children in their care clean and safe, at the very least.

Despite their shortcomings, day nurseries met a real need for the families they served. Day nurseries thus expanded, from only a handful in the 1870s to more than 175 by 1900. By 1914, there were more than six hundred day nurseries. Many of them joined a new organization: the National Federation of Day Nurseries. Yet studies of child care arrangements during the day nursery peak show that they served a small fraction of children—around 5 percent of young children with working mothers in both Philadelphia and New York attended a day nursery. Even as day nurseries multiplied, they never came close to meeting child care demands, and remained a less-preferred option by most mothers. Many mothers preferred neighborhood care and saw day nurseries as too institutional and too similar to orphanages. Surveys from the 1920s suggest that 80 to 90 percent of working mothers in Philadelphia used relatives or neighbors for child care.[21]

The combination of prizing the nuclear family, the rise of case-based social work, and the movement for mother's pensions eroded support for day nurseries in the 1920s.[22] By 1924, day nurseries in New York reported lower enrollment and smaller wait lists.[23] Another blow to day nurseries was the Johnson-Reed Act of 1924: a quota-based immigration law. It restricted immigration from Southern and Eastern European countries, and immigrants from these countries were the ones whose young children were primarily served by day nurseries. Migration to cities had not stopped—in fact, migration of rural southern Black people into northern and Rust Belt cities continued—but day nurseries largely denied entrance to Black children.[24] Given that public conversation about day nurseries centered on families in dire financial need and with potential problems, day nurseries were seen as essential for poor children. But they were also stigmatized by nonpoor working women in need of child care.

* * *

During the rise and wane of day nurseries, two parallel options for group care of affluent children under age six emerged: kindergartens and nursery schools. Starting in the 1860s, a transnational woman-based movement for kindergartens accelerated. Kindergartens were group experiences for children between ages four and six. They were designed with children's education and enrichment foremost in mind. Kindergarten teachers initially drew on pedagogy from Germany. The job of a kindergarten teacher actualized the ideal that women should have important roles outside the home. Becoming a kindergarten teacher was a way for women to do paid work within the confines of cultural expectations for feminized respectability.[25] Many kindergarten teachers were white women who were unmarried women, widows, or philanthropists. From the start, these kindergarten teachers were paid even less than public school teachers, foreshadowing a wage gap between private early childhood teachers and public school teachers of young children that would persist into the twenty-first century.

Unlike infant schools and day nurseries, kindergartens had a positive class connotation from the start, which may have spurred their popularity among affluent parents and their success in being integrated into the school system. But, like day nurseries, kindergartens tended to be racially segregated, especially in the South. When Black communities wanted to start kindergartens for Black children, they faced resistance. For example, when Frances Joseph, a National Association of Colored Women member, tried to start a kindergarten in New Orleans, she was rebuffed by white administrators who said there were no trained Black kindergarten teachers available. Under Jim Crow, Black teachers were necessary to teach Black children. By this point, traveling to Germany was not necessary to learn kindergarten pedagogy. American institutions—including Howard, Tuskegee, and other Black colleges and universities—now taught early childhood pedagogy to women who wanted to become kindergarten teachers.[26]

Yet even after Joseph recruited Black teachers trained in kindergarten pedagogy, the district refused to fund a Black kindergarten. Joseph raised money privately to found one herself.[27] Other Black communities from Washington, DC, to St. Louis to New York, started kindergartens for their children in the early 1900s. Some existing Black day nurseries, such as Hope Day Nursery, added kindergarten programs for their five-year-old children. The kindergarten at Hampton Institute taught Black children sweeping, dusting, and cleaning, in the vocational tradition of preparing Black children for agricultural or domestic work.

By 1911, kindergarten enrollment ranged from about 3 percent of five-year-olds in southern states to about 25 percent in states such as Wisconsin, Massachusetts, and New Jersey.[28] Most of these kindergartens were in urban areas with public school districts that had extra building space, and also were in places where parents lobbied the local government to offer kindergarten for their children. In 1913, kindergarten advocates succeeded in adding a kindergarten department to the US Department of Education.[29]

In contrast to kindergartens, which focused on children aged five and six, a movement for nursery schools designed more for children aged two, three, and four proliferated. The Rockefeller Foundation was hugely important to this movement; it donated money to universities to establish child study institutes. Many of these universities started nursery schools, places that fostered child development but also worked as research labs for scholars and as training institutes for aspiring early childhood teachers. As nursery schools multiplied in the 1920s and 1930s, their emphasis on child development and education drew middle-class mothers to them. Middle-class mothers' use of them helped decrease the stigma of institutional care and supported the idea that it was positive for an institution outside church and family to enrich young children. But these nursery schools served a limited number of children, and usually children who lived near a university. For example, seventy-four universities had created nursery schools by 1932, amounting to a total of five hundred nursery schools.[30]

Nursery schools both produced scientific research on child development and capitalized on such research. For example, Neighborhood Centre Nursery School in Philadelphia advertised itself as offering "a scientific investigation of the pre-school child, his capabilities, his development and his needs"; this was done through intelligence testing and psychological supports.[31] Historian Elizabeth Rose notes that while mothers applying to day nurseries emphasized their financial need to work, mothers applying to nursery schools emphasized the potential benefits for their children: "An analysis done by Neighborhood Centre staff in 1932 of forty-six families who applied to the nursery school shows that the most common reasons for applying were the need for 'habit training' (including social, emotional, eating, and physical habits), and the need for the companionship of other children."[32] Nursery schools advertised their ability to properly socialize children, and some suggested that they were especially popular with middle-class mothers of only children. The lab-based nursery schools further implemented their focus on scientific child development through parent education classes.

At the cusp of the 1930s, the recently created nursery schools existed alongside the day nurseries that had persisted from before the turn of the century. Up until this point, day nurseries were mostly intended as a short-term option for mothers who had to work due to extenuating circumstances.

The Depression was the first time when the federal government tiptoed into funding child care. As part of mobilizing President Roosevelt's New Deal, Congress funded an agency to meet the needs of the unemployed, called the Federal Emergency Relief Administration (FERA). FERA noticed the financial needs of unemployed teachers, service workers, and nurses, and asked Grace Abbott, the Children's Bureau director, to help create nursery schools.[33] Children aged two to five could attend. Helping unemployed teachers was the focus of these institutions, though the potential to support poor children was a benefit, too.

They were billed as temporary nursery schools rather than day nurseries. Many of them were started in settlement houses or were expanded from existing nursery schools. It was the nursery schools, and their educational rather than custodial aims, that made the project palatable to policy makers. Some applications to start programs were rejected because the programs seemed to be day nurseries rather than education-based nursery schools. Accordingly, what had been less than five hundred nursery schools before the Depression had quadrupled to nearly two thousand nursery schools by 1935. But even with this expansion, the FERA programs served less than 1 percent of children eligible.[34]

Scholar Emily Cahan contends that the mixed quality and limited number of these programs "reflect the nation's ambivalent attitudes toward both the poor and government-supported childcare outside the home."[35] These ambivalences were further tested during World War II. War production quotas recruited many mothers with young children into factories. At the start of the war, only one in thirty mothers with children six and under worked; by the end of the war, one in six of these mothers worked.[36]

Some government officials opposed mothers working. Some of them once again asserted that a mother's place was in the home. The secretary of labor, Frances Perkins, proclaimed, "Mothers of young children can make no finer contribution to the nation . . . than to assure their children the security of home, individual care, and affections."[37] Most mothers agreed. When Gallup asked mothers if they would work in a war plant if they could put their children in a day nursery for free, only 30 percent of mothers said yes.[38]

But still, a proportion of mothers needed and wanted nonparental child care. Distressing stories circulated about young children left at home. For example, a mother tied her four children to a post during her shift at a defense plant.[39] Some employers met the demand themselves. Kaiser Shipbuilding Company established a twenty-four-hour child care facility on site and hired skilled staff.[40]

The government met some of the demand for child care by converting closed FERA nurseries from the Great Depression into nursery schools. More than one thousand nursery schools opened in this way. Through the Lanham Act, President Roosevelt allocated some war emergency funds for communities to *plan* day nurseries, but not to actually *operate* them. Roosevelt and Congress made clear that the emergency day nurseries were to deal with a short-term crisis; they did not represent a long-term promise to fund the care and education of young children outside the home. The Lanham Act centers resulted in more than three thousand day nurseries. But these only provided care for 13 percent of children needing nonkinship care.[41]

When the war ended, the government swiftly withdrew funding. Because the Lanham Act was an executive order, this was easy to do. Communities wrote letters in protest of the decision, which prompted President Truman to ask Congress for $7 million to keep the day nurseries open a few more months, so mothers could find other, longer-term arrangements. Truman's response affirmed that the federal government did not want to be involved in providing broad, long-term support for child care so that mothers could work.[42]

Accordingly, group child care remained a marginal child care arrangement through the 1950s. The Children's Bureau surveyed parents in 1958 and found that 95 percent of children of working mothers with children under age six were cared for by a neighbor or relative in a home setting, 4 percent were in group child care, and 1 percent were unsupervised.[43]

The child care centers that survived the end of the Lanham Act were mostly designated for poor children and were run in major cities, including Philadelphia and Washington, DC. These child care centers were funded under the justification that they would get poor mothers off cash welfare.[44]

The Origins of Head Start

Though a fraction of poor children had attended the privately run day nurseries for decades, there was no national program intentionally designed for poor children. Project Head Start changed that. Project Head Start and the larger War on Poverty drew on arguments about cyclical poverty that were highly resonant in the 1960s. Culture of poverty arguments stressed that poor adults had character flaws that prevented them from succeeding in American institutions. These traits, when passed on to children, made poverty cyclical. This basic idea had been present for more than a century, evident in 1820s claims that infant schools would provide moral education that poor children were lacking.[45]

In 1965, Oscar Lewis published a book about Puerto Rican families that outlined the idea of the "culture of poverty." According to Lewis, poor communities had cultural traits that included "a strong present-time orientation with relatively little ability to defer gratification and plan for the future, a sense of resignation and fatalism based on the realities of their different life situation . . . and a high tolerance for psychological pathology of all sorts."[46] These cultural traits supposedly reflected poverty conditions but also supposedly explained persistent poverty because of the values they inculcated in children. Lewis claimed that the culture of poverty tended to "perpetuate itself from generation to generation because of its effect on the children. By the time slum children are age six or seven they have usually absorbed the basic values and attitudes of their subculture and are not psychologically geared to take full advantage of changing conditions or increased opportunities which may occur in their lifetime."[47] Lewis's view was that children would absorb values and attitudes of those around them.

The culture of poverty argument already had racist implications, but these were made more explicit in the Moynihan Report.[48] Troubled by his finding that both cash welfare enrollment and Black male unemployment were rising, Daniel Patrick Moynihan, the assistant secretary of labor, argued that the crux of the problem was the structure of the Black family: "At the center of the tangle of pathology is the weakness of the family. Once or twice removed, it will be found to be the principal source of most of the aberrant, inadequate, or anti-social behavior that did not establish, but now serves to perpetuate the cycle of poverty and deprivation."[49]

Specifically, Moynihan argued that rising numbers of female-headed households created deficient examples for children that left them ill prepared for the workforce. Moynihan's arguments included assumptions about children that resembled Lewis's: children would absorb the anti-social behavior that their parents exhibited, contributing to a "cycle of pathology."

Both of these reports popularized cultural deficiency as (faulty) explanations for poverty. However, an opposing scholarly discourse emphasized structural conditions, rather than the culture of individuals or communities, as perpetuating poverty.[50] After conducting ethnographic observations with a group of unemployed men in Washington, DC, sociologist Elliot Liebow concluded that "many similarities between the lower-class Negro father and son do not result from 'cultural transmission,' but the fact that the son goes out and independently experiences the same failures, in the same areas, as his father."[51] Thus, rather than poverty being the inevitable result of an autonomous culture, poverty reflected the combination of exclusion, oppression, and segmented labor markets that blocked opportunities for generations of poor people. The result was adaptive behaviors among some poor people that appeared culturally cohesive to anthropologists like Oscar Lewis.[52]

Though both the Moynihan Report and Lewis's book were cited and remembered for their arguments about culture, they did acknowledge the role of structural conditions. Lewis, for example, also described the culture as being, for some, an adaptation to structural conditions; sometimes people developed the individual traits of the culture of poverty because they were adapting to the the limited labor market they confronted.[53] Moynihan noted that female-headed households in part resulted in poverty because the institutions in the United States were modeled on a presumed two-parent household.[54] Ultimately, these two understandings of poverty—one that stressed culture and another that stressed failing institutions—both inspired the actions of the administrators of Head Start.

Further, ideas about children learning culturally inferior traits melded with mounting research on child brain development to paint a troubling picture. For example, in the 1960s, Benjamin Bloom had published an important book characterizing the research to date on cognitive skills and intelligence. Bloom argued that children developed half of their cognitive skills by age five, and thus, he advocated for the importance of early childhood education. This research, alongside culture of poverty understandings, made young poor children seem like ideal targets for antipoverty policy intervention.[55]

In January of 1965, the Johnson administration asked a pediatrician, Dr. Robert Cooke, to create a committee to plan a program to serve children from poor families. The twelve-person committee, known as the Cooke Committee, was mostly comprised of medical professionals who had worked on a previous panel addressing intellectual disabilities in children. Only three of the twelve members were educators.

The Cooke Committee drafted seven objectives for the program to help young, poor children. The seven objectives exemplify culture of poverty views about poor children. One objective addressed cognitive development and learning. A second objective addressed physical health. The remaining objectives addressed sociocultural aspects, using language resonant with culture of poverty concerns. Two objectives focused on improving personality traits in children: "helping the emotional and social development by encouraging self-confidence, spontaneity, curiosity, and self-discipline; and establishing patterns and expectations of success, which create a climate of self-confidence for future learning efforts." Three additional objectives emphasized the importance of reaching the child's family, calling for the program to strengthen family relationships and to "[develop] in the child and his family a responsible attitude toward society and fostering constructive opportunities for society to work together with the poor in solving their problems."[56] These themes of responsibility and solving your own problems echo the culture of poverty idea that poor people suffered from "learned helplessness." At the same time, they echo a sometimes-forgotten ethos of the War on Poverty, the emphasis on community action.

The Cooke Committee's objectives showed a strong interest in families. But rather than engaging parents in their child's educational endeavors by approaching families as they were, the objectives sought to change families. Head Start sought to increase the family's sense of dignity, feelings of self-worth, and responsible attitudes toward society—three things poor families were supposedly lacking. Changing families would impact adults but would also help messages from school "take" with the children because the messages would be reinforced at home. These culture of poverty–infused views of poor children were visible throughout the early years of the program. An early federal report justifying Head Start devoted two pages to comparing archetypes of the advantaged child to archetypes of the disadvantaged child. The description of the "child from a disadvantaged home" summarized evidence that these children had "significant differences in achievement motivation which were closely associated with the home environment" and that "important attitudes toward the possibility of success or failure in life were developing in the preschool years which could adversely affect performance in later years."[57] Only one of four bullet points about the disadvantaged child addressed cognitive and intellectual development.

In contrast, the description of the "child from the educated family" overwhelmingly emphasized intellectual and cognitive advantages. According to the report, the advantaged child had the ability to categorize stimuli, locate objects in space and time, show linguistic competence, and ask questions and gather information.[58] The report mentioned culture and institutions only briefly, to say that the advantaged child "has also developed a variety of motivational and behavioral characteristics that make him well fitted to begin his years in schools which were designed with children like him in mind."[59] The cultural advantages of middle-class children were so presumed that they affected programming. The Head Start planners wanted to keep poor children central to the program, but they did allow up to 10 percent of participants to be from nonpoor families. Describing this decision, an early official explained, "We did that with the notion that you wanted children from those [affluent] backgrounds to interact with low-income children and that that might be beneficial to both in social terms, but also—in learning terms—beneficial to the lower-income children. But the data for really establishing that firmly had not been very good. We did that on the basis of impressions and judgments."[60] Their assumption was that while social benefits went both ways, affluent children would help low-income children's learning.

On the basis of these presumed sociocultural, physical, and intellectual needs of poor children, the Head Start Planning Committee launched its first program. The Head Start Planning Committee disagreed on the ideal scale for the first program. The majority of the committee, including the researchers, wanted to offer a small, experimental summer program to ensure a quality program. But Sargent Shriver, who was in charge of Head Start and other War on Poverty programs, pushed for an immediate, large-scale implementation that would make headlines. In a meeting with the committee, he declared, "We're going to write Head Start across the face of this nation so that no Congress and no president can ever destroy it."[61] As a result, in February 1965, the committee decided to implement a large program that same summer across the nation.

Committee members diverged on their estimation of the costs of Head Start. Martin Deutsch, a child development expert, calculated that they would need at least one thousand dollars per child to run the summer program. Deutsch's calculation assumed that they would hire certified and trained teachers.[62] But Jule Sugarman, the first deputy director of Head Start, arrived at a much lower figure. In a subsequent interview, Sugarman recalled, "Mr. Shriver said to me, 'Now, what will this cost?' Of course, we hadn't figured the cost at all. I said, 'Well, I'll look into it and let you know.' He said, 'Fine, you have an hour!' So another fellow and I sat down over lunch, and we figured out what Head Start was going to cost in the summer. We estimated it would average $180 per child."[63] This low estimate, according to historian Maris Vinofskis, has had lasting effects on the program. During the first summer and in subsequent years, the need for a high volume of teachers willing to work for low pay led to the hiring of parents of Head Start children as substitute teachers and teacher aides—a practice that continues today.[64]

As Jule Sugarman described in a later interview, Head Start was designed to "keep deficiency from developing in the child which would therefore make it possible for him to achieve his maximum potential in later life. It was only in part a school readiness program, but really, I preferred the term 'life readiness program.'"[65] Head Start has always included a tension between educational goals and more sociocultural goals that reverberate with culture of poverty notions. Primary documents and oral histories reveal a hope, in part, that the program would affect the cultural orientations of both children and their families. These goals have existed uneasily alongside hopes for children's cognitive development.

Head Start has enjoyed consistent bipartisan support. The program has since expanded from an initial eight-week summer program to a mix of options for families. Families can enroll their children full-day and year-round, or they can enroll in part-day, part-year programs that are more akin to the way modern kindergarten is scheduled.

* * *

While Head Start enrollment was expanding in the 1970s and 1980s, affluent white families began to increasingly use group child care, too. Historian Elizabeth Rose argues that as white, middle-class mothers' employment rose in this era, the idea that daycare was only for poor, dysfunctional families was challenged.[66]

Since the 1970s, a steadily increasing proportion of children have enrolled in early childhood education programs. In 1970, 28 percent of four-year-olds attended preschool in a center, not including group care based out of a family's home. In 1980, 46 percent of four-year-olds attended center-based preschool. In 1990, 56 percent of four-year-olds attended center-based preschool. By 2000, 65 percent of four-year-olds attended, and enrollment has hovered around 68 percent since. To put it simply, in 1970, one-third of children went to preschool; by 2000, two-thirds of children went to preschool.[67]

Two important aspects of preschool education have not changed. First, preschool remains class and race segregated; the seeds of segregation sowed in the 1830s have only continued to bloom. Social class shapes the likelihood that a child will be enrolled in preschool. The more education a parent has completed, the more likely it is that a child will attend preschool. In 2015, 43 percent of children with a parent who had a bachelor's degree attended preschool, compared to 33 percent of children with a parent who had only a high school diploma. While Black, Asian, and white children attend preschools at similar rates, Hispanic, Indigenous, and Pacific Islander children are less likely to attend.[68]

While class and race shape who attends preschool in the first place, there is further clustering by race and class within preschools. One-third of four-year-olds from poor families who do attend preschool are enrolled in Head Start.[69] Head Start is class segregated by design; it prioritizes enrollment by children from poor or near-poor families. But other preschools are segregated in practice, clustering children by race and class. Early childhood education is more racially segregated than any other level of education that children experience. Research on children in center-based preschools in the early 2000s showed a high level of racial segregation, with 62 percent of Hispanic children attending predominantly Hispanic centers, and 91 percent of white children attending predominantly white centers.[70] An analysis of preschool classrooms operated within elementary school buildings found that about

50 percent of preschoolers attended classrooms with mostly poor children of color; about 30 percent of preschoolers attended classrooms with predominantly white, middle-income children; and about 20 percent of preschoolers attended classrooms with a mix of children from different race and class backgrounds.[71] Despite segregated conditions, preschool has tremendous benefits for getting children ready for academic success in kindergarten. Preschool attendance especially improves academic skills for low-income children.[72]

Second, child care in the United States continues to be structured as a private choice, rather than a public good. However, there is now a wide array of institutional types in the preschool market. Many of the laboratory university-based preschools from the early 1900s still exist, alongside nonprofit child care centers; small business child care centers; national, for-profit chain child care centers such as Bright Horizons and KinderCare; and preschools run out of public schools, sometimes called "four-year-old kindergarten."

The preschool market is also fiscally bifurcated, with publicly funded programs on the one hand and privately funded programs on the other. Nationwide, only 28 percent of four-year-olds attend publicly funded preschool. Some states offer public preschool but require income-based copays from families, with affluent families paying more per month for their children to attend. As more states push to fund public preschool, there are more opportunities for children to attend preschool offered by local school districts or funded by federal Head Start monies. Other children attend private preschools. Though "private" sounds like something only available to the affluent, many states, including Wisconsin, provide income-based subsidies for families to use in the private child care market. For a family earning below the poverty line, a private preschool and a public preschool might be similarly free or low-cost.

Statistics tell us that poor children of color and affluent, white children tend to be in different preschools. But what are children's and teachers' daily experiences like in these spaces? Given that licensing and safety standards have improved tremendously since the 1830s, perhaps the differences between these segregated spaces are minimal. Star rating systems exist in most states, attempting to quantify the quality of education that preschools provide to children. These star systems, in part, crystallize expert child-development knowledge as primary. As the field of child development has grown, preschools have also professionalized. Many states have licensing requirements that mandate that a teacher has taken child-development classes. States also incentivize further professional development of teachers, which can mean that they attend ongoing classes on "best practice."

Part of preschool's appeal is that it is literally "before school." Just before entering a twelve-year experience in formal public schooling, we can offer children an educationally enriching experience to help them be prepared to learn. Preschools are indeed separate from K–12 schools, even in states that offer "four-year-old kindergarten" within elementary school buildings. They have different licensing standards, parents find and pay for them differently, and access is not guaranteed except in a few states and cities.

Despite this specialness and separateness of preschools as institutions, what I outline in the following pages will sometimes be unsurprising to astute critics of K–12 education. As decades of education research have shown us, schools and teachers cannot solve all the problems of an unequal society.[73] To fully tell the story of the challenges of segregated preschool classrooms, we need to understand the cultural context of parenting today.

The Rise of Intensive Motherhood and Concerted Cultivation

The cultural context of parenting has shifted in recent decades to emphasize intensive mothering.[74] Intensive mothering is the idea that children have high levels of need that mothers are best equipped to meet. As sociologist Cameron Macdonald notes, "Intensive mothering ideologies are strongest in advice directed at mothers of preschool-age children."[75] Even though white mothers have increasingly balanced motherhood with paid work since the 1980s, the modern cultural ideal of "intensive motherhood" has only flourished. Intensive motherhood's influence is clear in studies of time use. Overall, mothers today work more hours outside the home than mothers in the 1960s, yet they also spend more time interacting with their children.[76]

Melding with intensive mothering is the rising expectation that parents perform "concerted cultivation" for their children. Introduced by sociologist Annette Lareau, this term refers to a parenting strategy based on the idea that children are unique individuals who can reach their full potential through tailored adult attention. In the concerted cultivation mode of parenting, parents spend time negotiating with children and shuttling them to adult-organized activities. Though in the early 2000s Lareau pinned this strategy to middle-class parents, more than twenty years later, sociologist Alex Manning and others have shown that concerted cultivation is now a dominant aspiration for parents across races and social classes.[77] However, poorer families struggle to realize their goals of enriching their children, given neighborhood-level inequalities, the high cost of some activities, and the time required to drive children to activities. Further, Black and Hispanic families also intermix concerted cultivation with cultural teachings and attempts to prepare their children to deal with racism.[78]

Successfully implementing concerted cultivation may reap benefits for children. Indeed, sociologist Jessica Calarco illustrated that when white, middle-class children are raised under concerted cultivation, they can activate their skills in elementary school to demand adult attention and to "negotiate opportunities" for themselves.[79] White, middle-class childrearing practices matter because children learn from these practices and use them to generate advantages for themselves in elementary school and beyond. Sociologists have long been concerned with the way that classed differences in parenting can make it even harder for schools—institutions that are often built around white, middle-class interests—to serve all children fairly.

Yet sociological discussions of concerted cultivation focus mostly on middle childhood—on children aged six to twelve. Preschool-age children are in a different life stage. Developmentally, three- and four-year-old children are more physically mobile and active than infants and toddlers. Social development is huge at this age, with a focus on understanding social categories like gender, ethnicity, and age. Children typically move from doing parallel play, wherein two kids do activities nearby each other but without actually engaging, to associative play, wherein kids join in activity together. Imagination also blooms, and many three- and four-year-olds love to do pretend play. Preschoolers are capable of learning numbers and letters, counting, and noticing the letters of their name, but these abilities sometimes need to be facilitated by teachers.

At the same time, children under five are considered to need close adult supervision for safety reasons. As children sort out cause and effect and learn to remember safety procedures, they are at greater risk of physical harm. Most states do not legally allow children to be on their own within their homes until they are older than age eight. Developmentally, children aged three and four need to be supervised and kept safe; to be reminded to eat, sleep, and go to the bathroom; and to be offered chances for rewarding social experiences.[80] Because of their age-specific developmental needs, the lines between required supervision and concerted cultivation are blurrier for this age group than for older children. When we talk about preschools, teachers figure heavily. Our evaluation systems reward modes of interaction that are reminiscent of intensive motherhood and concerted cultivation. Some researchers have investigated the role preschools play in modern forms of enrichment. Scholars Nelson and Schutz found that the style of supervision in two preschools differed, so that at a majority-white, middle-class preschool, teachers exhibited concerted cultivation approaches, while teachers at a majority-white, lower-income preschool did not.[81]

Four Ways of Talking about Preschools

There are dozens of ways that people talk about preschools. I want to highlight four discourses about preschools that are relevant to segregation. The first discourse highlights *teachers as key educators.* Policy makers and quantitative researchers often talk about preschool as nurturing children's academic and social development. These conversations center teachers' role, in a way that mirrors the cultural framework of intensive motherhood. Of course, same-age peers provide opportunities for play and social engagement. But teachers are ultimately entrusted with shepherding children's skills through direct instruction, warm conversations with individual children, and detailed assessments of each child. Quality rating systems exist for preschools and are somewhat akin to the grading and color coding that are done on some K–12 schools. These quality rating systems heavily emphasize teachers—preschools often get better quality ratings when they have lower teacher-student ratios (allowing for kids to get more direct teacher attention), teachers with more formal education and certifications, teachers with benefits and professional development opportunities, and teachers who respond in a certain way to children when trained observers visit. In this way, what preschools are presumed to do is reminiscent of intensive mothering. Preschools deliver enrichments through teachers—many of whom are college educated, white women with constantly evolving knowledge of "best practice."

The second and third discourses focus on family-school connections, but with classed assumptions. Poor parents and parents of color are assumed to be deficient by white, middle-class institutions. Accordingly, some people describe *preschool as compensatory* for children from poor families. Sometimes policy makers and the public clarify that family challenges trace back to scarce resources and to racism. But often, the narrative is simply that preschools can provide resources directly to children to compensate for the harsh conditions of poverty that affect families. Head Start programs and, in some states, preschool funding in general, are a means of delivering material resources to children. In this formulation, preschool also delivers a somewhat intangible thing to children: a more positive social environment. The idea that preschool is something that poor children especially need is predicated on the idea that poor children have inferior home environments and, without the intervention of preschool, would show up to kindergarten "unprepared." For these poor children, preschool would act as a one-time inoculation to give them the skills and experiences needed to succeed in navigating unequal institutions for the rest of their lives.

In contrast, for affluent parents, preschool is conceptualized as a form of early enrichment, a model that casts *preschool as a supplement* to positive parenting at home. At preschool, young children can learn to interact positively with other children. This social interaction is more needed for children who have no siblings or only one, and who spend minimal time hanging out with neighbors and cousins—conditions that are more likely for affluent, white families.[82] But unlike poor parents and parents of color, white, affluent parents who send their children to preschool have the luxury of their parenting being presumed to be adequate; preschool then supplements supposedly great parenting at home.

Beyond these three discourses, there is a fourth, sociological discourse, wherein we consider *preschools as sites of broad socialization*. Preschools are understood to be spaces that foster broader social learning about social class, race, and gender. Some research highlights children's different approaches to interacting with teachers, finding that affluent children interrupted and made more requests, while poor children deferred more to teachers.[83] But in general, sociologists tend to emphasize peers as socializers much more frequently than other considerations of preschool do. For example, in Debra Van Ausdale's landmark 1990s study of four-year-olds' racial attitudes at a preschool with a multicultural curriculum, children used racial categories and, in some cases, racial slurs to solve practical problems in their play.[84] Finally, sociologists have shown that children's practices in preschool reinforce gender conformity and heterosexuality.[85]

My approach comes out of this discourse of preschools as sites of broad socialization, though I use segregation as an underlying concept that connects children's socialization experiences to the broader structures in which we live. Race and class are always intertwining aspects of broader structures and people's experiences.[86] I also consider classroom-level conditions such as class size, teacher-student ratio, and teachers' rules as components key to children's unequal socialization. As the book unfolds, I will focus on teachers' experiences in classrooms but also on routines, pretend play, property access, and family-teacher relationships. Each of these topics is enmeshed in the four discourses of preschool described above. Underlining segregation throughout will lead to new insights on each topic.

Underlining Segregation in Young Children's Lives

When we segregate children by social class, we also concentrate poverty and classroom challenges, creating uneven pulls on teachers' time and attention. Teachers spread their time between doing paperwork, adjusting to turnover, and interacting most with the children who are externalizing poverty trauma. For the rest of the children, teachers are not close at hand to talk or play. At the same time, when we concentrate affluence, we concentrate family advantage and remove poverty trauma from teachers' workload. This frees up teachers to interact with children in ways that mimic intensive motherhood.

In the following pages, I show how segregation affected children's daily experiences within two segregated classrooms, showing important differences in children's daily routines, pretend-play skills, access to personal property, family-school engagement, and relationships with teachers.

In the United States, scholars, educators, politicians, activists, and parents are having important conversations about expanding access to preschools. New York City has pushed to fund universal preschool for four-year-olds, and now for three-year-olds, too. Cities and states around the country are having similar discussions. Yet while these discussions often reference "high-quality preschool" writ large, a silent issue is overlooked—the race- and class-segregated contexts in which much of preschool learning takes place.

False Starts reimagines the role of preschool in class inequality by examining how children experience the classroom. I wrote this book after spending two years closely observing, talking to, and playing with children. As an observer, I had a vantage point that parents, teachers, and policy makers do not have. By centering segregation *and* the children like Julian and Charlie who live and learn within these preschools, this book provides an urgently needed perspective for how we should envision preschools in such a way as to advance equity.

"IS THAT HOW WE BEHAVE?"

Routine Disruptions

During indoor play time at Sunshine Head Start, Shayla and I were playing school. Shayla had long brown hair that was usually a little matted at the ends. Shayla and her two brothers had been recently reunited with their mom after being in foster care. Her mom seemed to be slowly getting more consistent with having the kids at Head Start daily. This was Shayla's first experience in group schooling, and at first, she would spend hours each day not talking. The teachers were still trying to figure her out. Despite saying few words, her eyes were expressive, and it was clear to me that she had been observing the goings-on of the preschool. One day she played with me, demonstrating that she understood the key points of the classroom routine.

I sat cross-legged on the carpet, playing the child. Shayla sat in the teacher chair. I inched up dramatically to her chair. This was something I had seen the Sunshine Head Start kids do when a teacher was reading.

Shayla closed the book and placed it on her lap. She told me sternly to scoot back.

I scooted back and Shayla continued reading by talking about the pictures.

But then she paused and said, "I miss my mom."

"You miss your mom?"

Shayla nodded, frowning. "We just have lunch, outside, and then we lay down, take a nap, then she comes." She continued reading.

Shayla paused in a moment of play to recite the routine for herself. Like the other four-year-olds at Sunshine Head Start, she could not tell time. But she had memorized daily routine, which unfolded in the same order, every day.

At both preschools, kids and teachers followed a routine largely dictated by broader policies. A glance at their written routines indicates that the kids at Great Beginnings and Sunshine Head Start seemed to spend the day similarly. This was an artifact of both schools being highly rated preschools that adhered to the state's licensing requirements and followed play-based curricula. Licensing requirements are mandated by states to ensure safety for group care of children. Licensing requires a certain amount of classroom space, a daily nap time or rest period for children, and the offering of food every few hours. Licensing also dictates that kids should go outside twice a day, even specifying a temperature zone for when kids must be taken outside (if the weather is between zero and ninety degrees, and it is not raining).[1]

On top of abiding by state licensing requirements, both schools also followed play-based curricula, in line with the recommendation of the lead early childhood organization, the National Association for the Education of Young Children (NAEYC). NAEYC recommends "extended blocks of time in which to engage in sustained play, investigation, exploration, and interaction (with adults and peers)."[2] Together, licensing and play-based curricula heavily influence the way preschoolers spend their time.

However, as a federally subsidized program, Sunshine Head Start had additional requirements that affected the way time was allocated. Sunshine Head Start teachers had to keep track of who ate during each meal, complete developmental screenings of children at several points throughout the year, ensure that kids visited the dentist and eye doctor, and conduct two home visits during the year.

But even beyond the extra paperwork happening at Sunshine Head Start, the routines as described on paper did not capture the nuances of actual time use. Teachers at both preschools tweaked the routine in response to their students' needs and the other tasks on their plates. Because the classrooms were segregated, children's needs differed.

At Sunshine Head Start, teachers and children dealt with routine disruptions. The concentrated poverty in the classroom coincided with two things: children acting out after family trauma, and turnover in enrollment. These family traumas included eviction, homelessness, domestic violence, and parental incarceration. When kids experiencing trauma acted out by running through the classroom, hitting peers, or jumping off bookshelves, their behavior required special attention from the teachers. This prevented teachers from doing other things like reading to children. Poverty-induced events like eviction and foster care entry also created enrollment turnover. Some of these events meant that families would move away from the area and leave their classroom spot open. Sunshine Head Start teachers spent some of their time each month helping new children adjust to the classroom. When we concentrate poor children within a classroom, we increase the chance that multiple children will be facing the trauma and stress conditioned in contemporary American poverty.[3] At Sunshine Head Start, the result was routine disruptions to the daily routine.

On the other hand, at Great Beginnings, children and teachers counted on stability in the routine. Poverty-induced stressors were absent, and the classroom roster was extremely stable. I visited in February, and all the children had attended since September. Since orienting new students and dealing with big emotions were less common at Great Beginnings, the teachers were able to devote extra time to enrichment opportunities. Teachers counted on this stability when they added enrichments to children's learning above and beyond what they listed on paper. The enrichments ranged from extra reading to field trips to personalized activities.

While the overall guidelines for the two preschools were similar, the additional federal requirements and the impacts of class segregation shaped what was possible in each classroom, leading to deviations from the listed schedule that were frequent enough to be "routine."

Routine matters. Some scholars say that predictable routines have a stabilizing effect for young children, as routines let children know what to expect each day.[4] Children in poverty are more likely to face unpredictability in their family lives—from parents working service jobs with unpredictable schedules to events like incarceration and eviction that upend family life.[5] In a sense, then, predictable routines at school might be very key to these children. The Sunshine Head Start teachers emphasized their role in providing a safe, predictable environment for children. Routines are also the vehicle through which teachers deliver important things to children—opportunities to play with peers, to read, to connect with adults, and more. Intervention programs designed to enhance mindfulness, oral hygiene, or literacy also have to be folded into the existing classroom routine.

Finally, socialization and relationship building can happen in the small moments that are so routine as to be taken for granted in kids' lives. For example, race scholar and sociologist Margaret Hagerman artfully shows how white elementary schoolers make sense of race and racism on car rides to extracurricular activities.[6] Preschool researchers have noted some basic differences in daily routines and time use: for example, in majority-poor preschools, class sizes tend to be larger, so poor children spend more time "in transition" from one activity to the next.[7] When teachers prepare children to go outside, helping twenty children zip their coats takes more time than helping fifteen children zip their coats. Sending twenty children to use the bathroom takes longer than sending fifteen children to the bathroom. These disparities trouble scholars who underline the importance of the learning that happens during planned portions of the day. I think of all moments of the day as relevant to what children are learning. While children may not be practicing math and reading during these practical transitions, I would argue that they are learning how schools work as institutions. Segregation shapes differences in the way children spend time, not only within major time blocks but also across daily transition moments.

Morning Drop-Off and Breakfast: Multitasking and Meals

The morning period involved multitasking from teachers as children got dropped off. Drop-off was a busy time at Sunshine Head Start. Drop-off started a few minutes after the center opened at 6:30 a.m. and extended all the way through Circle Time. Families were not quite hurried but were efficient, as they were often on their way to work. Families were required to come inside the classroom and sign in their children. Most parents arrived in work uniforms. Jaden's mom wore scrubs required for her home health aide job; Isaac's mom wore her grocery store uniform; Dustin's mom wore her Walmart uniform.

Most of the time, moms dropped off children. Daniel's dad stood out as a father who always did drop-off. Daniel's mom was incarcerated, so his dad was solo parenting. Mia's grandma sometimes helped with drop-off; she lived close to her grandkids and was very involved. In the shuffle of removing coats, sending their child to wash hands, and signing their child in, parents discussed pertinent information with teachers—like whether their child had slept poorly or was recovering from a cold.

Because drop-off sprawled over an hour or two, the teachers greeted families while multitasking. Teachers were supervising kids, setting up activities, serving breakfast, or managing tooth brushing. If a child was dropped off late, in the middle of Circle Time, teachers quickly greeted families, because they were focused on keeping the kids' attention. During drop-off, kids were preoccupied with saying goodbye to their family. Once parents left, their child looked around for toys or people to play with.

Sunshine Head Start had already been open for an hour by the time I arrived. It was 8:00 a.m. on an October morning. There were three kids present, plus Ms. Julie and Ms. Camila. Ms. Camila was a teacher aide who had only recently begun work at Sunshine Head Start. Ms. Julie was an assistant teacher and a white woman in her fifties. She was the teacher most likely to be stern with the children, but she also relished when the kids offered her hugs and cuddles. I sat at a table where two boys were playing with magnetic blocks.

A kitchen worker brought in a utility cart with breakfast food. At Sunshine Head Start, the kids ate all their meals family-style, sitting around the three yellow, half-moon-shaped tables in the front of the classroom.

Seeing the breakfast cart, Ms. Julie announced, "Okay, it's cleanup time."

Dylan started to softly sing, "cleanup time in the preschool," as he transferred blocks to the bin, one by one.

Ms. Julie came from behind and said, "C'mon, breakfast!" attempting to hurry Dylan along. She went to the tables and wiped them down with disinfectant.

The kids and I put the bins away and returned to the tables for breakfast.

Most of the blue, kid-sized chairs were labeled with kids' names. Some of them were labeled with the names of kids who no longer attended Sunshine Head Start. The three bigger, yellow chairs were unlabeled, but these were for teachers. I searched for an unlabeled blue chair to sit in.

Ms. Camila took a toy that Bryce had brought from home and placed it in his cubby. Bryce started to cry.

Ms. Julie asked Bryce if he wanted breakfast, and he shouted, "No! I not hungry!"

For the first three minutes of breakfast, Bryce was crouched down in between the tables, howling, and repeating, "I'm not hungry." He occasionally mentioned the toy that Ms. Camila had taken from him. Ms. Julie talked to him in a low, matter-of-fact tone.

Julian entered with his mom and his little sister, who was in the toddler class at Sunshine Head Start. Julian's mom walked her kids to the coat rack and took off Julian's coat. When they came back toward the sign-in sheet, Ms. Julie asked, "How is Julian today?"

"He's good," Julian's mom answered for him, not missing a beat.

Kobe came in with a woman I had not seen before. She was talking quite loudly to him—not in a frustrated tone, but as if she was making an announcement to a group.

She said, "Let's go, Kobe. Is this your class?"

I locked eyes with the woman and smiled encouragingly. I surmised that she was new to dropping off Kobe in our class. She beamed back.

Bryce wandered by, on his way to the bathroom.

Looking toward Bryce, the woman said, "Kobe, there, look, it's your friend."

Neither of the boys said anything and Bryce walked on, unfazed, to the bathroom, to wash his hands. Adults often refer to kids as "friends" as a general moniker.

Bryce returned to a blue chair to find Julian sitting in it. He yelled, "He took my chair!"

Ms. Camila pulled out another chair for Bryce to sit in instead. The kids' chairs changed every few weeks, if a new kid joined the class or if teachers wanted to separate certain children.

Isaac entered with his grandma. She brought him to school sometimes, instead of his mom. Before departing, she scooped Isaac up with both arms, lifting him off the ground, and gave him a hug. She swung

Isaac down between her legs a few times. Isaac giggled loudly. Keisha and Dylan were watching this moment with wide, fond smiles on their faces. The other five children were focused on eating. Then Isaac joined breakfast. Breakfast was usually accompanied by conversation and laughter. There were sometimes breaks in this noise. Today, there were almost three minutes of complete silence while we ate. Eventually, Keisha broke the silence to announce that she had a pirate at her house. The conversation turned to Halloween.

Family-style eating offered closer engagement between teachers and kids. The aspiration for family-style dining was that in a quieter environment, teachers could converse with children while also reinforcing their table manners. But Ms. Lisa, a blonde assistant teacher in her early twenties, confided that this was her least favorite time of day—she was usually tired, and there were so many other things to help with and monitor. Children spilled milk, put their fingers in the shared serving dishes, and more. Furthermore, one of the three teachers would be doing the meal count during breakfast. Sometimes, if a child had come late, the teachers would be chatting with parents as well.

As kids finished their breakfast, they put their dishes in the dirty dish bin on the breakfast cart. Then the kids headed to the bathroom, an area next to classroom entrance. The bathroom had no door, but instead had a half-wall dividing it from the rest of the room. Licensing required teachers to always be able to see the kids. A teacher sat with a checklist, ticking off children's names after giving them a toothbrush loaded with toothpaste. Head Start mandates tooth brushing to support dental hygiene.[8] The school social worker also took the kids to the dentist, twice per school year. These health-related tasks took time from other parts of the day, but stem from Head Start's emphasis on supporting the "whole child" and on its aim to support the neediest children. While some kids may have already brushed their teeth at home and had families that took them to the dentist, at Head Start, daily tooth-brushing time was reserved to ensure that *all* the kids had clean teeth.

* * *

At Great Beginnings, the early morning went similarly. Parents were friendly but efficient and were on their way to work. Except for a surgeon dad whom I once saw in scrubs, parents were dressed in business casual clothing. They were teachers, technology professionals, and office workers. As parents signed in their children and greeted teachers, they likewise communicated any important information for the day ahead. The kids washed their hands and looked for their favorite toys and play-mates. A nearly even mix of mothers and fathers brought their kids, though Ruby's grandma brought her for a week when she was in town to help as Ruby's mom recovered from a surgery. Another grandma helped while both parents were out of town for business trips.

Before heading to breakfast, the teachers read a book to the class. Great Beginnings also ate breakfast family-style, serving kids food from shared bowls on the table. But rather than eat within the classroom, the children ate together in a large multipurpose room near the entryway of their school.

There was no tooth brushing or biannual dentist visit done by the school; these were presumably done at home. As a result, teachers did not need to dedicate time either to daily processes of tooth care or to the less frequent but more labor-intensive orchestration of trips to the dentist during the school day. Instead of supervising tooth brushing, the teachers read another book to the class after returning from breakfast. Sometimes teachers also set out a bin of books for kids to flip through as they waited for their classmates to finish eating. By the time both sets of kids were sitting down for Circle Time, Great Beginnings had read two books together, and Sunshine Head Start had not read together yet. In the time Sunshine Head Start used to promote oral hygiene and, on some days, deal with new families at drop off, Great Beginnings read several books.

Circle Time: Learning Body Management

At Circle Time, children sat in a group and listened while one per-son, often the teacher, talked. They sat on a blue, circular rug that had smaller shapes—triangles, circles, and squares—in primary colors along its perimeter. The teachers put masking tape labeled with a child's name onto each shape. Children sat cross-legged on these assigned shapes during Circle Time. Parents and community members might be pleased about the concepts, such as numbers, letters, and seasons, that children sometimes learned here. Implicit social learning happened at Circle

Time too. Children learned how to take turns in conversation and how to regulate their bodies to be still and quiet.

On difficult days, kids were physically active and were talking loudly. Sometimes the kids collaborated in misbehavior that interrupted the teacher's instruction.

During one Circle Time, Ms. Megan remarked, "This is Crazy Town." Many kids were talking, and some children were lying on their bellies. Fatima was a few feet from the Circle Rug. She was spinning around and wiggling her butt toward the Circle Rug. "Mia, look!" she said.

Mia egged her on: "Keep doing it, Fatima, keep doing it!"

Ms. Rebecca frowned at Fatima, saying, "No thank you."

Ms. Megan called out, "My friends, when the teachers are talking, your eyes need to be on the . . . ?"

"Teachers!" Fatima shouted.

Here, Ms. Megan scolded one child individually, but then admonished the whole class to focus on the teacher. This was typical at Head Start—on many days, there were enough children misbehaving that the group lesson stopped and the whole class was scolded. Ms. Megan's admonishments were delivered in a measured and confident voice. This was typical for her—she was a certified lead teacher who floated between Head Start sites when the usual lead teacher was absent. She remarked that she had a deeper well of patience with the kids at Sunshine Head Start because she only saw them a few times a month.

On a different day, one child's misbehavior recruited other children. The class was singing a song for Circle Time. Jace messed with the posters on the wall. He was the only child not sitting on the Circle Rug. The teachers ignored him. Mia said, "Ooooh, look at Jace!"

Two minutes later, Dustin left his assigned shape and joined Jace. The boys went to the exit door and then raced each other back to the Circle Rug.

"Jace, make better choices," Ms. Rebecca said firmly.

He did not respond. He started spinning his body off the Circle Rug. Then he ran to a play center and took out some toys.

Ms. Rebecca ignored Jace and instead scolded Dustin; he listened and returned to his shape for a minute. But then Dustin got back up, too. Dustin made exaggerated, silly faces at Henry. Henry started to whine about this distraction.

Ms. Julie instructed Henry, "Just look at me, okay?"

Though the teachers ignored Jace, his classmates did not. Mia highlighted his behavior, and Dustin decided to join Jace in acting out. At Sunshine Head Start, several children misbehaved in Circle Time daily, presenting their peers with the choice of how to react. Teachers, too, had to juggle their instruction with behavior management.

The teachers found the misbehavior frustrating, a feeling they sometimes expressed in the moment. During Circle Time, Sam exclaimed "fucker!" and "booty!" while he wiggled around on the rug.

The teachers ignored him, but a few kids chimed, "Ooh."

"Stay on your shape, Sam, or you need to take a break," a teacher said.

Ms. Julie and Ms. Lisa had a conversation above the kids' heads.

"Annoying," Ms. Lisa sighed.

"Why is he being like this?" Ms. Julie responded.

No one answered.

Among challenges, misbehavior, and interruptions, Circle Time was a time for teacher-led instruction. Notably, it always included a ritual of reciting the daily routine. The class did not recite the Pledge of Allegiance to the flag, but they did recite the daily routine.

At Sunshine Head Start, the children sat on their assigned shape around the Circle Rug, while Ms. Julie was pointing to a laminated poster listing the routine. After reviewing the fact that the class was currently at Circle Time, she asked, "And what's next?"

"Work Time!" the kids shouted enthusiastically.

A further implicit lesson of Circle Time focused on talk and attention. At Sunshine Head Start, the teachers often asked questions and let the kids shout out as a group, avoiding the complexities of hand raising and each kid speaking one at a time. Though raising one's hand was an important skill for the future, the teachers were first and foremost concerned with the kids being gentle and still with their bodies.

The Sunshine Head Start teachers saw these as important social and emotional skills that children would need in kindergarten, as safety was fundamental. Ms. Roxanne, the lead teacher charged with lesson planning and tracking child development, put it this way in her interview: "Social and emotional [skills] come first, and then the rest we'll piece together . . . because things intertwine, the math, the literacy, and the language, it all kind of interweaves, but you can't sit next to your friend and start beating the crap out of them. We've got to figure that out first." Accordingly, during Circle Time, the teachers reviewed the three official classroom rules: "Keep Ourselves Safe, Our Things Safe, and Our Friends Safe."

Head Start had up to seventeen kids at a time, some of whom were new to classroom settings in general, others of whom had been to preschool but were new to this class. With the routine disruptions of new children joining the class year-round, the teachers were always somewhat in orientation mode with the class. Getting all the children to be still and focused was a daunting task.

At the end of Circle Time, the teachers asked each child to "make a plan" for where they would play during Work Time. (Sunshine Head Start teachers called this time, when the children chose centers to play in, "Work Time," referencing the idea that children's play should be taken as seriously as adults' work.) In reality, the plan only covered children's initial choice of where to start the upcoming hour of indoor play. After the child told the teacher their initial plan, they had to "practice" a gentle touch with the teacher, either a handshake, a high five, or a hug. The idea was that children would then use these same gentle touches to safely engage with their classmates.

Ms. Julie was leading Circle Time. Julian had been grumpy this morning, and Ms. Megan had let him sit in her lap to get him to participate. When Ms. Julie called on Julian to share his plan and practice his gentle touch, Julian remained still in Ms. Megan's lap.

Ms. Julie asked a second time, "What gentle touch? What's your plan?"

When Julian didn't respond, Ms. Megan leaned close to his ear and repeated the questions in a soft voice.

Julian remained silent in Ms. Megan's lap.

Finally Ms. Julie said, "Okay, I guess you're not ready to plan."

Ms. Megan added, "Listen, you can either make a plan or sit here by yourself, but I gotta get up."

Julian was doing a "slowdown" and trying to avoid moving forward along with the routine. This bodily limpness was one of the few acts of resistance that kids had at their disposal. In moments like these the broader routine, with teachers as its facilitators, mattered more than individual children's feelings about the routine. Julian's resistance—

perhaps rooted in him preferring to sit quietly in Ms. Megan's lap—was deemed less important than the broader goal of moving the children along with the routine. Here the kids were learning something fundamental about being in a school. Children were scolded and praised as a group. Children were unable to change the pace of the ultimate routine. For Sunshine Head Start children, Circle Time emphasized that the rules of the group superseded an individual child's preferences for how to spend their time.

* * *

Instead of "Circle Time," Great Beginnings called their large group meeting "Group Time." As with Sunshine Head Start, teachers used the time on the rug to talk about feelings, the routine, the weather, letters, and other matters. Unlike at Sunshine Head Start, Great Beginnings teachers also read one or two books during morning Group Time. The children sat on assigned shapes on a rectangular rug.

On a Friday morning during Group Time at Great Beginnings, most of the children were sitting cross-legged on their assigned shapes, staring up at the book about sharks that Ms. Paula was reading. She had read this book earlier in the week, but the children seemed just as interested in the book today as they had been the first time. A pale girl with long brown hair rocked back and forth on her shape until Ms. Paula asked her to stop. The girl stopped moving.

At Great Beginnings, children's bodies were generally still. When a kid was squirmy, they stood out to me, and to the rest of the class. In contrast, at Sunshine Head Start, squirmy children were the norm rather than the exception.

In fact, sometimes kids corrected their classmates' behavior. The children sat cross-legged in rows, staring up at the book Ms. Paula was reading. Anna was seated behind Owen. Owen started staring off at other parts of the classroom, looking away from the teacher. Anna put her hands on either side of Owen's head and moved his head back toward the teacher. Owen removed her hands. Owen continued looking at the teacher for about two minutes, then began staring up absently at the ceiling. Anna put her hands on his head again and moved his head toward the teacher.

This time Owen said, "Stop it, Anna."

In these moments, children and teachers collaborated to manage minute, disruptive behaviors. This was possible because, in general, all the children were still and attentive at Great Beginnings.

Beyond the children having nearly mastered regulating their bodies during Group Time, Great Beginnings teachers emphasized having children speak in front of their peers. Kids played the part of both speaker and audience. When the teachers asked questions, the kids knew to raise their hands and wait to be called on before speaking. Some of these moments were planned, like the weekly Show-and-Tell, but other moments were spontaneous.

Ruby used black paper and glue to make a bat. When she showed it to Ms. Paula, Ms. Paula said, "That is very beautiful. Would you like me to show it to the class?"

Ruby smiled widely, nodding.

Later, at Group Time, Ms. Paula called Ruby to stand in front of the class. Ruby told her classmates, who were all sitting cross-legged and quiet on the rug in front of her, about her bat. Then Ms. Paula asked who else wanted to share something with the class; two boys volunteered.

Great Beginnings had many versions of these moments during Group Time, when kids commanded their peers' attention for a time. For example, sometimes the teachers added variety to their frequent reading by bringing out books on tape. They would choose a child to sit in the big teacher chair and turn the pages of the book when the audio book chimed. For Great Beginnings children, Group Time emphasized that individual children were each worthy of commanding the room.

At both schools, a visitor would see kids sitting on a rug and teachers talking through important things. But the Circle Time similarities ended there. Sunshine Head Start children were squirmy more often, and teachers asked questions and let the kids call out an answer together. In contrast, at Great Beginnings the children were still more often, and the teachers talked to kids and expected one child to answer at a time, or they gave children opportunities to command the room while all their peers listened. These routine moments accumulated over time, giving affluent white children more practice at the bodily skills of commanding the room. These different expectations of bodily skills are reminiscent of classed comportment that sociologist Peter Harvey observed among children aged nine to eleven.[9]

The time on the rug ended with Sunshine Head Start children heading off to their initial play center, according to the plan they had made, and Great Beginnings children moving to the play area indicated by the chart that teachers made. By the time both sets of kids were heading to play within the classroom, Great Beginnings kids had read four books, on average. The Sunshine Head Start children had not read together yet.

Center Time: Indoor Play and Population Management

At Center Time, kids spread through every corner of the classroom to play, do projects, and talk to teachers. The areas were similar at the two classrooms: there was a Science Center with magnifying glasses and bottles of liquid; a House Area (labeled "Dramatic Play," but rarely called that in practice) with costumes, a play kitchen, and dolls with varied skin tones; a Puzzles & Manipulatives table that was rarely used; and the Block Area with blocks for building. At Sunshine Head Start, the Block Area and House Area were popular choices.

The teachers managed children's movement during free play loosely. At the start of free play, children had to tell teachers about their choice for a play center. After that, the children could freely move between play centers for the next hour or so. Technically, each play center had a listed capacity of children. For example, the House Area had a sign saying "Four Friends Only." The children typically moved through three or four play centers during the hour, and teachers often allowed more children to play in the centers than was technically allowed. However, a teacher might tell a child to play elsewhere if the teacher decided a center was too crowded or if a conflict arose. Sometimes a newcomer to a center would take the toy another child had been using. After children cleaned up what they had been using, they decided themselves where to play next and what to do. They often did elaborate pretend play extending across the classroom.

When kids did pretend play, they would sometimes enact their routines at school. During Work Time, Mia initiated a game of teacher.

"C'mon, let's go do Circle Time."

"Are you my teacher?" I asked her.

She said yes. We sat on the Circle Rug. "Sit on your shape," she instructed sharply.

Ms. Lisa, who was walking by, overheard. "Mia, you don't talk to anyone like that."

Mia didn't respond. She continued instructing me: "That one, the one that says Mia. You are Mia." She was enacting a frequent Sunshine Head Start experience—teachers helping new kids understand where they were supposed to be as they adjusted to the classroom.

"Look," Mia said as she grabbed a bin of connectible plastic squares and then dumped them on the floor. "If I drop this stuff on the floor, is that a good choice?" Her tone—stern and matter of fact—reminded me of the way Ms. Lisa sometimes talked to the children.

"No," I answered.

"Good. If I drop this stuff on the floor, do I have to clean it up?"

"Yes."

She said, "Look, I'm cleaning it up," as she began scooping the squares back into the bin. Then she looked up and smiled. I turned around and saw that she had caught Ms. Lisa's eye.

"What?" said Ms. Lisa. "Why are you smiling like that?" I told Ms. Lisa that we were playing teacher. "Oh," she said, giving the slightest smile with raised eyebrows.

When Ms. Lisa looked the other way, Mia continued. "I'm a teacher so I'm drinking coffee." She had my purple travel coffee mug. "Look, if I take your coffee mug and throw it on the floor, is that being safe?"

"Yes," I responded, playfully.

"No," she said sternly. "Casey, if I take your coffee mug and I whack it like this, is that being safe?"

"No."

"What do you say?"

"Please stop!" I replied, invoking a phrase that teachers have been coaching the children to use for weeks. Instead of hitting or screaming if another child was being "unsafe," kids were supposed to say "please stop" while striking one palm on the other like a referee. If the unsafe behavior continued, the children were supposed to go get a teacher.

"Good," Mia said.

Mia showed her understanding of the teachers' coaching about behavior strategies they wanted the children to use to manage interpersonal conflict. These coaching strategies were important, because children were largely left to their own devices during Work Time. The

Sunshine Head Start teachers were broadly supervising the children, but they were most attentive to kids who were acting out.

Keisha entered the Block Area to play. She took out a bin of magnetic tiles and asked me to make a castle with her. We built a four-story castle with walls, different levels, and spires at the top. Lily entered the area, barreling toward a bin on the top of the shelf behind Keisha's head. Lily butted against Keisha's body as she wedged in to grab the bin.

"Arughff!" Keisha exclaimed.

Lily remained wedged in that corner, examining pieces in the bin.

"Heeyyy, Lily is making me mad!"

In response, Lily screwed up her face, and hit Keisha's head.

"Stop," Keisha said. "Please stop."

Lily hit Keisha again. Keisha started crying. Ms. Roxanne bobbed up from the neighboring Quiet Area, where she was talking down another kid who was angry. "Ms. Julie, can you?" she said.

Ms. Julie left the yellow tables where she was running an art activity and came to the Block Area. By this point, Keisha was standing up and shrieking at Lily in frustration.

"Use your words, Keisha," Ms. Julie said firmly. Eventually, Ms. Julie coaxed the two girls to play further apart. Keisha and I continued our castle. Lily made a Lego pad with little stacks of Legos on it. She put it on the bookshelf and said, "Birthday cake. Ha!"

Keisha deployed the teachers' favored strategy to solve a conflict when she declared "please stop." Her issue with Lily might have ended there, but when she cried, this elicited teacher attention that Keisha and Lily did not otherwise have. With the higher level of challenging behaviors in the classroom, the Sunshine Head Start children experienced routine disruptions to their play at Work Time. The Sunshine Head Start teachers sometimes spent the whole hour of Work Time helping children through these routine disruptions. They fit this in while multitasking. Teachers were standing at the "teacher counter," organizing materials for small group lessons. They were cleaning up messes, breaking up conflicts, helping kids deal with big emotions, and they were doing assessments, like the Gold Notes—observational notes on each child, for thirty-eight objectives, that the teachers were required to write up at three points during the year.

* * *

Meanwhile, at Great Beginnings, the morning indoor play period was called "Free Choice Time." I found this name ironic because children's choices were highly structured by teachers. At the start of Free Choice Time, the teachers chose two kids per center. Then teachers set timers for ten to fifteen minutes, signaling when kids could rotate centers. Great Beginnings had all the centers that Sunshine Head Start had, plus a dedicated Writing Center.

Free Choice Time at Great Beginnings was much quieter than indoor play at Sunshine Head Start. The classroom had twelve children, compared to Sunshine Head Start's seventeen. But also, because teachers managed play so closely, they usually allowed two or three kids to play together. These groups rarely became as lively as when five or six kids played at the House Area at Sunshine Head Start. Adding to the quiet, the Great Beginnings children often elected to do puzzles, books, and simple board games.

Like the Sunshine Head Start children, the Great Beginnings children sometimes pretended they were teachers in their play. During Free Choice Time, I approached the Science Area, where Chloe, Anna, and Amanda were playing. Chloe and Anna played teachers. They told me and Amanda to be kids. We sat cross-legged on the floor while they sat on two stools. Anna began reading me a book. She noted the author and illustrators. "It's a singing book," she added. Anna started singing about animals to a Christmas tune.

Amanda sat quietly and listened to the story. Mimicking the interruption I sometimes had observed at Great Beginnings, I raised my hand and asked if I could go get a drink. They said yes, and I went over to the drying rack and pretended to drink from there. When I returned, Chloe was smiling in amusement.

Anna finished reading the story and told us, "I am having a day off in Milwaukee!"

"So you will be with me," Chloe added.

Amanda asked if that meant we would get another teacher.

"Well you have me," Chloe repeated.

In Great Beginnings children's reenactment of their teachers, the teachers calmly read a book, responded to children's raised hands, and shared information about their lives and plans in Group Time. This was congruent with what I observed on most days. The constant attendance of teachers and children at Great Beginnings was part of the stability at their preschool—when one child or teacher was missing due to sickness, it was discussed throughout the day. When a child or teacher had a vacation or day off planned, they might discuss this in advance. This was in stark contrast to Sunshine Head Start, where it was more unusual for all children to be present, and it was not common for children to be absent because of a planned vacation.

As indoor play time ended, teachers at both preschools called children to the rug to prepare to go outside. They were then dismissed one by one to simply line up in the summer, or to start the long process of suiting up for the cold in the winter.

Outside Time: An Equalizer of Experiences

While indoor free play was quite different across the two preschools, Outside Time was quite similar. Unlike indoor free play, where teachers subdivided the space and monitored (to different degrees) where kids went, during Outside Time, there was no limit to how many kids could play together. This was the time of day when both groups of children had the most control over what they did.

Some kids liked to keep to themselves outside. At Sunshine Head Start, Julian liked to dig for worms. Sam liked to take his shoes off in the sandbox (which was not actually allowed). Omar liked to shoot hoops. Riding tricycles was a favorite activity, and due to limited bike supply, children often had to wait to use a bike. There was also a climbing structure and a framed playhouse. In the back corner, there was a raised garden bed with vegetables that the kids liked to examine.

Outside Time also allowed for dynamic, larger group play that spanned across the playground.[10] During one Outside Time, Jasmine called me into the playhouse that was next to the bike path.

"I'm the mom, and you're the daughter," she said.

"Okay."

Alicia entered and pointed to Jasmine, telling me, "That's your sister."

Jasmine handed me a small plastic bucket and said, "*Galletas de princesa* [cookies]."

"Oooh," I said, while I mimed eating cookies.

Omar entered.

"Okay, you can play," Jasmine said to Omar.

"I'm the dad," declared Omar.

"No," replied Jasmine, shaking her head.

"Okay, I'm the grandpa."

We sat in silence for a moment. Then Jasmine said she was going to the store to get more *galletas*. She grabbed a piece of snow that had been hardened into a disc by a footprint. Jasmine said we should all go out together so we could get more cookies.

We left the playhouse and searched the surrounding snow for more cookies. We put the cookies we had found in the bucket held by Omar. We followed the bike trail out to near where a kid-sized gas pump was. Then Alicia shouted, "Hurry, it's raining!" We screamed and ran back to the house.[11]

This play scene is notable for the wide use of space and number of kids in the play. But the play scene is also similar to what the Sunshine Head Start children were already able to do during their indoor play time.

* * *

At Great Beginnings, the outdoor space was three times bigger than at Sunshine Head Start. There were several rolling hills, three separate play structures, and a climbing section with tires. In comparison to Sunshine Head Start's simple, frame playhouse, Great Beginnings had a large outdoor kitchen with a sink basin, pots and pans, and a pretend stove. The garden had several raised flower beds. There was also a small hill that the kids used for sledding.

Though the two spaces were quite different, Outside Time still allowed for similar play among the kids. While Great Beginnings teachers ran a regimented Free Choice Time, Outside Time was lax. The teachers backed off, and kids played in groups of various sizes, sometimes with six or seven children. For the Great Beginnings children, Outside Time was the only time when the kids were potentially out of direct earshot of teachers. It was a moment in the day that gave the Great Beginnings children similar latitude for play as what Sunshine Head Start children experienced in both indoor and outdoor play.

In the summer, both classes went outside for as long as possible, often doing this by cutting the indoor play period short to start Outside Time sooner. At Sunshine Head Start the teachers would bring bubbles, kiddie pools, popsicles, chalk, and whatever they could think of to entertain the kids outdoors. But Outside Time rarely ended early or late—the classes liked to head inside close to 11:30, just in time for lunch.

Reading and Lunch

At Sunshine Head Start, after returning from outside, the teachers sat the kids down on the Circle Rug and read a book. This was the one stated time in the routine for reading. Ms. Roxanne said she liked to read a book at this point, because the kids had gotten their energy out from the playground and were more likely to be calm.

Ms. Roxanne was reading a book about Goldilocks. At the same time, a social worker was tapping kids to come to the back of the classroom and have their body weight measured for some health information.

Luz and Dylan began jabbing each other in the ribs. Their jabs got harder and harder and settled into a rhythm. Both kids were laughing. This continued for one minute before the social worker paused her task and came to break up the hitting, while Ms. Roxanne finished the book.

On this day, Ms. Roxanne finished the book, but not without managing disruptions. On many other days, she did not finish because there were too many interruptions from child behavior. Further, this day included a semi-frequent disruption unique to Head Start—the collection of health information to meet Head Start's whole-child mandate. While each individual activity that Head Start incorporated had a rationale and an outcome in mind, for the teachers and kids they accumulate and require classroom time.

After the book, Sunshine Head Start kids sat at the yellow, half-moon-shaped tables for lunch. Just like breakfast, lunch was served family-style. Lunch food was almost always hot, and often handmade by the school's kitchen staff. The kids ate things like spaghetti and meatballs, meatloaf, vegetable soup, teriyaki chicken, and grilled cheese.

Meal times had a logistical component of getting food to each child. But during this transitional time, children socialized.

At lunchtime, Lily said, "Casey, come sit with me."

I agreed and pulled my chair next to her. I asked Lily what we were supposed to do.

"Nothing. We wait like this."

Anthony picked up the plates and started handing them out to kids. This was usually an adult's job.

"Oooh Anthony, don't!" said Mia.

Anthony continued. The children at his table looked to Ms. Lisa for her reaction. She ignored it and continued singing a song about rolling your hands and putting them in your lap.

From the neighboring table, I overheard Julian say, "I lost my spider, it's out there somewhere."

Rather than follow along with Ms. Lisa's song, Ben shaped his finger like a gun and shot at me. "Pow," he whispered. He was very quiet and subtle about it; I couldn't tell if others noticed.

Ms. Lisa finally began doling out the food, but Mia was still talking and playing with her cup.

"Mia, you need to listen so you can be passed food." Looking around at the adults in the room, Ms. Lisa said, "I feel like I'm being mean, but they need to listen."

"Yeah, I always feel like I'm being mean," Ms. Julie responded.

As Lily had pointed out, the kids spent some time "waiting" for their lunch to be served. But what was happening daily was complex. The children were conversing, pushing boundaries between adults' and children's roles, and in some cases, breaking classroom rules with weapon play.

Once food was served, children and teachers were busy eating. This sometimes created a temporary silence that the teachers welcomed.

Ms. Roxanne served food to the children at her table. But the milk pitcher was empty before Gabe could pour his milk, so Ms. Roxanne refilled the pitcher at the food cart. Then she lingered, holding the full pitcher. She sighed softly.

After a few seconds' silence, I asked, "What?" I was wondering if something was wrong.

"Soaking up the silence," she said.

Ms. Lisa nodded.

"Yup," Ms. Julie agreed.

"You gotta enjoy it while it lasts," Ms. Roxanne said, sitting back down. "The thing is, it's really the calm before the next storm."

The Sunshine Head Start teachers appreciated the quiet change that lunch brought. Given the bustle they were used to during Work Time, Circle Time, and even during the reading period just before lunch, lunchtime's quietness was special.

* * *

Like Sunshine Head Start teachers, Great Beginnings teachers read books to the class before lunch. However, during my month of observations, I never saw the teachers be unable to finish a book. Great Beginnings teachers also read books after lunch. One day, teachers read books to the children after lunch for thirty-two minutes straight, while the children listened quietly. The Great Beginnings teachers could do this, in part, because of the relative stability in children's classroom behaviors by February. They had worked as a group and one-to-one with children to acclimate the kids to quietly sitting during reading time. And the teachers were able to be so successful in this that it was presumed by the whole class that they would finish a book they started—both in the after-lunch reading period and in the other, unlisted times when the teachers read books.

Nap Time: Quiet Children and Breaks for Teachers

Teachers began preparing for nap time while the children were finishing lunch. The teachers dimmed the lights and put on music—slow flute melodies or instrumental versions of Disney movie soundtracks.

As lunch wrapped up at Sunshine Head Start, one teacher referenced the list of kids and invited each child to use the bathroom. After a child used the bathroom, they went to their mat: small, blue, mesh beds, raised up about an inch from the ground by plastic legs. The teachers stretched hand-sewn fitted sheets over each mat, and each child had a canvas bag with a blanket and possibly a pillow from home.

While most children simply lay on their mats and rested until falling asleep, nap time occasionally fostered other activities. Though teachers did not allow children to bring toys with them to their mats, some children would sneak special objects to hold during nap time. Julian brought a small action figure to his mat for a few days; Luz brought her sparkle ring to her mat and played with it one day. At other times, children would play with their clothing or blankets during nap time.

Jasmine was fiddling with her sparkly Mary Jane shoes, which she had placed next to her mat.

"Jasmine!" Ms. Julie said sharply. She got up and crossed the room to come to Jasmine's mat. Ms. Julie moved Jasmine's shoes and jacket further from her mat, sat down next to her, and started to rub her back.

Children also had whispered conversations at nap time. Luz and Jasmine discussed stickers; Hannah invited Keisha to her house after school; Julian and Isaac talked as if they were superheroes. After I knew some of the children better, they would ask me to rub their backs during nap time.

The ideal nap time, from the teachers' point of view, was when all the kids fell asleep. The next-best case, however, was when most kids were sleeping and a few rested quietly. To achieve this, the teachers carefully decided which children could sleep next to each other. The teachers changed the sleeping arrangements throughout the year if they felt something was not "working" in terms of getting kids to fall asleep.

Once nap time arrived, teachers spent up to an hour helping get all the children to sleep. Their main method was sitting next to a child's mat and rubbing the child's upper back in slow circles. This usually helped calm the child into falling asleep. As soon as they got one child to sleep, they would move on to another child who was still awake.

Nap at Sunshine Head Start included logistical complications when the teachers had to help new children acclimate to the class. Kids had different temperaments about nap time. Hannah rarely napped. Jayveon always did. Sam would only fall asleep if you rubbed the bottoms of his feet gently.

It was Shayla's third day at Sunshine Head Start. During nap time, she was messing around on her mat.

Watching her, Ms. Roxanne told Ms. Julie, "I think it's best to I-G-N-O-R-E it. I think it's just attention seeking."

"Ah. Maybe she is showing her true colors," Ms. Julie replied.

Though nap time was the calmest part of the day for the teachers, when new children joined the classroom, this added to teachers' work. They had to get to know the new child, including their sleep habits. On days when most of the children were sleeping or quiet, nap time was down time for teachers. The teachers would sit at the tables, far away enough from the sleeping children to have whispered adult conversations but close enough to loosely supervise the children. The teachers sometimes browsed on their cell phones, organized materials for class activities, cleaned, or ate lunch.

However, at Sunshine Head Start, even nap time was not dependably free from disruption. On some days, children's misbehavior reoriented all of nap time.

As nap time started, Ms. Roxanne called in two school staff to lend support. The front desk worker, Ms. Ashley, sat by Dylan and Jayvon. She let them run their fingers through her long red hair because they found it relaxing.

Isaac and Julian were wrestling on the carpet, unchecked. Then Julian walked around the bookshelf while Isaac remained on the other side. The boys jumped up and down, peeking through the bookshelf while yelling and joking with each other.

Linda, the school social worker whom Ms. Roxanne had asked to help, said, "Do one of you want to help them?" She looked at Ms. Roxanne, who was sitting by Bryce, and at Ms. Paige, who was sitting with Sam. These two boys had been acting out during nap time all week.

Ms. Roxanne said, "Nope. This is what it is. Every day. We either stay here and hold these ones down so they're not running around, or I go deal with that. So this is what I choose. That's why I called in for help, 'cause I just, I can't."

While Linda scolded Isaac and Julian, Anthony got up and ran gleefully through the classroom, passing through every play area. On the way, he stepped on Jasmine's calf, and she cried out in pain. Then he nearly stepped on Gabe's head, but Gabe dodged it. Anthony weaved into the Quiet Area, where Lily had just barely fallen asleep. We could not see what happened because of the bookshelves, but we heard him hit Lily, and heard Lily cry out angrily.

Ms. Roxanne jumped up and grabbed Anthony within seconds. She held his arms by his sides.

Linda and I were both frozen, having watched Anthony's movements with shocked disbelief.

"Did you see that? He just stepped on people and then kicked her!" Linda said.

"Yeah, I know, I did see it," Ms. Roxanne said tersely as she walked Anthony back to other side of the room.

"Terrible, Anthony, that's terrible." Linda shook her head disapprovingly.

Ms. Roxanne's intuition that she had too many children misbehaving to be handled well by the three regular classroom teachers—plus me—is telling. Even after bringing in two additional support staff, this day at nap time included Anthony stomping over children. On good days, nap time was a restful period for children and teachers alike. On tough days, the contrast between peaceful, sleeping children and children who were acting out was stark.

* * *

At Great Beginnings, the children also tried to whisper to each other and enjoyed playing with objects at nap time. However, teachers allowed each child to bring one "lovey" object with them to their mat. For most children, this was a stuffed animal. Great Beginnings children would try to play and talk to their toys, and teachers would scold them and implore them to rest and relax. The teachers kept track of who slept and who just rested quietly, writing children's names on a chart by the front door, so that parents could reference the chart at pick-up time. After my two years at Sunshine Head Start, I was surprised that teachers were able to offer parents this level of detail about children's activities. It was evidence that teachers in general considered each child in the class individually, on a day-to-day basis. At Sunshine Head Start, a few parents at a time might be interested in how their child napped and could ask the teachers at pick-up and see if the teacher remembered on the spot. But routine reports about napping for every single child in the class were not expected.

As kids woke up at Great Beginnings, they headed to the classroom tables to play quietly with puzzles and toys while waiting for their peers to wake up. Like Sunshine Head Start teachers, the Great Beginnings teachers used nap time to take a short break, lesson plan, or talk among themselves.

Snack and Outside

At Sunshine Head Start, the class always transitioned from nap time into Snack Time. The teachers mostly allowed the kids to wake up on their own and would have them play with quiet toys at the tables while they waited for classmates to wake up. Shawn often slept the longest, snoozing past the point when teachers turned on the lights to encourage the final kids to wake up. He did not always sleep well at home, as his mom worked both a day job and a night job.

Once most of the kids had woken up, the class cleared the tables to prepare for Snack Time. The kitchen staff brought snacks in on a cart. The snack was usually a fruit or vegetable, plus crackers, pretzels, or another crunchy item. It was around 3:00 p.m. now, and one or two kids got picked up at this point, while the class was eating snacks. While kids ate their snacks, as with all other food, a teacher marked on a clipboard who had been offered food.

Then the class cleaned up their snacks and prepared to go outside again. This was the second required outdoor play period. When the weather was very cold or very hot, going outside was unpleasant.

On a twenty-degree day, Julian resisted putting on his coat.

"You're gonna be really cold out there," Ms. Paige said.

By the time we got to the doors leading outside, she was holding his coat and he was just in his t-shirt. "Come on, put it on before we get out there."

He still did not want to.

On his way out, he said, "I don't wanna go outside!"

"I know," Ms. Julie replied. "It's not my choice. If it was my choice, we would stay inside."

After the class made it outside, Julian started crying loudly and hugging himself. Ms. Paige eventually coaxed him into his coat, but he remained next to the door crying for two more minutes.

A few moments later, I asked Ms. Paige why we had to come outside. "It's required," she said.

"By who?" I asked.

"Well, to be accredited. So, we have to take the kids outside for twenty minutes, two times a day, at least. Unless the weather's, like, terrible."

"Do you think they [the kids] like it?"

"I think it's important for them, they like need it. And also, for some of them, this is their only outside time, 'cause their parents don't take them out really in the winter. So then at least they get to play in the snow and stuff."

Ms. Paige recounted that when she was in school, she hated recess. "I would just stand by the door until it was over."

Outside Time was tricky in Wisconsin's weather. Ms. Roxanne agreed that outdoor play time was critical. She made this clear one morning when we chatted about the lack of Outside Time resulting from weeks of frigid weather.

When I entered the classroom, a few kids shouted half-hearted greetings. The class was eating cereal, milk, and bananas. Ms. Roxanne was scolding Alicia—"*Enough*, Alicia, okay?"

She turned to me with raised eyebrows and an exasperated expression. "What? What's wrong?"

"It's been a rough morning," she said. "Everyone's just hitting and kicking and upset. This morning it was constant, like 'he did this,' 'she did that,' oh my gosh. And it's just . . . you know what I think it is, we haven't been outside in like weeks! Except for that one day. It's just been too cold."

Instead of going outside, the class had been using the multipurpose room, which they called the Big Room. Ms. Roxanne hated it; she much preferred going outside. "I mean, you put them in there with only a few things, and of course they're gonna get in fights. You're like setting them up to fail, honestly."

"Oh yeah, and what happened to that basketball hoop we used to have?"

"I don't know," she shrugged, dismayed. "Someone probably broke it or took it. And we don't have the key to that big cupboard, so we're locked out of that. It's just . . . kids need to run. They like *need* it. We're all going stir crazy, I think, because we're all cooped up."

While Ms. Paige saw outdoor time as compensatory—giving children experiences like snow play that she assumed they lacked at home—Ms. Roxanne talked about outdoor time as essential to managing children's high levels of energy.

* * *

Great Beginnings also had a second outdoor period. But before heading outside, the class gathered on the rug to read another book. When the weather kept them inside, they played in their multipurpose space. This space had permanent indoor playground equipment, as well as some of the toys that Sunshine Head Start kids had—hula hoops, gymnastics mats, and indoor tricycles. I observed several days of forced indoor play during February—which is a particularly cold month in Wisconsin. The kids and teachers approached their curated indoor play area with excitement rather than dread.

The weather in Madison was experienced equally at the two preschools, but their resources and indoor equipment to cope with it differed. While Outside Time was one of the most similar parts of the day for the two groups of kids, things shifted on days of inclement weather. When the children were forced inside, Great Beginnings' superior indoor play space offered them a more pleasant experience than the Sunshine Head Start children had.

Pick-Up Time: Conversations with Families

At 4:30 p.m. at Sunshine Head Start, the class went back inside. The classrooms closed at 6:00 p.m. The kids played casually while they waited for their families. Teachers were cleaning up and tidying from the day, but the energy was lower and calmer in the room. With each child who left, there was less for the teachers to do.

Families and teachers discussed pertinent information, such as whether a kid had fallen outside or had had a bathroom accident. For Sunshine Head Start parents, informal conversations at pick-up were the primary form of communication. Sunshine Head Start also wrote a newsletter to families, but amid their hefty paperwork, the newsletter only seemed to get written every few months.

At pick-up, families and teachers generally had more time to communicate. Instead of being on a time crunch to get to work, most families were heading home for the day. Dustin's mom, a single mother of five boys, sometimes pulled out a chair and chatted with teachers for ten to fifteen minutes. She said she enjoyed the adult conversation. She knew the teachers well because she had sent her two older sons to Sunshine Head Start.

* * *

At 4:30 p.m., across town, the Great Beginnings children went inside. Some children stood by the floor-to-ceiling window that revealed the walkway to the classroom door, hoping to see their parents or a classmate's parents on the way in. Some children were picked up early by parents or babysitters a few days a week, so that they could do extracurricular activities like swimming, gymnastics, or soccer. While they waited for their parents, the kids played. For this part of the day, the teachers at Great Beginnings did not set timers or assign classroom centers to the children.

Unlike Sunshine Head Start, Great Beginnings did more frequent, formal, and tailored communication with parents about what their kids were doing. For daily communication, Great Beginnings had a whiteboard at the front of the room. The teachers would write a sentence or two about what the children did that day (i.e., "went on a walk," "learned about polar bears"). Next to it was the whiteboard describing how each child had napped. Great Beginnings had a newsletter that seemed to happen monthly without fail. The newsletter included reminders about seasonal clothing, upcoming field trips, or special babysitting nights for families. The teachers sent a weekly email to parents, typically on Fridays, with information about what the class was learning, and with some pictures of the kids.

How Inequality and Segregation Shaped the Routine

On paper, the two schools' routines looked similar. This was an artifact of the external pressures for routines—from licensing rules, curricula, and industry "best practices" to the necessary time involved with getting a group of four-year-olds to eat and use the bathroom. But apart from the listed routine, the children's experience of time differed in important ways. Overall, Sunshine Head Start children experienced disruptions to the routine in the form of conflict or adjustments to the presence of newly enrolled children. Though these might have seemed to be random occurrences, after observing for two years, I see them as consistent enough to be *routine disruptions*. While both sets of teachers had to work lesson planning and tracking the children's development into their day, Sunshine Head Start teachers managed more intervention programs and tracking requirements, meaning they spent a substantial amount of time on paperwork.[12] The listed schedule did not include this kind of important, time-consuming work that teachers had to juggle, from minute tasks like tracking who was offered food to sprawling tasks like making developmental notes. More intensely, the unpredictability of who was enrolled and who would attend on a given day added work, and sometimes contributed to classroom chaos. As a result, some parts of the daily routine that policy makers might hope for—like consistent use of various interventions and curriculums— occurred sporadically. Even daily reading by an adult was sporadic. Sunshine Head Start read an average of one book per day, spending about five minutes on reading.

Across town, Great Beginnings children were used to stability in who their classmates would be, in general good behavior, and in compliance with each part of the day. The teachers used this stability mostly to add in reading time. Though the routine posted on the wall listed two reading periods, in practice Great Beginnings teachers read an average of six books per day as a group, spending about thirty minutes on reading. They offered children baskets of books to peruse individually during other transition times and quiet moments. Great Beginnings children had other routine experiences that were not listed on the paper schedule but that enriched the children in various ways, such as parties, library visits, and field trips.

In addition to these distinct differences peppered throughout the day, Circle Time and Work Time differed substantially. At Circle Time, Sunshine Head Start children experienced more group conversation and behavior correction from teachers; Great Beginnings children experienced more silent listening to teachers or peers. At Work Time, Sunshine Head Start children experienced more autonomy over their play, while Great Beginnings children experienced less autonomy over their play. I discuss this extensively in the following chapter.

In one study, early childhood researchers were dismayed to find that in a public pre-kindergarten program, a large portion of time was spent transitioning between various activities, rather than being spent on "instructional time."[13] I indeed saw these same challenges at both Sunshine Head Start and Great Beginnings. But deeper transitions—of kids moving in and out of classrooms or adjusting to family changes made likely by poverty—should trouble researchers too. This is deeper transition time that is required when poverty means instability, as it often does in the United States. Transitions and unpredictability add to teachers' workloads and capture teachers' attention. This work is multiplied when we group poor children into one class. Segregation is relational. When poor children are grouped in one preschool, other preschools can be free of children facing poverty- and racism-conditioned challenges, and instead can have a concentration of advantaged families. A solid routine was unable to create two equivalent preschools for rich and poor children. Inequalities in race and class meant that in segregated classrooms, routine disruptions were common for poor children of color, and stability was common for white, middle-class children.

Shayla, for her part, slowly adapted to the routine disruptions at Sunshine Head Start. Within a few weeks, she had made a friend. But she was still sorting out who sat where in the classroom.

Keisha was doing a sorting activity with small jewel pieces at the yellow tables. Shayla approached her and asked, "Keisha, you my friend?"

"Yes, we friends," Keisha replied.

Then Keisha turned to me and said, "We [Shayla and I] are friends. You not my friend!" I frowned but said nothing. The girls sorted jewels for a while until Shayla went to another table. Keisha came and pulled the chair out from under Shayla. Shayla crouched to stop herself from falling.

Keisha said, "You're in my seat." Keisha bent over to locate the picture on the back of the chair. She confirmed that the chair was hers and nodded. Keisha sat down in her chair and Shayla silently took the neighboring chair. The girls cut paper together.

Three months later, Keisha and Shayla were still friends and Shayla was now comfortable in the classroom—including with the notion of transitions in enrollment. Sunshine Head Start had three new kids enroll on the same day, and at breakfast, the chairs had been rearranged to accommodate the new kids. Noticing the difference in the chairs, Shayla declared, "Here, this is Luz's chair," and she pushed the chair back over to Ms. Roxanne's table. Ms. Roxanne interjected, "No, Luz, this is your seat now. You're sitting at that table." Shayla nodded and returned to her breakfast, unfazed by the change.

One month after this, Shayla's mom moved the family to a cheaper apartment on the other side of town. The school social worker was trying to get the kids a spot at a Head Start site closer to the new place. Shayla would soon be transitioning from Sunshine Head Start, too.

PLAY TIME

The Privileges of Pretend Play

During Outside Time on a cold day at Sunshine Head Start, I joined Isaac at the sandbox. Isaac had light brown skin and straight brown hair. His bangs were often grown out to the point of touching his eyes. He was scooping up nearly frozen sand and pouring it out. I started to fill up a bin.

We sat in silence until Isaac said, "I am just filling up my truck. It's almost full."

I nodded.

"I am just putting chocolate in here because my mom and my grandma say I can't have it till I am a big boy."

When the truck was almost full, he added, "I'm gonna put all the chocolate in here, because I can."

Isaac relished control over his play. Free from sanctioning eyes and some of the rules of an adult-controlled world, he could pretend to have all the chocolate he wanted. He had relative autonomy—freedom from external adult influence.

In early childhood education, children are said to learn best through play. This notion is reflected in licensing and accreditation guidelines, which require children to have daily opportunities to play with peers and classroom toys in open-ended ways.[1] Open-ended play can provide an opportunity for autonomy. Children exert control over an imaginative realm, bringing in other children and material objects according to their discretion. How does segregation shape the degree of autonomy that children experience during free play times?

When preschools segregate bodies, they also segregate and concentrate resources like teachers' attention. This affects how much autonomy teachers ultimately extend to children. At Sunshine Head Start, teachers gave their poor students of color more autonomy over play in practice, in part because of strains on their attention. In contrast, at Great Beginnings, teachers gave their white, middle-class students less autonomy over play in practice—these teachers had more free time and attention to spare, and they used it to control and comment on kids' play. The Great Beginnings teachers also intermixed their belief in play-based learning with practices that cultivated well-rounded interests in their students.

Sociologist Alex Manning argues that we are now in an age of concerted cultivation: more than just a middle-class parenting style, as Annette Lareau asserted in the early 2000s, concerted cultivation has become the benchmark across race and class lines. Concerted cultivation is a parenting style wherein parents seek to enrich their children's unique talents through adult-organized activities. Yet while this is a benchmark by which parents—and mothers in particular—are judged, concerted cultivation is predicated on resources necessary to achieve a particular vision of childhood. The Great Beginnings teachers' approach to intimate involvement in structuring children's time corresponded to concerted cultivation. Importantly, these teachers had the resources—time and attention—to deploy for this effort. The Sunshine Head Start teachers did not. In this way, preschoolers' time use mirrors inequalities observed in time use of older children, where middle-class children experience more concerted cultivation than poor and working-class children do.[2]

I augment these conversations about inequalities in parenting by zooming in on free play within preschool classrooms. The free-play time period is mandated and incentivized to be similar across preschools—making it a ripe case study through which to see how segregation might create unintentional inequality. During free play, it is teachers, rather than parents, who are organizing children's time.

Segregation meant that the constraints and opportunities on the way people spent their time were different in each classroom. This affected the way teachers set up pretend play. While we often assume that time, autonomy, and behavior are more thoroughly monitored for low-income people and people of color, the opposite occurred at these two preschools. Sunshine Head Start children's daily lives adhered more to the principle of autonomy over play. They managed a creative, child-based system for accomplishing peer play. But with their autonomy, boys sometimes jeopardized girls' space and play, and children's play included more conflict. Some of these poor children of color practiced behaviors that might be stigmatized or devalued by future white, middle-class teachers.[3]

By contrast, the actively managed children at Great Beginnings accomplished pretend play by using adults' techniques. They played like miniature adults. At the same time, teachers' naturalized control over children prevented peer conflict, with the result that these white, affluent children had fewer chances to practice managing their own activities and solving conflicts with peers. However, the children were accustomed to adults' interest in even their basic, conflict-free activities, reinforcing a sense of entitlement to adult attention. These white, middle-class children ultimately practiced behaviors that align with white, middle-class teachers' expectations for them.

Paradoxically, the autonomy over play lauded in early childhood can exacerbate inequality by fostering social skills like creativity and independence in children of color that their elementary teachers may undervalue in the future.[4] Though autonomy might be thought of as beneficial, in the preschool context, it may undercut preschools' ability to foster upward mobility for poor children.

Play at Sunshine Head Start

Upon entering Sunshine Head Start in the middle of indoor free play, one sees groups of three to five children in each play center. A few children are moving around the classroom, crossing the invisible boundaries between play centers. The curtains are open, and daylight streams through floor-to-ceiling windows, intermixing with fluorescent overhead lights. There is a symphony of laughter and talk, mostly from the children. To an unfamiliar observer, the scene might appear chaotic. But there is an underlying coordination to the children's movements.

Play time started out with some adult coordination. As explained earlier, Sunshine Head Start teachers called play time "Work Time," alluding to the idea that children's play should be taken as seriously as adults' paid work. At the start of Work Time, the teacher dismissed each child from the Circle Rug. The child had to "practice a gentle touch": either a handshake, a hug, or a high-five. Then they told the teacher their plan, explaining in which area of the classroom they wanted to play, and with whom. The teacher almost always approved the child's plan, except for times when too many children had chosen the same area. Then the kids managed their own play and movement across play centers for the full hour of Work Time. Meanwhile, the Sunshine Head Start teachers were often occupied with two or three children who were dealing with challenging behaviors and emotions. The other fourteen children played with relatively little adult control—they managed their movement across play centers, chose whom to play with, and chose how to play with objects.

With the ability to manage their time, the children developed a collaborative, child-based system for how to do pretend play. This involved constant decisions about how to incorporate the ideas their peers proposed, almost the way an improv troupe would do. The children knew how to get pretend play going and then continue to coordinate it, even with large groups of peers.

The Sunshine Head Start children's system was that the child who initiated the pretend play could then control who joined afterwards, and how they would play. The initiator of play had the right to refuse newcomers to the play and to refuse other children's suggestions. The kids accomplished this while keeping the imaginative pretense intact.

I was observing kids play in the House Area. Luz, Jasmine, and Julian were talking by the play kitchen.

Julian was bending over the table. "I need money though; I need money though."

Jasmine opened her black clutch purse and peeked inside. Turning to Luz, she said, "Mamí, *el* Julian *dice que* needs money" (Julian says he needs money).

"*Pero no tengo no* money," Luz replied. (But I don't have money.)

Julian turned and headed off. As he was walking away, Jasmine checked her purse again and said, "I have, though." She looked up, saw that Julian had gone, and shrugged.

Later, Julian returned, but he stopped at the boundary between the House Area and the Block Area. "Ding dong, ding dong," he chimed, five times in total. He threw in a "knock knock" and then returned to saying "ding dong," his voice rising and tempo quickening, communicating increasing urgency.

The girls did not respond. They went about their business, tending baby dolls. I started to feel uncomfortable that Julian was being ignored, so I called out "come in, it's open" from where I sat at the kitchen table. This was the first time I had spoken since entering the area.

"I'm not talking to you," Julian said. "Ding dong," he repeated a few more times, but still got no answer from Luz and Jasmine. Finally, Julian said, "I guess there's no one in there," and he headed off to the Science Area.

The kids had developed their own rules for pretend play, and in this case, they all followed the rules. To Julian, Luz and Jasmine started the play, and so they had control over how the play progressed and who could join. I was an observer rather than an initial participant in the play, and so when I tried to include him in the play, Julian ignored my overtures.

To rejoin, Julian rang the doorbell. This was the Sunshine Head Start kids' default strategy for joining play—implicitly accept the existing players' pretense and hope to be included by the kids in charge. What Julian did not do, and what I saw less often from all the children, was try to join by asking explicitly, "Luz and Jasmine, can I play here with you?" The Sunshine Head Start teachers recommended this explicit asking strategy to children, but the children rarely used it. Rather than playing the way adults sometimes dictated, the children were comfortable participating in the creative worlds of pretend that their peers created. They also used their peer control over play to solve potential interactional problems—in this case, a child wanting to play, but other children not including him—on their own. These poor children of color were practiced at using their creativity and at autonomously managing peer interactions.

Once children got play started, they continued it so long as other players accepted the context of the game. One morning, multiple children and I collaborated to create play about running from a fire. Sam started the play, so he was in charge.

I was in the House Area with Sam, Shayla, Hannah, and two other children. Suddenly, Sam shouted, "Fire!! There's a fire in here!"

"Oh no," Shayla said. Shayla looked at me pointedly, and said, "Fire! C'mon, fire!"

We all jogged to the Science Area. Shayla started setting out chairs; a few kids sat in them. Shayla instructed me to sit in one of the chairs.

"Did anyone call the fire department?" I asked.

"I did." Sam jogged over to the House Area, selected a plastic fork, and mimed putting out the fire. "No fire! No fire!"

"Is it safe?" I asked.

"Yeah," he replied. We all returned to the House Area.

We repeated this sequence five more times. Someone called fire, and then we evacuated to the Science Area to sit in the chairs. I assumed these were seats in a car, though nobody confirmed this verbally.

At one point there was a stall in the announcement of a fire.

Then Hannah attempted, "Fire, another one!"

"No, there's no fire, look," Sam insisted. There was a pause.

The play had stalled because Sam rejected Hannah's proposal for more play. But eventually, another kid affirmed the proposal of another fire, which Sam did not veto. So the play continued.

"Fire!" another child yelled.

"Yeah, fire!" a third child affirmed.

"Fire, fire!" Hannah repeated.

We all ran to the Science Area again.

Five children and I worked together to make this play happen. We ran across two classroom areas, and all together participated in responding to a fire, calling the fire department, and putting out the fires. It took collaboration to make this happen, and it occurred without close monitoring or facilitation from teachers. The Sunshine Head Start kids created a marvel of autonomous play. Without intervention or support from adults, they accomplished creative play with one another.[5]

Generally, when Sunshine Head Start children's play was peaceful, it was unusual to see teachers involved in it. They did not often comment on the kids' creativity, or suggest plot lines, or ask the children to include others. This was, at least in part, because the teachers' attention was pulled toward other aspects of their jobs, as discussed earlier. Ms. Roxanne was often lesson planning, doing assessments, checking the attendance log, or leading small group activities. Ms. Lisa and Ms. Julie were often paired one to one with the children exhibiting the most challenging and potentially unsafe behaviors, while keeping a general eye out for other conflicts or problems that might require their assistance.

In the handful of times when I saw teachers join children's play over my two years of observations, the teachers usually brushed past children's rules for play, which diminished the creative, peer-led nature of the children's rules. Teachers often approached play through democratic decision making and very explicit communication about how to play. In these moments, the separateness of kids' and teachers' activities was apparent.

During Work Time at Sunshine Head Start, Keisha put on a tiny toy fire hat. "Look, I'm a fireman!"

Ms. Megan said, "Oh yeah, you want to make a fire truck?"

Keisha pointed to the toy car ramp and said, "There's one there!"

Ms. Megan said, "Yeah, but let's make our own. We can use the chairs. You want to?"

"Okay," said Keisha.

Ms. Megan turned to Bryce. "Bryce, you wanna make a fire truck with us?

"No thank you," he replied.

In this example, Ms. Megan flouted the children's usual practice of having the initiator of play set the terms. Keisha initiated the play when she declared herself a fireman. Yet Ms. Megan took over the role of deciding the play and inviting newcomers.[6] She did this through explicit invitations ("let's make our own"; "you want to?"), rather than addressing Keisha as a fireman and moving the play forward under a shared pretense. When teachers played with children, they tended to assume that decision making would be shared across participants in the play. Teachers also encouraged kids to automatically include their peers. But ultimately, children and teachers at Sunshine Head Start had different systems for play.

The Sunshine Head Start teachers' relaxed system, which allowed children to roam the classroom and enter and exit play at their discretion, created dozens of small decisions for the kids to make. With the autonomy to manage these decisions, the children developed their own practices for how to play, and most of the time, the children managed these interactions peacefully. The Sunshine Head Start children decided how to incorporate peers into their play often, and without intervention from teachers. By having frequent chances to control their own activities, the Sunshine Head Start children developed important skills: they managed their own play and collaborated with larger groups of five or six children. These skills, however, might be the same ones that poor children who spend significant leisure time "hanging out" with peers are able to develop at home and in their neighborhoods.[7] If segregated preschools like Sunshine Head Start replicate and enhance play skills like autonomy and creativity only for poor children of color, there may be unintended future consequences, depending on how future institutions recognize their skills.

The children were largely allowed to decide whom they played with, where, and for how long within Work Time. Sunshine Head Start teachers most often intervened during play to reprimand the kids for playing in the wrong place or in the wrong way.

Teachers intervened occasionally about how children used toys. But these interventions were inconsistent and sporadic. Isaac, Julian, and I were playing in the Block Area. We were using blocks that had a colored film in the middle. We used them as pretend "clown eyes," staring at each other through the blocks, so that the classroom appeared to be red, or yellow, or blue.

The two boys left with their clown eyes and walked around the classroom, looking at different things and narrating the colors they saw.

They got to the half-moon-shaped tables where Ms. Roxanne was seated. "Boys, those are for building things, okay? They are for the Block Area."

The boys returned to the Block Area.

"These are for building," they told me. "We have to build something with them."

The boys listened to Ms. Roxanne's admonishment that they should use the blocks to build within the Block Area. But I saw many other cases where children only partially modified their play to fit teachers' expectations.

I headed to the Circle Rug. A teacher had set out bins with toys. Alicia and Shayla were already on the rug; I stayed to the side to observe.

Alicia barked like a dog. Shayla petted Alicia's hair and laughed. Alicia crawled around on all fours and barked some more.

"Alicia," Ms. Julie admonished. "Alicia, we are playing with toys. That's what I put out."

Alicia crawled like a dog over to the toys. She paused for a moment, still on all fours, but silent. Then she barked—more quietly than before—and resumed the dog game with Shayla. The girls never touched the toys.

Ms. Julie clashed with Alicia and Shayla over their play choices. Ultimately, the girls ignored the boundaries the teacher tried to impose on their play. This might have been an opportunity to applaud the girls' creativity. Instead, the teacher admonished the girls for playing "incorrectly."

These simple reprimands accumulated and subtly shaped Sunshine Head Start children's experience of play. On the one hand, the poor children of color at Sunshine Head Start had many opportunities to dictate the terms of their play. However, teachers' involvement in their play often consisted of behavior corrections such as those shown above, falling short of positive feedback on the kids' creativity. Over time, this sent a message that teachers are indifferent to the creative, positive details of kids' play.

A further consequence of the autonomy that Sunshine Head Start teachers offered children was that play was uncensored at times. For example, there was a curse word epidemic that spread at the school. I heard kids curse dozens of times, usually during Work Time when teachers were busy doing other things. The children also used pretend guns and swords in their play, which was against the classroom rules. I was most troubled, though, by children hitting peers during Work Time. Being hit by a classmate intrudes on the enjoyment of autonomy over one's play. Hitting happened several days per week at Sunshine Head Start.

In one instance, the hitting was so rampant that a teacher halted Work Time. Her response was to limit the autonomy of the whole class.

One morning, Ms. Lisa became frustrated during Work Time. Some of the kids were hitting or throwing toys at each other. Ms. Lisa called the whole class back to the Circle Rug. Once the kids were seated and quiet, she said, "Look at my face right now. I am mad. Do you know why I am mad?"

"Because we were hitting each other," Mia replied confidently.

"Yep. And my friends were throwing things. Do you think that is keeping yourself safe?" Her voice was stern, but not harsh or loud.

Several kids shook their heads.

"Yep. What are our rules? We keep ourselves safe, we keep our friends safe, we keep our things safe. And it's the teachers' jobs to keep you safe. So when you don't follow the rules, you get teacher plans. And today your plans are to go make [your nap] mats and read books until lunch comes. Does that sound like fun?" she asked, almost rhetorically.

"Noooo!" the kids chorused. Some of them shook their heads, looking dismayed.

Ten minutes later, when the children were settled on their nap mats, Ms. Lisa approached Ms. Rebecca and me. "Yeah, I'm sorry," she said. "But if they're not being safe, then we can't."

Ms. Rebecca shrugged.

In response to dozens of peers hitting each other—small infringements on autonomy—the teacher's reaction was to limit the autonomy of the entire class. Her statement of their behavior having forced the consequence of "teacher plans" held great symbolic weight because of the relative autonomy to which children were accustomed.

Autonomy in a group setting is complex. While it often allowed for creativity and joy in children's pretend play, it also meant that children had more opportunities for physical harm. Because Sunshine Head Start teachers were detached from the minutiae of most of the children's play, they responded to bad behavior from a handful of children by punishing the whole class. This subtly diminished children's individuality.

Autonomy also allowed more peer conflict. The kids were so used to dealing with smaller-level peer conflicts on their own that they often went to peers for comfort or help.

Isaac and I were reading books at the Puzzle Table.

Julian jogged over and said, "He toppled my blocks. I was just building it!" He frowned and gestured to the Circle Rug, where a few boys were playing.

Isaac shook his head and said, "I'm not playing that game anymore. I'm reading a book." He turned slowly back toward the table. "Now I'm a book reader."

Julian shrugged and left.

His response to peer conflict was to seek help from a friend, rather than from a teacher. Isaac did not address his problem, but Julian let it go.

In addition to relying on peers for help, I also observed that children sought out friends for comfort. Alicia and Jasmine had been carefully collecting the scattered autumn leaves from across the playground. Alicia brought the leaf bucket to the picnic tables where I was already sitting. Anthony grabbed her bucket and tipped all the contents out. Alicia started wailing, open mouthed.

Gabe came over and patted Alicia on the back. He inspected the bucket and saw that it was empty. He frowned angrily. Wordlessly, he swatted the back of Anthony's shoe.

Then the teachers called the class to line up. As Alicia walked to the line, tear tracks lined her cheeks. "Mommy, Mommy!" she wailed. As we waited for the final kids to join the line, Gabe hugged her, saying, "Don't cry." Luz came and grabbed Alicia's other hand, forcing her into a hug. Afterwards, Luz and Gabe held Alicia's hands all the way back to the classroom. She eventually stopped crying. The teachers did not intervene or comfort Alicia during any of this.

The Sunshine Head Start children practiced solving problems with peer support, rather than with teachers. This is evidence of resourcefulness and self-sufficiency.

The Sunshine Head Start children used the same reliance on peers for help in dealing with a gendered form of peer conflict. I often saw boys invade girls' play space. The result was a gendered chase-retreat pattern in which boys forced themselves into a play area, and girls reacted by asking the boys to leave, or by retreating to another area.[8]

At the art table, Luz made elaborate pictures for her mom, her grandma, and me. After she showed the pictures to me, we discussed going somewhere else. Luz chose the Block Area, so we jogged over there. Luz pulled the plastic car ramp off the shelf and selected a bin of plastic toy people while I grabbed the bin of plastic animals.

Before we could play with the toys, Gabe came to the Block Area and started ramming cars into our toys.

Luz scrunched up her face in irritation. "*Vamos al otro lado*" (Let's go to the other side).

I nodded, and we ran over to the House Area. Gabe followed.

"Noooo, Gabe, *no juegas con nosotras*," Luz declared. (No, Gabe, don't play with us.)

But Gabe wouldn't leave.

Then Luz and I went to the Science Area. Luz wanted me to read her book, but after I told her I couldn't read in Spanish, she took the book and motioned for Gabe and me to sit on the rug while she sat on the teacher's chair.

"*Los niños sientan aquí*" (Kids sit here), she said, while she smiled shyly. I nodded, hoping to communicate that I was okay with Gabe playing with us.

"*Bueno, vamos* Gabe" (Good, let's go), I said. "*Siga siga siga*," I told Luz, urging her to keep reading.

The same autonomy that allowed children to play creatively across play centers also allowed Gabe to enter and disrupt Luz's play. Luz signaled for us to sit on the rug, saying "*los niños*" to indicate that multiple "children" should sit in front of her, inviting both Gabe and me to play. Gabe's deference to Luz in this instance showed that he knew how to enter and play appropriately, even though he had not done so earlier, when he chased us across the classroom. Luz solved the problem by including Gabe in her play.

At other times, a boy would invade girls' space, the girls would resist, and the boy would listen.

Keisha, Shayla, and I were coloring at the table. Keisha went to the bin of papers. She called back to Shayla, "Want purple or pink, purple or pink?"

"Purple," Shayla said.

"Here, you have this one," said Keisha, handing Shayla the purple paper.

Gabe approached the table and grabbed the bin of crayons.

"No! You can't play with that!" Keisha shouted at him.

Gabe left.

In this instance, Gabe entered and took materials from the girls. However, when Keisha told him no, he left. Keisha still had to deal with the intrusion on her play, but she also solved her problem without the assistance of adults.

In fact, in the few cases where I did see teachers intervene in gendered chase-retreat, they ignored the boys and punished the girl involved. In doing so, they supported the system of boys' entitlement to disrupt girls' play.

We were at the yellow tables playing with toys. Dustin was sitting next to Hannah, and Dylan and Isaac were building things across the table.

Hannah built a structure with magnetic tiles. "This is a house."

"No, it's a poop," Isaac said.

"No!" Hannah shouted, in a whiny voice. "No it's not!" Her brow was furrowed, and she looked upset.

Dustin took her magnetic tile.

"I'm ignoring you," she said. "I'm ignoring you."

Isaac said, "Look, he took your Magnatile." His voice was measured, but his slight smirk implied that he was taunting Hannah.

Ms. Megan interjected, "Hannah, they are trying to bother you, you should ignore them."

Hannah moved her house over, further from the boys. She asked me for some pieces to put on it. I gave her some magnetic tiles.

Then Dustin smashed his hand into the house and the other two boys laughed. Hannah started to cry loudly.

"Hannah, come here," Ms. Lisa said. Head bowed and still crying, Hannah shuffled over to Ms. Lisa. She continued: "You need to take a break for a while, you're all worked up. We told you to ignore those kids."

Julian was passing by as he wandered the classroom. He commented, "Dustin broke her toy."

Ms. Lisa kept talking in a low voice to Hannah, while she sobbed. Hannah went to the Quiet Area and lay on a beanbag, still crying.

Hannah labeled her structure a house—exercising her autonomy to determine the content of her play. While Isaac calling Hannah's house "a poop" may seem an insignificant statement, it was a serious intrusion on Hannah's play. Deciding the pretense for an object is a delight of autonomous play. Recall Isaac's joy at calling sand chocolate. Accordingly, rebutting a child's pretense for an object is a form of interactional violence. Isaac's rejection of the way Hannah had animated her toys was an intrusion on her autonomy over her play. He then took her toy, physically preventing her from using it. When Hannah moved her house over, out of the boys' reach, she minimized her claim to classroom space. This was a rare time when teachers were close by to witness conflict erupt in real time. Yet they intervened to reprimand Hannah for not suppressing her emotions, rather than to punish the boys for infringing on another child's play.[9]

Teachers were complicit in compromising Hannah's creative autonomy. They effectively let the boys have the autonomy to trample on girls' space. The teachers heavily encouraged self-sufficiency. When Hannah failed to demonstrate it, she was punished by being removed from her play. When the teachers punished Hannah for failing to just ignore the boys, they reinforced a pattern in which girls could not fully enjoy their play. The occurrence of gendered chase-retreat illuminates the fact that autonomy was not equally enjoyed by all children. Instead, some boys used their autonomy to infringe on the autonomy of their classmates.

The Sunshine Head Start children's approach to play had several implications. First, it meant that when children talked during play, it often took the form of pretending to be a character. Children showed their creativity and role-taking strengths in these moments. These are complex interactional skills. Second, the children organized play by often allowing one person to be the leader. These instances amounted to many small moments in which to practice deferring to authority, but to peer authority figures, rather than to adults. The children were mostly comfortable sharing the role of leader, although there were conflicts every few months when children felt that one or two kids were "bossy" and claimed the leader role too much. Finally, it mattered that teachers were detached from children's method of play. Teachers were usually uninvolved in play that was progressing without conflict. If they did participate, they did so according to their preference for explicit negotiation and shared decision making. These were moments of misalignment between teachers' preferred modes of interaction and children's preferred modes of interaction. These four-year-old children from poor families of color exhibited creativity and problem solving frequently—but it was not praised by their teachers. During my time at Sunshine Head Start, I did not see an issue with the separate spheres of adults and children during play time. However, after observing the connected, affirming approach that the white, middle-class children at Great Beginnings experienced, I saw potential consequences for inequality.

Play at Great Beginnings

After two years at Sunshine Head Start, where children played in large groups, pushed the boundaries of what objects should be used for, and had a creative, child-based system for their pretend play, I observed Great Beginnings. When I watched indoor play for the first time, what struck me the most was the difference in the way the classroom felt. Children played in groups of one or two. A few children were by themselves, working on puzzles or reading books. There was happy chatter from children, peppered with comments from teachers. The environment was quiet, calm, and controlled. After observing for a few days, I noticed that play was highly scripted by the children.

Great Beginnings called their play time Free Choice Time. Free Choice Time started with teachers sending children to play centers. The teachers assigned an even number of kids to each play area, making sure each center had two kids before adding a third child to any center. I never saw teachers send more than three kids to a center. Teachers continued to manage where kids went throughout Free Choice Time. They did this by setting a timer for fifteen minutes or so. When the timer beeped, the children would rotate with their original playmates to a new area of the classroom. This meant that children always played in multiple areas of the classroom during Free Choice Time.

In timing and orchestrating play, Great Beginnings teachers activated their interest in making the children well rounded. The teachers wanted to expose the children to different activities and make sure that the kids played with different classmates. Ms. Erica explained their approach during her interview:

> [To start], I will pick the two kids and I will let them pick their center. I will say, "Lucas and Owen, you guys are going . . . Where would you like to go?" They have to conference together, and they pick their center. That way it gets a little bit of the girls who just want to play with the girls to play with other people. Really, they find that they [the boys] are not that bad. Ivy and Lucas have been playing quite a bit outside together. She played cat lady [with Lucas] two days ago and I have never been more proud in my life.

Ms. Erica's explanation seems simple but it exposes a deep familiarity with the children. She knows whom they prefer to play with. She knows what they are playing (cat lady), and she uses some of her energy to curate children's playmates, in ways that she hopes will advance their social development.

Beyond teachers' deeper motivations for organizing playtime, the timer system did a lot of work to structure children's play. The timer system exposed the kids to a variety of toys and activities. Otherwise, the teachers told me, some kids would play with blocks every day, but never go practice writing.

In addition to cultivating well-rounded skills and interests, the timer system prevented peer conflict. Children could not cross centers without teacher permission. When they did cross centers, the teachers kept an eye on their movement. What this meant was that children could start pretend play, and usually continue it without dealing with intrusions from newcomers.

In this quiet, more teacher-controlled environment, the kids' default practice was explicit negotiation on what and how to play. Just as at Sunshine Head Start, one child usually initiated the play and then decided what could happen next. But to decide, the children had explicit discussions about the play. These discussions took place outside the pretense of their pretend-play scenario.

At Free Choice Time, I sat with Katrina and Ryan in the Math and Puzzles center. Katrina was building a tower with magnetic tiles. Ryan was playing a board game with penguins. It was quiet; though each child occasionally narrated things to themselves in a low voice, there were also periods of no talking at all in the play center. After Katrina and Ryan played separately like this for a few minutes, Ryan asked to merge their two games.

"Can the penguins come to the house?" Ryan asked. He waited for Katrina to say yes before he moved his penguins in.

Adding to the game, Katrina asked, "Ryan, this penguin can be a monster, right?"

Ryan agreed. The kids continued playing, frequently asking each other before adding elements to their pretend play.

Ryan's explicit request to join was emblematic of the way the Great Beginnings children usually initiated shared play. At Sunshine Head

Start, the children rarely started play by explicitly assigning parts. At Great Beginnings, children's method involved starting play with talking and questions.

Great Beginnings children continued to ask questions during their play, sometimes in the form of suggestions with a rhetorical "right?" tacked onto the end. Their playmates did sometimes disagree with these suggestions. In another form of scripting, I observed the Great Beginnings children giving each other ongoing backstage instructions—such as whispering, "Katrina, pretend you are the mom and say you are going to work"—and the other child would repeat the suggested lines. Teachers supported the method of asking explicit questions before joining and during play. They further wanted children to share the power to decide how the play progressed.

During morning Group Time, the class was sitting quietly on the rug, listening to Ms. Erica. She was holding a brown hand puppet. She animated the puppet, which said it was having a problem with friends.[10] Ms. Erica asked the class, "What could a kid do who wants to join a game that other kids are playing?"

Three kids raised their hands. Ms. Erica called on a child. The child explained that the kid could just ask the other kids if he could play.

"Good idea," Ms. Erica affirmed.

"And do you think it's fun though if you wanna play, and someone just tells you 'Okay you do this and then say that,' and doesn't let you share your ideas?"

"Noooo," the class chimed in response.

"Has that ever happened to you?" Ms. Erica asked.

"No," a few kids replied.

"Really?" Ms. Erica smiled doubtfully. "Because I think I have seen you guys do that before. Well, do you think if someone's trying to play with you, you should let them share their ideas?"

"Yesss," the class answered.

The method of pretend play that Ms. Erica encouraged requires extended talk and discussion, done outside of the pretense of play. This strategy is attuned to small group play but would be tricky to execute with larger groups of peers. For example, if the Sunshine Head Start kids had taken this approach with the five kids playing fire truck, they would have gotten very little play done.

Sunshine Head Start children's pretend play could be likened to the interactions of an improv team, and the Great Beginnings children's pretend play could be likened to a staged play with multiple directors. The skills kids practice in their play mirrors these terms: the poor children of color at Sunshine Head Start practice creative collaboration with their peers; the Great Beginnings kids practice directing their peers and following directions.

At Great Beginnings, teachers' broader organization of play meant that they had consistent control and supervision over the play process. This included teachers influencing how children incorporated newcomers to play. At Great Beginnings, the teachers' rule was that children could switch centers outside of the official system, but they had to ask teachers. Sometimes teachers said yes, sometimes no. This rule limited newcomers to play and meant that teachers were monitoring when a child tried to join existing play.

During Free Choice Time, Luke, Owen, and Gavin were on the floor in the Block Area, building something large with wooden blocks. I sat at a table nearby, absently playing with some plastic people. Ms. Paula, who was a few feet away, asked the boys what they were building. They told her it was a castle. They continued playing. A few minutes later, Ms. Paula asked the boys if it was still a castle. They told her that it was now a ship.

A new child came into the center. Before the child got close to the toy ship, Luke asked the child, "Did you ask the teacher if you could change centers?"

I saw Ms. Paula watch this exchange. The new child said yes. The boys let the new child play, and they all played together with the ship they had built.

Ms. Paula showed interest even in the children's conflict-free play. Her interest intermixed with a tight classroom system for moving between centers, ensuring that a new child could enter smoothly. The teachers' control over which children played together was seen as natural by the children. Ultimately, the basics of who played with whom occurred on teachers' terms. As a result of teachers' close supervision and control, children rarely entered play spaces and had to work things out on their own. Children had comparatively fewer moments per day to solve problems among themselves.

The Great Beginnings children's approach to play had several implications. First, it meant that the talking those children did during play took the form of discussion as often as it took the form of pretending to be a character. These discussions amount to many small opportunities to practice negotiating with peers, complementing the negotiation with adults that sociologists have documented among middle-class children.[11] Second, it meant that, while the children still improvised and deployed their autonomy to create imaginative realms, this creativity was measured and involved group decision making at each step. The pace was slower. It took longer to develop a play scheme when children discussed and negotiated each piece. Finally, it mattered that teachers supported children's method of play. Teachers endorsed the explicit, democratic notion of play, and the children largely used this method. These moments of alignment between teachers' preferred modes of interaction—even peer interactions when the teachers weren't necessarily involved—constitute an early experience of affluent, white children having their behavior endorsed by authority figures.

While Sunshine Head Start teachers sometimes intervened in play to correct children for defying rules of space, these types of reprimands were rendered unnecessary at Great Beginnings. Great Beginnings teachers' system of control precluded most of these conflicts. The children's movements were also so controlled that I did not see actual hitting between children during my month of observations. However, I did see Great Beginnings teachers reprimand students to correct aggressive play toward inanimate objects.

Katrina, Sarah, and I were playing in Dramatic Play. Katrina had a stuffed orca that she was playing, and Sarah had an owl that the girls were calling the baby. Katrina said, "How about the orca chases the baby, right?"

"Yeah," Sarah responded. Katrina had the orca chase Sarah's baby owl all around the Dramatic Play Area. At one point, Katrina hit her orca and said, "You need to listen, orca."

Seconds after Katrina hit her orca, a teacher called Katrina over and talked to her for a minute. I hadn't even realized that a teacher was watching the play. Katrina returned after talking to the teacher. She was frowning.

"She says I can't play here anymore," Katrina said to us.

"Why not?" I asked.

"I was being rough," Katrina answered, her head bowed. She took her orca to another center.

As was typical at Great Beginnings, the teacher kept an ear out for what children were doing. She was watching closely enough to see a girl hit a stuffed animal, and immediately stop the behavior. The consequence the teacher doled out was to send Katrina to play elsewhere. She did get to keep her toy with her, though. In this moment, the teacher ensured a performance of innocence, keeping an aggressive moment out of school—even one that arose in the context of pretend play.

Thanks to their practice of evenly spacing children throughout the room, a smaller group size overall, and few children needing special attention, the Great Beginnings teachers were able to keep an eye and ear out for moments when children enacted violence in their play.

At Great Beginnings, the children could not cross classroom play centers during play time. This prevented more wide-ranging gendered chase-retreat, as happened with Luz at Sunshine Head Start. I did not observe gendered conflicts over space among two or three children playing in the same center, despite looking for it every day for my month of observations.

How the Teachers Managed My Time

The difference in teachers' approach to managing other people's time was clear even in the way they managed me as an observer. The Sunshine Head Start teachers viewed me as a resource that could compensate for some of the individual attention they wanted to provide to each child. One morning, Ms. Roxanne came over and said, "You know, I think you are the best volunteer we've ever had. You really let the kids climb all over you and get down with them. And that's great, because that's what they need, we just can't." Ms. Roxanne saw opportunities for adults to get on children's level—therefore giving them attention—as something that children needed. She contrasted my more personal relationships with the children to the teachers' broader supervision of children.

In addition to being on kids' level, Ms. Roxanne thought that the time I spent talking to children one on one was important.

Ms. Roxanne and I were chatting about my upcoming schedule. I told her that I planned to come in three days a week.

"I'm not gonna tell you no if you want to volunteer more," she said. "It's great to have you here."

"Oh, I'm not that helpful." I was feeling embarrassed, thinking of how I had been intentionally unhelpful to the teachers.

"Yeah, you are," she insisted. "Even just to have someone to sit and talk with Luz. And Shayla's clearly attached to you."

"Oh, sad," I replied. I was thinking of the custody battle that Shayla's mom was dealing with. I wondered if Ms. Roxanne meant that Shayla being attached to me was inappropriate.

Before I could explain what I meant, Ms. Roxanne continued, "No, it's not sad, it's good. We just have so much going on, it's hard to sit with them like that."

Ms. Roxanne articulated a core challenge of her job. Some of the children needed an adult to talk with one on one, and yet teachers had too many demands on their plate to do that. I had indeed been spending a lot of time with Luz and Shayla. Both girls asked me to play often and would sit and talk with me. They also had specific needs that were important but not physically unsafe, like those of some of the children whom teachers often paired up with.[12] Luz had been teasing the other two Spanish-speaking girls in the class, and then, in turn, had been excluded by them. Luz spoke some English, but was far more talkative in Spanish, a language that I spoke, unlike the teachers. Shayla had seemed to struggle to adjust to preschool. She peed her pants frequently and was shy with most people.

Ms. Roxanne singled out these children as examples in these two conversations. But Ms. Roxanne and the other teachers had never asked me to pair up with these girls, or even encouraged the connection outside this one moment. Much in the same way the teachers let the children be autonomous over their play, the teachers let me be autonomous in choosing whom to spend time with during my observations.

The Sunshine Head Start teachers' more global supervision of children's play was not quite an expression that they thought children only needed generic supervision. Rather, the teachers—and Ms. Roxanne especially—saw individual attention as valuable and necessary. She did not have the resources available to actualize her ideals for individualized attention. Instead, her attention was oriented around responding to the results of family disadvantage. She prioritized children who were acting out at school—often concurrent with traumas made routine by racism and poverty.

In contrast to the autonomy that the Sunshine Head Start teachers afforded me, the Great Beginnings teachers viewed me as a resource that could enhance the individual attention they already provided for each child. From the beginning they were more directive about sending me to pair up with certain kids, resulting in me being managed as an enrichment resource for the children.

Upon entering the classroom after a bathroom break, Ms. Paula immediately told me where to go. "Oh, Casey, maybe you can go to the writing table and help those guys?"

I sat at the writing table with a few children who were drawing quietly. Half the class was outside with the other teacher. Then the kids who had been outside came back, and their classmates prepared to switch. I asked Ms. Paula if she wanted me to go outside, so that I would remain with the group of kids I had been with. "Actually, can you stay in? Because otherwise it's just Ms. Jessica." She explained that I could help by giving the other kids inside some one-on-one time.

This moment was instructive because Ms. Paula was explicit about wanting to use me as a resource to offer one-on-one time. Implicit in Ms. Paula's instruction was that she wanted to offer children the enriching experience of undivided adult attention.

The Great Beginnings teachers seemed uncomfortable with me sitting back to observe at times, and sometimes sent me to specific children.

Ms. Paula came over to Luke, who was looking at emotion cards. The cards depicted kids making different facial expressions and had emotions written below.

With a small gasp of excitement, she said, "Oh, Luke, why don't you show Casey how to play those?"

"Okay," Luke replied. He brought the cards over to me. We took turns guessing the emotions.

Ms. Paula did not share her reasoning for sending Luke to me, but the result was that Luke had one-on-one adult time. Ms. Paula also communicated her delight at what Luke was doing in his play, giving Luke the experience of a teacher being interested in his play.

Ms. Erica also sent me to work one on one with children. During morning play time, Ms. Erica suggested that I go and play with Ryan, who was building something with blocks by himself. I asked Ryan how to create windows with the building blocks. He didn't know, so we figured it out together.

Teachers at both schools held some similar ideals for adult involvement in children's activities. Like Sunshine Head Start teachers, the teachers at Great Beginnings saw me as a resource for the kids. But at Great Beginnings, the teachers directed me, much in the way that they directed kids to the play centers. Sometimes, as with Ms. Paula, their directions showcased the kids' learning and capabilities. At other times, they moved me around to ensure that as many kids as possible got one-on-one time with an adult. The kids they sent me to varied. Rather than seeing me as compensating for something that teachers were unable to do, as Ms. Roxanne put it at Sunshine Head Start, the Great Beginnings teachers saw me as enhancing the one-to-one attention they already tried to offer to their students.

Great Beginnings' granular management of children's play was more than an indication that they could deploy adult intervention in children's activities to a deeper extent. These teachers had the time and attention available to actualize their ideals for how preschool should look. Their time and attention resulted from family advantage among their students. They had no children experiencing poverty-related disruptions and traumas within their families. Most years, they had one or two children with challenging behavior. But their affluent families typically marshalled medical expertise and services to address these behaviors. With the further benefit of families who rarely moved and who tended to keep their children enrolled consistently all year, the teachers were able to support children with difficult behaviors. Typically, the most difficult children improved in their behavior over time. The Great Beginnings teachers' initial reaction was to prioritize their attention by directing most of it to the child with the most intense behaviors, just as the Sunshine Head Start teachers did. But after a few months of dedicated work with that child, they moved on to enrichments and control over Free Choice Time.

The Paradox of Autonomy over Play in Preschool

Autonomy over play is thought to be liberating and enriching. But for the poor children of color at Sunshine Head Start, this autonomy came at the cost of distant relationships with teachers and more conflicts with peers. The affluent, white children at Great Beginnings sacrificed autonomy over their play but gained a deeper relationship with authority figures and less conflict with peers. The poor preschool children of color at Sunshine Head Start experienced more autonomy over their play. But this autonomy can have contradicting consequences. These children experienced teachers as uninvolved in the mundane, creative aspects of their play, and unavailable to help with conflict, including protecting girls from gendered intrusions on their space. The dynamic here is reminiscent of a pattern highlighted by sociologist Victor Rios. Observing how Black and Latino boys experienced police presence, he noted that they experienced overpolicing that punished them, but underprotection in cases when they wanted adult intervention to keep them safe.[13] In the Sunshine Head Start classroom, children experienced sporadic reprimands for their use of space, but also sometimes experienced a lack of teacher support when they were being hurt by other children.

Segregation created practical issues that facilitated teachers' different approaches to structuring play time. While the Great Beginnings teachers sat calmly, monitoring their timers and poised to overhear even hints of aggression in children's pretend play, the Sunshine Head Start teachers were multitasking. They alternated between completing paperwork, helping new children adjust, and staying close to boys and girls enacting the most unsafe behaviors. The group of less supervised children, who creatively did pretend play and solved most of their own conflicts, was of lower priority to receive Sunshine Head Start teachers' attention. Instead, the tasks preoccupying teachers' attention were rooted in poverty and structural racism. For example, when children experienced eviction—something that is more likely to happen to kids of color—and then acted out at school, that was a consequence of structural racism.

Segregation is an important, relational process that undergirds children's experiences at *both* schools. The Sunshine Head Start classroom had a high number of students dealing with the fallout of structural racism because few children of color attended other preschools—such as

Great Beginnings. When poor children of color are segregated in some classrooms, white, affluent children in other classrooms are insulated from challenges that poor children and children of color experience in an unequal society.

These structural and institutional features influenced the degree of autonomy that children experienced. It may be surprising that in this case, it was poor children of color who experienced a condition—autonomy over play—that is pitched as ideal by experts. Work Time, as it was experienced by the poor children of color spending formative years at Sunshine Head Start, gave children practice managing their own activities and not expecting teachers to intervene in mundane moments of play. Unlike the Great Beginnings children, they were not accustomed to constant teacher attention.[14] Free Choice Time, meanwhile, gave the white, middle-class children at Great Beginnings practice at experiencing teachers' oversight of play and prevention of peer conflict. Teachers' control over kids' activities was constant and naturalized. This allowed those children to develop a sense of entitlement to a school environment tailored to their preferences. Yet while this resulted in scripted, somewhat dull play, it had up sides for these children's future schooling: they will be practiced at censored play and at feeling entitled to teachers' attention, even regarding their ordinary pretend play.

The different expectations that preschoolers are developing toward their teachers can reinforce inequality. In her ethnography of a mixed-income elementary school, Jessica Calarco found that middle-class students often asked their teachers for help, while working-class students often struggled through assignments on their own. When children activated class-based strategies for behavior at school, the middle-class children secured advantages for themselves that working-class students missed out on.[15] The Great Beginnings children were learning to expect adult structure for their time and peer interactions, something that may lead them to elicit close relationships with their teachers in the future. The Sunshine Head Start children were learning to play creatively and solve their own peer disputes—positive skills that may be overlooked in segregated elementary schools where teachers are not looking for them in poor children of color.[16] Similarly, these skills might be overlooked in mixed elementary schools if teachers are busy meeting middle-class, white children's high expectations for personalized teacher support.

Through a close look at how adults differentially organize "unstructured play time," the paradoxical potential consequences of autonomy over play become visible. Though autonomy over play is thought to be ideal in preschool, when this ideal is deployed in segregated contexts, it might result in deepening class and race inequalities.

Isaac had attended Sunshine Head Start since he was a baby. He was adept at managing conflict. This was clear one day when he instructed me on how to behave. We were sitting at the yellow tables, building cars out of plastic stick pieces.

I brought my car up to Isaac's.

"Hey, nice to see you!" he said, animating his car. "Come to my train."

"Okay," I agreed.

Isaac took our cars and placed them on a tray in front of him. We continued adding to our cars. Isaac made his car into a fire truck and then into a Batmobile. I declared that mine would be a tractor car.

Bryce appeared, seemingly out of nowhere, and took my car away from me. I was surprised and sat staring blankly at the table.

Isaac frowned at Bryce. "Hey, she made it. She made it. Give it back!"

"It's okay, I'll make a new one," I interjected quickly.

"I'll get it back for you!" Isaac insisted.

But I talked him down and built a new car. Ten minutes later, Bryce returned again and broke Isaac's car. Isaac tried to snatch it back, but Bryce hit him. Isaac began crying. This got Ms. Julie's attention, and she came over to console him. After the teacher left, Isaac commented to me, "I'm going home with my mom to tell her how Bryce hitted me. Don't hit me. I went on the Ferris wheel with my mom and Cassie."

I nodded.

Then Isaac said, "If you were sad when Bryce broke your toy, you should have cried."

On my bus ride home, I thought about Isaac's advice. In general, he had a knack for putting complex things into words. And as a seasoned Sunshine Head Start kid, he was right—the way to get teacher attention and help was to express loud emotions. Otherwise, the teachers would assume that the kids could solve the problem themselves.

TOYS IN CUBBIES

The Power of Objects

During nap time at Sunshine Head Start, we sat in the dark glow of light that filtered through the blue curtains, listening to the tonal lullabies that teachers played on the radio. Sam's eyes were droopy. He seemed to be on the verge of sleep when he whispered, "My mom's got money."

He said it so quietly that I repeated it to make sure I heard it right.

"Yeah. My mom has money for my Hulk now."

Sam was a boy with pale skin, freckles, and blonde curls that delighted the adults he met. He had been asking his mom for a Hulk toy for weeks. His Mom, Paige, was a single mom who prided herself on being resourceful and thrifty. She joked about buying generic treats for Sam since he didn't yet know the difference (in her words, instead of Oreos, she bought "Poor-e-os").

But the Hulk that Sam wanted had to wait until payday, which Paige simply told him when he asked. In fact, as much as Sam longed for this toy, he would be unable to play with it at preschool. His preschool forbade personal property; teachers hoped to downplay the material scarcity some children faced at home. Across town, the white, affluent Great Beginnings preschool celebrated personal property; teachers created institutionally supported ways for children to enjoy some of their abundant personal property while at school.

These different property rules trace back to the practical realities of teaching within segregated classrooms. Structural racism and conditions of poverty percolate, creating the institutional conditions in which teachers and children experience their daily lives. With property, the concentration of material hardship among Sunshine Head Start families made teachers wary of having kids bring in personal objects, and the concentration of material abundance among Great Beginnings families made teachers comfortable inviting children to bring in personal objects. In this way, the property rules that each group of kids experienced *reflected* race and class inequality. But property rules also *reinforced* race and class inequality through two avenues. First, under each property regime, children accumulated countless small moments of being either able or unable to customize their classroom experience. They developed a sense of what it means to be in an institution. Poor children of color were prevented from customizing their experience of school through personal property, inculcating a sense that customizing school through property is subversive. Affluent white children had their personal property celebrated, inculcating a sense that customizing school through property is supported by the institution. Most of these children will then confront future schools that operate under white, middle-class sensibilities that reward the sense of entitlement to customization that the Great Beginnings kids have developed. Second, quests to enjoy personal property became a source of racialized, gendered discipline that disadvantaged boys of color. This was a subtle way in which kids of color—at age four—were already being pushed out of schooling.

How Children Customize School through Property

I realized the importance of personal property through taking children's concerns seriously. Several months into my observations, I noticed children sneaking in special property from home, and treasuring items like rocks, snowballs, barrettes, and Hulk toys. I began to track every instance when I saw a child designate an object as special.

Children prized personal property despite the many classroom things available for them to use. At both schools, the classrooms had multiple play areas with abundant objects: books, crayons, paper, play dough, large wooden blocks, magnetic building tiles, plastic toy people, baby dolls, dress-up clothing, a play kitchen area, magnifying glasses, a sand table, a water table, and more. Large supply closets filled with toys and art supplies were on a monthly rotation to ensure variety throughout the year. The two schools had comparable amounts of objects available for children to use daily.

But these classroom objects differed somewhat from things children brought from home.[1] For example, the classrooms had no "character toys" from children's shows and movies. Instead, classroom property was often open-ended items with many interchangeable pieces, like blocks. The more distinctive objects were things like dress-up clothes, where there might be three aprons, each with its own pattern. In contrast, objects children brought to school or deemed personal varied. Some were found objects from nature like rocks or leaves. Others were action figures representing favorite characters. Finally, some objects were significant because someone special had given the object to the child.

Personal property resonated differently from classroom property. In both cases, using property allowed children to control some aspect of their school experience. But when kids brought personal property into school, they could both control and *customize* their school experience.

Yet children were not free to bring in any object they wanted. They had to contend with their classroom's rules. While both preschools confronted the problem of children wanting to access their property at will, they did so within the constraints and opportunities that segregated classrooms afforded. With their students' poor families in mind, the teachers at Sunshine Head Start enforced rules that constrained children's access to their personal property. These rules removed an opportunity for kids to customize their experience at school, and, for the boys of color, became a pathway to punishment. Meanwhile, at Great Beginnings, teachers did not have to consider families' material scarcity. Instead, they counted on families' material abundance. The Great Beginnings teachers created three avenues for kids to bring personal property to school: they hosted a weekly Show-and-Tell, encouraged kids to bring books from home, and allowed children to bring in a stuffed animal for nap time. The teachers did not control the fact that they taught segregated groups of children. Yet the rules they made, with their segregated groups of families in mind, had the effect of giving affluent white children secure access to property, and giving poor children of color precarious access to property.

Classroom Rules Restricting Personal Property at Sunshine Head Start

For the Sunshine Head Start children, being able to access the property they prized while at school was difficult. The children's quest to enjoy personal belongings at school brought them up against classroom rules. Though Sunshine Head Start families were similar in that they all lived near or below the poverty line, families differed substantially in the toys they gave their children. Some children, like Sam, talked about toys they desired but that their parents said they could not afford. Other children got new toys often and talked about their new toys at school. Still others were facing extreme material hardship, including homelessness, eviction, and job loss.

But ultimately, in a classroom that concentrated children from poor families, teachers always kept in mind that families had strained resources for toys and other property. The Sunshine Head Start teachers created rules to deemphasize personal property. Children were not supposed to bring personal property to school. If a child did bring personal property, it was to be stowed in the child's cubby until the end of the day. The teachers said that forbidding personal property at school both avoided jealousy and avoided prized property being stolen or broken, which could be especially disappointing to families that had worked hard to acquire objects.

Despite the classroom rules, some children still brought special property to school. Of the thirty-six children who attended the classroom over my two-year observations, thirteen children brought special personal property to school.

Julian brought special personal property most often. Julian was the tallest boy in the class. He had brown skin, and he wore his hair in close-cropped curls. Julian was obsessed with bugs and superheroes. In October he brought two books. In February he brought a small metal car. That March he brought a big Spiderman with him for a few days in a row. When he showed it to another boy, the boy examined it carefully and said, "Yeah, it's so big, it's like the biggest one! Ask your mom if I can have your toy?"

Julian said quietly, to himself, "My mom's in jail."

Julian's mom's boyfriend, Adrian, brought Julian and his two sisters to school while his mom was in jail. In April he brought a Bumblebee (from the movie *Transformers*) action figure—not the knock-off version but the real one. In May he brought a red plastic spider, the kind you get from coin-op machines at the grocery store. In June he brought two plush Ninja Turtles, a yellow plastic airplane, and plastic nunchucks. In the final months before kindergarten, he brought a collapsible frisbee, a slimy sticky hand, and a laser pointer. Julian carried this property with him through days of boredom, moments of friendship, moments of excitement, and changes in his family.

At first, when Julian brought special belongings to school, he showed them proudly to teachers and peers alike. It was possible for Julian to show his property to teachers because, initially, the teachers' rule was that children could keep special property either in their pockets or in their cubbies. In January, over several days, Julian brought the same toy to school. Classroom rules about personal property limited how much he could enjoy it. While sitting down for breakfast, Julian tugged at something in his pocket. He struggled because his pocket was compressed. He finally extracted a red figurine. Holding it out, he said, "My Iron Man hungry. My Iron Man hungry. My Iron Man wants to sit down." He moved Iron Man's arms as if preparing him to eat.

"In your pocket or cubby," said Ms. Julie, who was sitting next to him. When Julian did not answer, she continued, "School rule. Everyone follows it, not just you."

He returned the figurine to his pocket and kept eating.

About an hour later, at Work Time, Julian chose to play at the Water Table. Keisha and the mental health counselor, Ms. Susan, who visited a few times a month, were also there. "Wanna see my Iron Man?" Julian asked Ms. Susan. He held up the figurine so she could see it.

"Oh, that's cool," she said. "Is that yours from home?"

"No. My uncle bought it."

"Oh, that was nice of him. Where can you keep it so it's safe? Cubby?"

Julian walked over and deposited Iron Man in his cubby.

"Good choice," Ms. Susan said. As he was walking back over to her, she held up both hands, inviting a double high-five. Julian did not oblige. She wrapped her arm around his side instead; Julian stood still during her embrace. As he sat back down at the Water Table, I heard him mumble, "I want my Iron Man . . ."

About three minutes later, Julian went to the cubbies again. He climbed on the bottom shoe shelf, gaining the extra height he needed to reach his yellow cubby on the top. He took out the Iron Man and pocketed it.

While property was indeed "safe" when stored in cubbies, as Ms. Susan claimed, property was also inaccessible to its owner. The cubby area contrasted with the rest of the classroom, where nearly everything was child-sized, to the point where I often felt like a bear in a dollhouse trying to play with the kids. Though the cubbies became a holding place for forbidden property, they were really intended to hold extra clothes, artwork, and things that parents and teachers shuttled between school and home. Even Julian, the tallest boy in the class, could not reach his cubby box without standing on the shoe shelf below—something he was not supposed to do.

Further, the act of retrieving something was conspicuous; cubbies were in the front of the classroom by the teachers' prep counter and the activity tables. Teachers were often on that side of the classroom. The cubbies were also not touched for most of the day. Unless it was drop-off, nap time, or pick-up—the three times of day when people re-trieved or stored items there—the cubby area was empty. Accordingly, these moments, when Julian and other children were retrieving their property from cubbies, were quite visible.

Ten minutes later, a teacher from a neighboring classroom entered. She approached another teacher and talked about dismissal time. Julian showed her his Iron Man.

"Very cool!" she said, smiling. "But you should keep it in your cubby."

About twenty minutes later, Julian went to an activity table. Alicia and Mia were a few seats over at the same table, working on a puzzle. Julian went over and stood behind Mia's seat, removing Iron Man from his pocket. "Iron Man will hit you," he said. He extended the toy's arm and hit Mia on the shoulder. Mia's face remained drawn as she continued her puzzle. She did not respond to Julian. He walked away a few seconds later.

Then Julian approached Gabe, who was working on a penguin matching activity at the yellow tables. "Wanna play with me, Gabe?"

"What?" said Gabe.

"Wanna play with me, Gabe?" Julian repeated. Gabe didn't answer; instead, he stood up and went to wash his hands.

Julian headed back to Mia and Alicia's table. "Wanna play with me?" Mia answered that he could play with them.

"We're coloring," Alicia added.

As he sat down, Julian said, "Have you seen my Iron Man? Him cool." Alicia kept coloring.

Julian leaned over and tapped her. "Look, my Iron Man."

Alicia nodded and turned back to her paper.

Julian walked away, pocketing Iron Man. Then he doubled back, saying, "Alicia, Alicia!" He picked up his pace and the Iron Man fell out of his pocket. He stopped and quickly picked it up. Then Julian sat back down at Alicia's table.

"My name's not Alicia, it's Malicia."

"Can you write my name?" he asked her. They began to chat and color.

Julian showed his Iron Man to adults, offering a chance to connect with them around something that was special and interesting to him. But, without exception, the adults' response was to quickly acknowledge the toy and then direct Julian to put it in his cubby. With other children, Julian used the Iron Man toy to various ends. First, he used it to hit Mia, on his behalf. Then he returned to play with Mia and Alicia, this time showing the toy to Alicia, twice, until he got her attention. But his display of Iron Man did not lead to them playing with the toy.

Two days later, in the middle of Work Time, two maintenance workers came in. This was a rare event, and so within a few seconds, seven of the twelve children present that day were crowding the two workers, pointing to their toolboxes, and asking them questions. One of the men stood on a chair to fix a high cabinet.

Julian went over and held out the Iron Man, extending his arm fully. "Look, my Iron Man," he mumbled.

The man didn't respond.

Julian repeated, clearer this time, "Look, my Iron Man."

Ms. Lisa said, "Oh, Frank, look, he's showing you his Iron Man."

"Oh, cool," Frank said, glancing down at the figurine.

Julian turned and walked to the front door, waiting. The second maintenance worker entered and paused in the doorway; he was at least six feet tall and filled the door frame. As the man stepped inside, Julian stretched his arm out and said, "Look, Iron Man."

This man didn't answer; he headed back to his project in the bathroom. Julian followed him to the bathroom and tried again. The man still didn't answer. Julian wordlessly stowed the Iron Man in his pocket and sat at the table next to Ms. Julie.

Julian had internalized the cubby-or-pockets rule. After Julian failed to get the second worker's attention, he sat down and pocketed his toy, needing no prompting from the teachers to do so. Under the cubby-or-pockets rule, poor children of color like Julian were unable to customize their school experience by enjoying personal property. Instead, they were experiencing preschool, an important, early institution, as indifferent to their personal preferences. The most Julian could do was quickly show his special toy to others, before pocketing it.

The Iron Man toy was a significant personal object to Julian. He took care of it, animated it, and showed it to others. Teachers and other adults were largely uninterested in Julian's special toy. Their reaction was usually to quickly acknowledge the toy and then steer Julian to put it in a cubby. Ms. Lisa's reaction was one exception; she helped Julian by alerting Frank. However, her polite assistance stopped short of genuine interest.[2] Julian also showed his toy to his peers, but he failed in trying to use it to connect with peers.

Personal property was scarce under this regime, and though usually kids who snuck property in did so without peer conflict, occasionally there were fights. In the next field note, what started as a struggle between two kids became a moment of conflict between a child and a teacher.

In February, Julian and another boy were standing on the blue Circle Time rug, fighting over a toy motorcycle, each tugging to gain hold of it. After Julian won, he clutched the motorcycle to his chest, crying.

Mr. Alex approached the boys and addressed Julian. "That's why we don't bring toys from home. So you know what? I'm going to put this in your cubby."

"I wanna put it in my pocket," said Julian.

"Well, you can choose, I can put it in your cubby, or you can put it in your cubby."

"No, I wanna put it my pocket," Julian insisted, sounding more desperate.

"I wanna keep it safe for you in your cubby."

"In my pocket."

"I know. I heard you say that. I heard your words."

"I wanna put it in my cubby by myself," Julian said finally.

But when he didn't move, Mr. Alex grabbed Julian's hand and pulled him toward the cubbies. Julian started crying louder. He made his body go limp, and Mr. Alex pulled fruitlessly at Julian's arm. Then Mr. Alex released Julian, and Julian's arm snapped flat to the ground. He kept his arms clenched at his sides, immobile. "I want it in my pocket," he said.

Another teacher approached. "Should I go get my cars so you can play with some cars?" she asked. Julian agreed to this. He gave his motorcycle to Mr. Alex and then played with the cars that the other teacher gave him.

Under the regime of cubby-or-pocket, Julian preferred to keep his property in his pocket. This allowed him to keep it close and take it out of his pocket to enjoy—sometimes privately, sometimes with peers. But for these same reasons, teachers began to favor cubbies for storing personal property. This way, children were less likely to play with their objects and cause problems of distraction, jealousy, or damage.

The teachers further emphasized the division between institutional property (allowed at school) and personal property (not allowed at school) when Ms. Lisa offered "her cars" to Julian. This was a gallon bag full of small, cheap cars that she kept high up in the teacher cabinet. Instead of supporting children in accessing their toys from home, the teachers introduced "safe" institutional property.

The rule forbidding personal property from being used at school sometimes led to conflicts with teachers. For Julian, this added to the other ways in which teachers were highly involved in managing his behavior. On some days, Julian came to school upset, and would hit his peers, or jump off bookshelves. Accordingly, teachers often paired up with him so that they were close by to make sure he was "being safe."

As winter receded into spring, the teachers modified their rule about personal property. After dealing with children—mostly boys—bringing property to school and arguing about cubbies, the teachers began putting kids' toys into a new "teacher bin" at the start of the day. It was a clear plastic tub that they stored on a high shelf. This new rule sharpened the message that personal property was not for enjoyment at school.

Even with the new rule, some children, Julian included, continued to bring personal property to school. By the summer of 2015, Julian was five and about to leave the preschool to attend kindergarten in the fall. By this point, Julian had become practiced at maneuvering his personal property around teachers' gaze, so that he could enjoy his property at school.

I walked into the classroom and saw that kids were tossing their plates from breakfast into the dish bin. Julian came up to me and said, "I brought a Frisbee."

"Oh? Is it little?" I assumed it must be, because a regular-sized frisbee wouldn't fit in his cubby.

He pulled it out of his pocket. It was a polyester, collapsible Frisbee; when opened, it was the size of my hand. There were superheroes on the front.

"You wanna play with it outside?" he asked.

"Okay," I replied, "but we should probably ask the teachers. Because I bet you they will notice."

"I don't wanna do that. I don't think they will see."

Julian was planning to play with his property outside and had already calculated that he could avoid teachers. He showed me his Frisbee and had a plan to enjoy it later. He was right; he played with it for a few minutes on the playground, without teachers addressing it. Bringing things he liked to customize his experience of school had become subversive. Julian had learned that he could not keep his stuff with him anymore unless he purposely concealed it from his teachers.[3]

That summer, Julian brought a laser pointer even after teachers told him not to.

Julian spotted me on the playground. He asked me if I would play. I agreed.

"Let's play zombies," he said. "I'm the leader."

Before we started playing zombies, Julian showed me a small metal tube that lit up red when he pressed the button. He called it a flashlight. Then he returned it to his pocket.

Later, as his class was lining up to return to the classroom, his teacher saw the object. She said, "Julian, you're gonna give that to me. We told you not to bring that laser to school. You could blind somebody."

This moment was the first time when I saw Julian bring something that teachers specifically asked him not to bring. The teachers viewed the laser as dangerous, stating that he could "blind somebody." In Wisconsin, it is a misdemeanor to point a laser at a police officer.[4] Since lasers are included on some guns, lawmakers classify lasers as "weapon-adjacent." In future school situations where he was less known to teachers, these behaviors might be labeled and stigmatized, as can happen for boys of color.[5]

Even after his experiences of having to sneak his property into school, Julian felt attached to Sunshine Head Start. He made this clear as kindergarten, and the end of his time at Sunshine Head Start, drew nearer.

Julian was sitting near the teachers after Circle Time, lagging behind after the other kids had gone off to play. "I was sad last night," he said. "I want to stay here."

Ms. Megan told me, "Yeah, I heard he's been sad; he doesn't want to go to kindergarten. Such a sweet boy."

Later, as Julian was sitting at the picnic table during Outside Time, he said, "I don't like that school [his future kindergarten] anymore."

Ms. Megan said, "Well, I'm sorry to hear that."

"I just want to stay in this preschool forever."

For all the struggles between Julian and teachers about property, Julian liked Sunshine Head Start. The teachers liked Julian, saw him as sweet, and attempted to affirm Julian's interests via certain property. One day in the spring, Ms. Roxanne had caught a bug that she saw near her apartment. She knew that Julian loved bugs. She put it into a plastic bug catcher and brought it in to school for him and the other kids to use. The teachers later went a step further to support Julian's interest in bugs—they got a big, clear tub and let the kids put worms that they found outside on the playground into the tub to observe.

These moments show the care and interest that Sunshine Head Start teachers took with Julian in mind. However, they stopped short at incorporating his property into the classroom. At Sunshine Head Start, the sense was that the classroom held abundant toys for kids to use, so personal property could be checked at the door. Overall, the Sunshine

Head Start children either experienced the classroom as depersonalized compared to home, or as a place where they had to sneak personal stuff in if they wanted to enjoy it.

Gendered, Racialized Access to Personal Property

Though boys brought personal property to school more often, the girls at Sunshine Head Start brought special things too. But what happened to girls and their property afterwards differed sharply. Keisha's experience illustrates this. Keisha had dark brown skin and liked to have pink pompoms at the end of her braids. She was a quiet child at the start of the year, but she became more talkative as the year went on. Keisha's grandma was raising her; Keisha called her mom.

During breakfast, Keisha entered with her mom. "Look it, look it my dress," Keisha said excitedly to the class at large. She hurried to unzip her sweater and remove her thick black snow pants to show us the dress underneath. "I got a blue dress! My mom got it for me!" Keisha pointed to the blue and silver star on the middle of the dress.

Julian's mom was nearby, signing in her son. "Yes, very nice," she said absently.

Keisha's mom laughed a little.

For Keisha, this dress was special. She used it to start a conversation with her peers. Both boys and girls occasionally highlighted clothing that was special to them—Spiderman pajamas, new shoes, sparkly skirts. When Sunshine Head Start children prized clothing, they were able to keep it on their person all day and showcase it to others whenever they wanted.

Keisha also sometimes brought outfit accessories to school. I only saw girls bring accessories at Sunshine Head Start, such as bracelets, headbands, and ponytail holders. These items were in a gray area relative to the classroom rule—they were not toys per se, though I did see girls play with them as such. They were also not clothing, and girls would sometimes keep them in their pocket, more like a toy or a trinket than a part of an outfit. Yet I never saw teachers take these personal objects from girls.

On a frigid January morning, my bus was late. By the time I arrived, the class was already eating breakfast.

As I hung up my coat, Keisha told me, "I got a pink headband."

"Where is it?" I asked.

"In my pocket."

"Why aren't you wearing it?

"'Cause I am at preschool," she replied. Keisha struggled to extract it from her pocket, which was sealed tight because she was sitting down. She pulled it free and held it up for me to see. It was what I would call a cloth "scrunchie" ponytail holder.

I nodded approvingly and she returned to eating.

"You can't touch it, it's my pink headband," she said. "Ms. Julie, I have a pink headband."

Ms. Julie didn't respond.

Just as Julian prized his Iron Man toy, Keisha prized her pink headband. Like Julian, she showed her special object to adults, who were mostly uninterested. She also stored it carefully in her pocket. But this happened without incident or struggles with teachers wanting her to put it in her cubby.

When girls brought something special from home, it was almost always clothing or an accessory like Keisha's pink headband. Accordingly, they could put it in their pocket or on their wrist and keep it. My count of all instances when I observed children bring personal things to Sunshine Head Start revealed a gendered pattern. Boys brought action figures most often, followed by games, books, and toy cars. In all but one instance, girls brought outfit accessories.

Keisha kept the headband in her pocket for most of that day, pulling it out at various times to admire it, or to show others. The battles that Julian and other boys experienced while trying to enjoy their personal property at school were notably absent for the girls in the class. The result was a system of punishment toward boys of color. Nearly 70 percent of the time, boys who brought property had it taken away.

Race was linked closely with gendered punishment, reinforced by the classroom demographics wherein most boys were boys of color. Of the two white boys in the class, one—Sam—was punished for bringing in property. Overall, struggles over personal property moments resulting in behavior correction affected boys of color disproportionately.[6]

Girls may have had special toys that they wanted to bring but did not, in which case they heeded the classroom rules more fully than boys did.

However, in having the means to bring personal accessories to school, the Sunshine Head Start girls were afforded some small chance to customize their classroom experience—they brought a personal emblem to school that they could use to display to peers, to play with absently, and to keep as a special token throughout the day.

Classroom Rules Allowing Personal Property at Great Beginnings

When it came to classroom experiences of accessing property, the Great Beginnings teachers made rules that were possible because of families' resources. The schools' understanding of their families as affluent was apparent with the monthly fundraisers they did. In February, the school fundraiser was a toy and coat drive for the Head Start preschools in the city.

While the class lined up next to the donation area, I noticed three boxes overflowing with toys and winter coats.

A child commented on the many toys.

"Yes," Ms. Erica replied. "Do you know who those toys are for? Did you know some kids don't have toys to play with?"

The kids stared up at her.

"And don't you think every kid should have a toy to play with?"

Several kids nodded. Others said, "Yeah."

"Yeah," said Ms. Erica. "And since you have a lot of toys at home, we are being helpful and giving these toys to other kids."

"My mom told me that too," Esther said.

Smiling slightly, Carter said he did not have a lot of toys at home.

"Oh, I bet you do," Ms. Erica replied, returning his smile.

Ms. Erica assumed that the children had ample toys, enough to donate to needier Head Start families. The Great Beginnings children were not experiencing extreme material hardships like eviction or homelessness. But despite this obvious difference, their parents likely had a different orientation to buying toys. For these families, choices to not buy toys were likely about values or clutter rather than about sheer inability to do so.

Sociologist Allison Pugh found that affluent families practiced "symbolic deprivation," sometimes denying their children's requests for toys in order to show moral worthiness.[7] Here, the preschool's fundraiser underlined moral worthiness of a different kind—not just that these affluent families avoid material excess but that they give some of their abundance to others.

Given the material abundance among their students' families, Great Beginnings teachers did not express worries about jealousy from kids who had no toys. Instead, they created three teacher-approved ways for children to enjoy personal property at school. First, teachers held weekly Show-and-Tell. Children had to bring in something that matched the letter of the week. After displaying it and talking about it with their peers, the kids could take the object along with them throughout the day to play with it. Second, the teachers allowed each child to bring a stuffed animal from home during nap time. The kids would cuddle and sometimes quietly play with these during nap time. Third, the teachers encouraged children to bring books from home, which the teachers would then read to the class.

Personal Property as Celebrated

Though children's access to personal property was still supervised and controlled by teachers, these white, middle-class children experienced their preschool classroom as inviting them to customize their school experience through property. In fact, rituals like Show-and-Tell celebrated children's personal property.

Show-and-Tell allowed each child to stand in the spotlight and display an object they loved. During this ritual, a teacher called on each child individually. When they heard their name, the child skipped to their cubby. Hiding their item behind their back, the child shuffled carefully back to the rug, where they beamed as they revealed it to their peers. The class then asked questions about the object. After that, the child could choose to bring their object with them throughout the play centers. Show-and-Tell let children practice being in the spotlight and having the stage in front of their peers. It fostered a particular way of being in the world—and a sense that children's personal property was worthy of individual recognition.

The celebration of personal property that began with Show-and-Tell then extended into enjoyment of that property throughout the day. In this way, one day per week, the children had the pleasure of using a special object while at school.

Katrina brought a stuffed orca whale. She asked the teacher if she could put it in a center.

Smiling conspiratorially, the teacher said, "What do you think I will say?"

"Yes?" Katrina replied, with a shy smile.

"Yes," the teacher confirmed, still smiling warmly. Two other kids asked if they could bring their Show-and-Tell items with them to a center, and the teacher said yes.

The kids' questions were rhetorical here; on Show-and-Tell day, the teachers always allowed all the kids to bring their property to centers to play with throughout the day. The Show-and-Tell ritual went beyond what Sunshine Head Start children could do with their snuck-in personal property. The class had extended, teacher-facilitated conversations about each child's property. Then, the kids played with their personal property under the approving eyes of teachers.

Sometimes the celebration of personal property reinforced connections among the children. In three of the four Show-and-Tells I observed, there were some children who brought the exact same object.[8] For example, during "O week," three kids brought the same thing: stuffed owls. For "N" week, Ryan brought a wooden tool set and showed the nails to the class. Charlie said he had the same toy at home. When children brought in identical items, Show-and-Tell promoted peer connections about their shared possessions. Bringing the same property is an instance when kids customize the school environment and find another commonality with a peer. At Sunshine Head Start, these types of moments were precluded by the rules forbidding personal property.

Children's sense of entitlement to customize experiences through personal property was clear one morning at drop-off, when Ryan forgot his Show-and-Tell item.

Ryan's father made an extra trip home to get something for him. Since the letter of the week was "O," Ryan's father returned with an ocean-themed playdough kit.

"That's not the one I was thinking of," Ryan said.

A teacher stepped in. "Well, Ryan, it was very nice of your father to go all the way back home to get it. Maybe if he has time, he can stop back for something else. But right now, he has to go to work. You can also bring in the other thing tomorrow."

Ryan's father changed his routine to accommodate his son, something not possible for shift workers—many of whom are poor or working class—who need to "clock in." But Ryan was still dissatisfied; the teacher then negotiated another possibility for Ryan. While Ryan did not get everything he wanted, he experienced his father and teacher taking time to ensure that he had the chance to bring a personal object to school. The teacher even offered Ryan the chance to bring in his toy outside of Show-and-Tell day. Adult authority figures slowed down and changed the rules to ensure that Ryan had the chance to customize school with the object he wanted.

Most of the Great Beginnings children brought personal property through the three teacher-approved channels. Even the rule allowing a stuffed animal at nap time created an opportunity to bring something special. As the class was settling onto their mats for nap time, Gabby said, "Chloe, you have a unicorn dolphin [stuffed animal]?"

"Yeah," Chloe replied.

"I do too. I'll bring mine tomorrow when I come, and you bring yours too."

Overall, the Great Beginnings children enjoyed two teacher-supported pathways to bring treasured personal items to school. All the Great Beginnings children were able to bring a nap-time object that they could switch out during the year, and every week they chose something personal to bring in.

Personal Property as Supported

Despite looking out daily for moments when the Great Beginnings children snuck in personal property outside these channels, I did not see that happening. However, one child, Owen, talked about personal toys a lot, and sometimes brought things in outside of the usual channels. However, he did it in full view of his parents and teachers.

Owen was a wiry boy with pale skin and inquisitive brown eyes. His mom traveled a fair amount for work and tended to bring him things when she returned from these trips. Owen was also reprimanded more than most of the other children, after behavioral missteps like poking a kid during Group Time and distracting other kids while lining up.

With the opportunity afforded them by teachers encouraging kids to bring books, Owen and his mom communicated that they were working on his behavior. At drop-off one day, Owen approached Ms. Paula and showed her the book he was carrying. "It's called *Know and Follow All the Rules*," he said. Owen's mom told Ms. Paula that they had been reading it at home. Ms. Paula said they would read it at school that day, too.

Owen's family was attempting to solve his problem through buying an object—a book. He then showcased this item at school, and the teachers supported his ownership in it by reading it to the class. This moment shows a family trying to save face but also a family able to acquire property to solve problems.

But while Owen's family acquired a book to demonstrate that they were working on his behavior, some of the teachers believed he had too many possessions in general, and that this explained some of his misbehavior.

I joined Owen at the art table. I had heard him mention a brother before, so I asked him if he had a brother.

"I have a brother and a sister. But not people ones. They are cats."

"Oh, cool," I said.

Then Owen told me that one of his cats had to have surgery because it swallowed one of his toys and they had to go in and cut it out. His mom had to have surgery too. The baby in her belly died and she had to have surgery to take it out.

Ms. Paula came over and told him to put his name on his art. He wrote his name.

"Where is your mom right now?" Ms. Paula asked.

"She's home."

"I thought she went on a trip?"

"She did, but she came back last night when I was sleeping. She brought me Legos and some more toys because I was good. And she gave me lots of candy too."

"Oh," replied Ms. Paula.

Later that day, Owen mentioned to a friend that he had lots of new toys. I overheard one teacher comment to another, "Yeah, and that's why he is the way he is."

Owen stood out as talking about toys and gifts he received frequently. Nonetheless, the teachers participated in letting Owen showcase his toys to friends. They still recognized his personal property as important.

One day, Owen brought a toy to the classroom, sparking an extended, teacher-approved discussion about his property.

Owen entered with his mom, toting an elaborate Lego toy the size of a shoebox. Ms. Paula told him to go show it to his friends so that his mom could take it home.

"Yeah," his mom confirmed, "show your friends the features."

Owen brought the toy to the table where Ruby, Chloe, and I were working on a hundred-piece puzzle. Ruby was really interested in the toy. "Let me show you the features," Owen told her. "This door opens, and this one."

As he was showing Ruby the toy, Gavin came in with his dad. "Hi, Owen, I have to tell you something. Remember that toy you got me for my birthday?"

"Yeah," Owen replied.

"I don't really play with that yet—"

"Is it the Pirate Legos?" Owen's mom interjected.

"Yeah."

"We love those," said Owen's mom. "We give them to a lot of kids."

Owen continued showing Ruby the features, while his mom stood over the kids, waiting to take the toy with her and go to work. "You got that with your allowance, right? For doing chores?" she said.

"Yeah." Owen glanced at Ruby and said, "I got this with my allowance."[9]

This moment sharply contrasted with the indifference that adults at Sunshine Head Start displayed toward kids' property. Here, both a parent and a teacher indulged in an extended conversation about a child's toy. This was the only time I saw a Great Beginnings kid bring in a toy outside of Show-and-Tell. Owen's teacher encouraged him to show it to others before taking it home. However, the teachers' support of Owen's enjoyment of the Lego toy had limits. Ms. Paula did not allow him to keep it all day; she made that clear by instructing his mom to take it with her.

At Sunshine Head Start, Julian was the analogous child—he often brought new and impressive toys to school, as well as other property. Yet Owen and Julian could not have had more different experiences. Julian had no teacher-approved ways to bring his personal property to school. Without being able to label his property to fit the letter of the week, or to declare a toy his nap-time companion, he could choose to leave property at home, or to sneak it in. He snuck it in. This meant that when Julian enjoyed his personal property, he did so while hiding it from teachers. When Great Beginnings kids like Owen enjoyed personal property, it was with their teachers' blessing.

Under the vastly different property rules in each classroom, kids' struggles to enjoy their personal property ultimately resulted in Sunshine Head Start children—all from poor families and most from families of color—being forbidden from customizing their school experience by bringing their personal property into school. In contrast, the middle-class, white children at Great Beginnings had scheduled, teacher-approved times to enjoy their property at school—showing it to teachers and peers, indeed with a captive audience at Show-and-Tell, and then playing with it in their own way while at school.

The Consequences of Unequal Property Access

Class and race segregation concentrated family scarcity within one classroom and family abundance within another. Responding to these conditions, teachers created disparate rules about personal property. For Sunshine Head Start children, being unable to bring property to school with teacher approval led most of them to not bring personal property at all. Other children, mostly boys of color, reacted to the strict classroom rules by repeatedly sneaking items in, which they sometimes had taken from them. In contrast, teacher-approved rituals like Show-and-Tell celebrated property at Great Beginnings. These white, middle-class children largely used these institutionally supported rituals to enjoy their property.

Some developmental psychologists advocate for the use of what they call transitional objects—items that children deem special and that can be used both at home and at school.[10] A transitional object symbolizes bonds with home and can be used semi-autonomously by toddlers as they navigate transitions between home and school. But these scholars typically focus on one resonant object—such as a pacifier, beloved stuffed animal, or blanket. The perspective of developmental psychologists shows that early in children's short lives, attachment to a personal object may be highly significant. Scholar and early childhood teacher

Colleen Goddard advocates that teachers and parents not force children to give up these objects, and instead set boundaries for how the children can enjoy their transitional object while doing classroom activities.[11] In my observations, some children prized personal property longer into early childhood, but with different degrees of institutionally supported access.

Though the children could not access their personal property at school, they technically had access to a wealth of classroom toys. But as I discussed in chapter 2, children's access to the blocks, dress-up property, baby dolls, crayons, and other classroom supplies was ultimately controlled by teachers. Teachers controlled when free play time happened and how long it lasted. When it was over, the children had to put the communal toys away. These toys and supplies then sat enclosed in bins until teachers specified another time to play. Ownership of classroom property was ultimately shared across children, and access to this property was mediated by teachers. Further, though I saw children favor certain toys and declare the toy "theirs" for the free play period, this property was not personal to the children. Classroom property did not symbolize children's tastes and identities in the same way as Keisha's sparkle dress, Julian's Iron Man, and Owen's Lego toy.

These kids' experiences expand our understanding of unequal childhoods. Sociologist Annette Lareau contends that poor and working-class children are given more control over their time, while affluent children spend more time in adult-controlled activities.[12] When we turn to control over property at preschool, children's unequal experiences occurred differently. At Sunshine Head Start, poor children of color were denied the autonomy to control property. They were instead controlled and held to institutional rules. The affluent, white Great Beginnings kids were also held to institutional rules—but these rules were designed to recognize, and even celebrate, their personal property. Ultimately, the Great Beginnings children had a greater degree of control over property.

Despite the construction of preschool as compensatory for poor children's "inadequate" home environments, in the case of property access, preschools are operating similarly to classed home environments. Affluent, white children are being recognized as individuals with unique interests to be supported, and teachers do this through adult-sponsored activities like Show-and-Tell. Poor children of color are recognized as needing to ultimately conform to the rules of the classroom when it comes to property. When we recognize that personal property can be a means to customize the school environment, then the fact that poor children of color face limits to their ability to personalize an institutional experience is not surprising; poor people of color face these experiences in K–12 schooling, workplaces, and other institutions.[13] Here, we see this process starting at age four.

More integrated preschools might reshape the pressures and opportunities that shape teachers' policies. Short of desegregation and eradicating child poverty and structural racism, though, teachers working in segregated classrooms could consider different approaches. Teachers could adapt Show-and-Tell to cater to children with few personal possessions. Children could be encouraged to display anything they find special, including found property from outside, their favorite classroom toys, and property from home. This would offer an institutionalized pathway to enjoy access to property and may inculcate poor children's sense of entitlement to some personalization and control over the school experience. Meanwhile, preschools serving middle-class children might consider more concrete ways to curtail children's entitlement to property. Show-and-Tell could feature found property in nature so that middle-class children spend less time showcasing toys that people had bought them.

While these preschools' rules about property reflect class segregation and the corresponding differences in families' resources, children's experience of these divergent contexts *reproduces* class and race inequality. Other sociologists have shown that while poor and working-class children defer to and accommodate institutional rules, middle-class children tend to negotiate these rules to meet their individual needs. When schools—often middle-class, white institutions in their orientations—respond well to entitlement but not to deference, then white, middle-class children accrue advantages.[14] Early experiences of property access in these two preschools only played into these inequalities.

Paige and Sam gave me a ride to Sunshine Head Start. I sat in the front seat.

"Casey, look!" Sam called from his car seat in the back. He showed me a book and a small yellow plastic figurine. "I got a book and a Bumblebee [a *Transformer* action figure]. I can read this book. I can read it to you."

Paige told me, in a low voice, "It took him a few days to realize [the action figure] was fake."

On the way into Ms. Roxanne's class, he showed the book and Bumblebee to Ms. Ashley at the front desk. Paige quipped awkwardly to Ashley about the action figure toy being fake. Inside the classroom, Sam showed Ms. Roxanne his book.

"Cool," she remarked.

After that, Sam informed me, "I'm gonna put it in my cubby and we can take it out later." As we prepared the tables for breakfast, Julian arrived. He was clutching a giant Bumblebee toy. The real one. It was the size of a college textbook and twice the size of Sam's toy.

The boys talked for a minute about how they had the same toy.

Ms. Roxanne interjected, "Okay, I need Sam and I need Julian. You guys need to put your stuff in the bin."

They whined a little bit but ultimately complied.

Sam sat back down next to me at the breakfast table. He was frowning. "It's gone, the book is gone," he said.

"The book is gone?"

"Yeah."

"When do you get it back?"

"If I am a good boy, I can have it back after school."

DON'T TALK ABOUT DISNEYWORLD

The Surveillance of Families

Briana, a Black woman who either was quiet or speaking quickly, had enrolled three children at Sunshine Head Start over the years. Her youngest child, Shawn, now attended. For years, she had been a job coach for people with disabilities. But when Shawn was three years old, her car broke down and needed a six-thousand-dollar repair. She also moved to a new house, adding to her bills. So Briana picked up a night shift job as a home health aide to catch up. She told me about this during an interview at the close of my observations at her son's preschool. She said, "It was really hard, because I would work from 10:00 p.m. to 6:00 a.m., come home, get Shawn dressed, and then bring him here, and then go to my 8:00 a.m. to 2:00 p.m. job."

I asked her when she would sleep.

"I didn't. I would doze off maybe from 3:00 a.m. to maybe 5:00. I just, I needed to do what I needed to do."

But because Sunshine Head Start had income-based copays, the extra income from her second job had a financial ripple effect for Briana. She told me,

Once I started the other job, my daycare went ridiculously high. I'm still in the hole with them, the lady, the new lady [the social worker], she's actually trying to fight it to where either I don't have to pay . . . It was like thirty-five dollars a week, and I was working both of those jobs, but all that money was spoken for. But they've been really good with working with me I think because I've been here so long, and I've never really been behind until last year, like everything just started happening, happening, so that's how we ended up.

"Yeah, because what do you usually pay?" I asked.
"It's about fifteen dollars a week."
And Briana had another cost to contend with.

Then, in the process of everything, this really sounds not good, but I went through a travel agent, and I was planning a trip to Disney[world]. So because I did it before the car broke down, I still had to pay. Because I'd already been five hundred dollars in, and the money would have been gone, and our plane tickets—I had to pay that in full—that would have been gone too. So I kept the second job until I got the car fixed, paid the Disney trip off.

I've been feeling more stressful lately. I'm not sure if it's because of the holidays, or because of my mom [passing away], but yes, I am very stressful now. It's just everything, I just feel like if it's not one thing, it's another, like I can never get ahead. Like we don't really have nothing, so it's like I really can't afford to try to issue out more money for anything until after we get back from this trip [to Disneyworld]. I don't want to get down there and be like . . . You know I probably would never be able to take them again, so I want them to do whatever they want to do while we're there. I don't want to be like no, we can't do this because I don't have the money.

"So much responsibility," I said.
"It sure is. I'm stressed, believe me," Briana said.
Briana asked me not to tell the teachers about her Disneyworld trip, though she assumed they would find out afterwards. She felt she had to hide the fact that she was planning a fun trip because she was behind on child care copays. In my two years at Sunshine Head Start, this was the first time I had heard anyone talk about Disneyworld. Because we were in Wisconsin, traveling to Florida for an amusement park trip was

a luxury to offer one's children. With Christmas and her Disneyworld trip coming up, both joyful but financially straining occasions, Briana was swimming in stress.

A few months after I interviewed Briana, I was observing the children at Great Beginnings. We were seated around the table, eating breakfast that was served "family style," meant to mimic the feel of a meal around a family dinner table. While I dished out food for the kids, Gabby mentioned something about Disneyworld. I asked her if she had been there.

"No," she said. "I just know about it."

I asked the other kids at the table if they had been. Kyle, Ruby, and Chloe—half of the kids at the table—said they had been before.

On a different day, Ms. Paula was letting the kids take turns talking about whatever they wanted in front of the class.

Kyle raised his hand and asked for a turn. Once he was standing next to Ms. Paula, looking down at his classmates seated on the rug, he said, "We are going to Disneyworld to go to Jedi training camp. Last time we went on a plane, but this time we are going in a car."

Ms. Paula prompted the class to ask Kyle questions if they wanted.

Ruby, who had been to Disneyworld herself, asked where he would eat breakfast. Another child asked how he would defeat the Jedi.

* * *

Preschool classrooms are communities that draw together teachers, children, and families. They are embodiments of the village it takes to raise a child. For many families, the preschool is a key partner in raising their children. Storytelling and sharing information knit a fabric of connection between families and school. In a real village, communities talk about disruptions to the ordinary routine, celebrate together, and come together to share space.

Each of these things happened in the two preschools. But each preschool was an institution and had rules and practices that set the terms for family engagement. At Sunshine Head Start, family-engagement practices were embedded in larger policies of scrutiny directed at poor families of color. The result was distance between children, families, and teachers in talk, in celebrations, and in decisions to share space. At Great Beginnings, the preschool's family-engagement practices were based on parents being presumed adequate at raising children. The result was relative openness between children, families, and teachers in talk, in celebrations, and in opportunities to share space.

Briana's experience of Disneyworld illustrates the challenges of open conversation in her segregated village. Her trip was a disruption to the normal routine, albeit a happy one that she had worked hard to create. Her son was sure to talk about it when he returned. Yet even this joyful event became something she felt she could not talk about, given the deeply layered policies for the subsidy she received to send her child to Head Start. She decided to hide these upcoming happy plans from her son's preschool.

In contrast to Briana's uncomfortable silence about her upcoming, once-in-a-lifetime vacation, the four-year-olds at Great Beginnings talked openly and with relish about repeated trips to Disneyworld—not just casually at mealtimes, but in front of the whole class and with their teachers' support. This kind of open talk was possible because their families' finances were not required to be under scrutiny by the preschool.

The different terms under which families and schools engaged with one another stemmed from two connected issues. First, race and class inequality meant that Sunshine Head Start families more often experienced disruptions to their routines that were stigmatized—such as incarceration, domestic violence, and housing instability. These things happen more often to poor people and people of color because of inequality. Segregation divided unequal families, so that there were many stigmatized disruptions to family life at Sunshine Head Start, and few stigmatized disruptions to family life at Great Beginnings.[1]

Second, the two segregated villages were under different layers of classed, racialized policies. Policies for poor families operate under the auspice of protecting children but often require surveillance of families to assess whether they truly "deserve" help. Such policies of surveillance intermingle with structural racism, which has included decades of residential segregation and racial profiling.[2] Structural racism further pushes Black, Hispanic, and Indigenous families into poverty at higher rates than white families.[3] Given segregation and structural racism, even middle-class Black families have family and neighbors who are experiencing material hardship. This means that the specter of state intervention in family life—through policing, courts, eviction, or child protective services—is more likely to be woven into the stories of families of color.[4]

Some Sunshine Head Start families brought this knowledge to their interactions with the preschool.

But Head Start also had multilayered policies designed to support children in some cases, and to prove families' worthiness to funders in other cases. This resulted in an institutional source of scrutiny of families. The "whole-child" approach of Head Start, designed to holistically benefit children, can have the side effect of whole-child and whole-family surveillance. Head Start families have a preschool that knows about parents' working hours month to month, their child's dental hygiene and physical health, and the state of their housing. Part of the social contract of Head Start involves minimum participation standards that give the preschool a view into family life. Beyond this minimum participation, if families wanted more connection to the school and the teachers, they could get this through whole-hearted involvement in school-sponsored events and in mandated home visits.

In contrast, Great Beginnings operated privately and under the presumption that children's families were competent to provide for their children's general well-being. This resulted in institutional indifference about holistic aspects of family life. Great Beginnings families had a preschool that assumed parents were working as they needed to, that they were brushing their children's teeth at home, and that they had safe, adequate housing. Parents could choose to use Great Beginnings for child care without divulging specifics of their family life. If families wanted more connection to the school and the teachers, they could get this through hiring teachers to work as babysitters within their homes. These families had the luxury of either enjoying privacy or seeking additional closeness on their own terms.

By tracing the pathways of conversations about disruptions to family life—from vacations to breakups to moves—at each school, we can see how segregation and inequality are, once again, at play. Inequality affected the types of family disruptions at each school, and segregation concentrated these family disruptions in one school but not in another.

Fractured Talk about Family Disruptions at Sunshine Head Start

Sunshine Head Start was dealing with the challenge of families having disruptive, stigmatized life events. These took place amid policies of scrutiny.

All teachers are mandated reporters of child abuse or neglect. If teachers see signs that indicate a child might be experiencing physical abuse or neglect, they are supposed to call a hotline to alert Child Protective Services (CPS). CPS decides whether they believe the report warrants further investigation. Because of inequality and segregation, however, institutions like Sunshine Head Start that serve high numbers of poor families are more likely to confront concerns of neglect and to be in the position to make a report.[5] In this way, the state's mandated reporting policy felt closer to home at Sunshine Head Start than it might for an affluent preschool.

The four-year-old children at Sunshine Head Start partially discussed or enacted family disruptions. Families kept some information private from teachers. Teachers, however, avoided direct talk with children about family disruptions, though they did gossip among themselves when bits of information came through.

At Sunshine Head Start, children enacted pretend-play scenes that depicted family challenges. Jasmine was a four-year-old girl with dark brown hair down to her waist and large brown eyes that sparkled when she talked about her little sister.

Jasmine took a portable phone and went a few feet away from the House Area. Alicia remained in the play kitchen and called Jasmine from there.

"*Amiga*," Alicia said. (Friend.)

"*Yah?*" Jasmine replied.

"*Yo no tengo comida.*" (I don't have food.)

"*Mi tengo comida*," Jasmine said. (I have food)

Alicia asked, "*Puedo venir?*" (Can I come over?)

"*No, mi casa esta cerrado*," said Jasmine. (No, my house is closed.)

"*Bueno*," said Alicia. (Okay.)

"*Amiga?*" Jasmine said. (Friend?)

"*Yah?*

"*Oye, esta lloviendo*," Jasmine noted. (Hey, it's raining.)

"Okay, *no puedo venir porque esta lloviendo.*" (Okay, I can't come because it's raining.)

Jasmine and Alicia mentioned real-world problems of not having food, their house being "closed," and staying home to avoid the rain.

Children drew on their family experiences in pretend play, sometimes with improvisation. I saw the Sunshine Head Start kids act out breakups, not having milk, not having lights, going to jail, and having no money for the bus. In some cases, I knew that these were real-world challenges their families had faced. The children did not censor these family hardships out of their play. This shows that the kids saw their family stressors as worthy of mention at school.

However, there was a distance between children's mention of family hardship and adults' direct conversation about it. Teachers generally did not discuss family challenges with children—even events that children brought up. Instead, when teachers would overhear or observe something that flagged a concern about children's behavior, they gossiped.

During a nap time in early March, I was sitting between Luz's and Mia's mats. Jasmine came over and sat on my lap. I told her that she should go to her mat to sleep. But instead of returning to her mat, she told me a story. "When I was little, only one year, I used to sleep in the bed with my mom and my dad. But then one day I told them there was a monster in my room. And so my mom got up and told the monster to go away."

"Did it work?" I asked her.

"No."

"The monster is still there?"

"Yeah."

Luz piped in, "No, silly, it's just a dream."

Ms. Lisa was seated across the room, with her back to the wall behind the Circle Rug. She was rubbing Sam's back. In a rough whisper, Ms. Lisa asked, "Casey, is she talking to you about her mom?"

"Not really, she's telling me about a bad dream."

About a minute later, I told the girls they were too chatty and so I was going to leave. I moved closer to Sam, who was now asleep, and Ms. Lisa. "Yeah, she wasn't really telling me about her mom," I repeated.

She raised her eyebrows significantly. "Yeah, well, there's stuff going on."

"What happened?"

"She hit the girlfriend of the D-A-D, and she's in jail right now." She paused and looked over at Jasmine, checking that she was not listening. I looked, too.

"So mom's in jail, like right now," Ms. Lisa continued. "She went a few days ago."

"Oh? So who's taking care of the kids?

"Well that one [Ms. Lisa pointed to Jasmine] is being watched by her D-A-D. But I think mom wants the little one [Jasmine's younger sibling] to go with her brother."

"Dang," I replied. I couldn't think of anything else to say.

"Yeah," Ms. Lisa said grimly.

Teachers used spellings and whispering to ensure that kids didn't overhear. In this way, they censored talk about family hardship from the children.

A week after that nap-time conversation, Ms. Roxanne brought up Jasmine's family events. I came in around lunchtime. Ms. Roxanne told me that things had been dramatic that morning. "Luz hit Alicia. Jasmine and Luz were saying they weren't friends with each other, then nobody was friends with Gabe. Yeah, and I guess some pretty intense stuff is going on with Jasmine," she said. "Like apparently her mom put herself in front of the car door of her dad, so that his girlfriend wouldn't come out. And so that makes sense. 'Cause I noticed she's been acting different for about two weeks. And I thought it was just 'cause of . . .'"

"The friend stuff?" I finished.

"Yeah. Or like things happening between the kids. But it would make sense that if things are going on at home, maybe her parents are being a little violent or something."

Another week later, the class was on the playground for morning Outside Time. It was almost spring, and we could see the woodchips peeking through the snow for the first time since the fall. The teachers were talking about Jasmine, Luz, and Alicia being mean to each other. Ms. Julie said,

It's been like a week of this. It's funny—Luz is being mean and even Jasmine is mean. They're excluding Gabe. But the good thing is that he at least goes and gets a teacher. You know, the school social worker told me that she saw something happen here one morning with Jasmine's mom and dad, where the mom wanted to talk to the dad, but he didn't want to, and the girlfriend like had her body blocking the door and wouldn't let her through. So I'm thinking that if she's seeing that at home, maybe that's why she's acting . . . I don't wanna say aggressive, but like, meaner.

The teachers were often searching for explanations for children's behaviors, and so when they did get bits of information about home stressors, they seized on these details. Being attuned to children's home lives is thought of as good teaching. Yet often what I observed was that teachers sought information about family traumas through gossip rather than through direct conversation.

Parents sometimes selectively managed the information that Sunshine Head Start had access to, choosing only some aspects of their lives to submit for potential scrutiny. Jasmine's family incident stood out because it took place in the school parking lot, so the teachers and administrators had an unusual, full view of what had happened. But normally, teachers were afraid to ask parents and children questions about challenging family events for fear of seeming prying. They articulated this as a vague fear of "trouble." And so instead of open conversations with families, the teachers speculated among themselves—especially if they suspected that something negative at home explained children's challenging behavior at school. While sitting down to interview Ms. Julie in the staff break room, I asked her, "If you feel like you know what's going on—like you know someone's in a housing transition, or a parent went to jail—does that make it any easier to deal with [the difficult behaviors]?"

Ms. Julie replied, "No, because if the kids, you know, aren't talking about it, I don't feel comfortable asking the questions, because it could be leading. And I don't know if it could possibly get back home, and in trouble. So unless they actually say something to me, or I'm told by the parents, or somebody I work with . . ."

"Is that kind of rare that you get the details like that?" I asked.

"Yeah."

Ms. Julie implied that if kids were already talking about family events, that would be an opening for her to ask further questions. However, I observed several moments when kids talked openly about family challenges—having the lights turned off, a grandparent sent to jail earlier in the week, etc.—and teachers brushed past it. In two years, I never observed a teacher engage in an open conversation with a child about a family challenge.

Further, Ms. Julie invoked a vague notion of "trouble." This illustrates the sense of distance baked into Sunshine Head Start's communication with poor families and its layered programmatic requirements. Teachers worried that children might repeat incomplete details of a conversation. Then, parents might assume bad intentions on the teachers' part—such as that they might be implying the parents were neglecting their child or that something was wrong at home. This is a genuine possibility with four-year-olds, who can be eager but sometimes unreliable narrators of conversations.[6] The teachers expressed a desire for open flows of information, but their actions showed reluctance to come off as monitoring families. At the same time, families may have been reluctant to share information about family challenges given the long history of poor families being monitored and even punished by institutions.[7]

As a result, information sharing about family disruptions was incomplete at Sunshine Head Start. Family disruptions become teacher-to-teacher conversations—whispered during nap time, or with key words spelled out (such as saying "J-A-I-L" instead of "jail") to avoid kids overhearing and repeating the information at home.

Teachers applied a loose lens of "concern" for children but did not use such concern to have open conversations with families. The issue of teachers' loose concerns and families' desire to not be seen as warranting concern is especially clear in the case of absences from preschool. Head Start programs are required to track each child's attendance. If a child has more than two unexplained absences, the program must do a home visit or make contact with a parent. Children are not supposed to miss more than 10 percent of school days.[8] This rule meant that families must account for daily disruptions to their child attending school. Families cannot just inform the preschool that they are not coming; they need to explain and justify their daily decisions to Sunshine Head Start.

Occasionally, I witnessed families go beyond a phone call and come into the preschool to explain absences. In these moments, families attempted to control the narrative of their child's absence and, hopefully, the scrutiny that teachers and administrators would apply to them.

Late into the morning, when Work Time was well underway, Isaac and his mom entered. His mom was wearing a t-shirt and jeans, instead of her work uniform. Isaac was wearing his favorite Spiderman rain boots. He was crying softly.

"Hi, Isaac!" Ms. Julie said cheerfully.

He didn't answer.

Isaac's mom began talking quietly to Ms. Julie. She explained that Isaac hadn't gotten much sleep the previous night, and that he was going to stay with his grandma that day, but that she just needed to talk to the front desk person first. Then his mom said goodbye and the pair left.

Later, Ms. Roxanne asked Ms. Julie if Isaac was coming back and what had happened. Ms. Julie repeated the story: "Mom says that he didn't get much sleep last night so he's staying home with Grandma."

"Hmm," Ms. Lisa intoned, looking skeptical.

Ms. Roxanne added, "That was weird. I've never seen him act like that, crying so much." Later in the day, this story was repeated among teachers and staff a second time.

I do not know what happened that night or why Isaac's mom wanted to talk to the front desk staff. But her hesitation made sense considering Head Start's attendance requirements. Isaac's day home with his grandma, whom he adored and saw regularly, could be understood as important family time. But instead, teachers interpreted it as a cause for concern about Isaac's well-being. Notice, also, teachers' subtle suspicion about Isaac's mom's explanation for his feelings.

The Sunshine Head Start teachers did not talk directly with Isaac or his mom about their concerns. Instead, they talked around the concerns with one another.

A related incident happened with Ms. Paige, who was Sam's mom and worked as a teacher aide in his classroom. Ms. Paige was thus both a worker at the preschool and a scrutinized single mother. She was a white woman from a majority-Black neighborhood in South Bend, Indiana, that she described as "rough." Paige once saw me walking from the bus station to the preschool. She took pity on me and offered me rides sometimes, as she commuted from a similar part of town. One morning she picked me up at 8:45 a.m., about an hour later than usual. As I approached the car, Sam rolled down his window to greet me.

As she pulled away from my house, she said, "Sam is sick. I knew something was up. He was a little funny at the lake yesterday. We went after school and he was playing and stuff but then he'd stop and come up to me and just stare. And then he knocked out [fell asleep] last night. And today he told me he doesn't feel good. But I was like, well, let's go to school, let's just try. That way they can see it for themselves."

"Yeah, good idea," I said. "'Cause they'll totally be different about it if it's their idea [for Sam and Paige to stay home]."

I entered the classroom, but they lagged behind.

Ms. Lisa said brightly, "Hey Casey! You're missing two people. Paige and Sam?"

"Oh yeah. They're just behind me. Sam's sick."

"What?"

"Yeah, you'll see in a second," I replied.

Sam and Paige entered, but Sam stopped just beyond the front door. He stood quietly—unusual behavior for him.

"Hi, Sam, do you want to have some breakfast?" Ms. Roxanne asked.

Sam remained quiet for a few seconds. Then he burst into tears. Paige crouched down to his level and asked softly, "Oh buddy, what's wrong?"

Ms. Roxanne turned her chair around to face Sam and echoed, "What's wrong?"

"Like I don't know what your professional opinion is," Ms. Paige said, a slight edge to her voice.

"Well, he doesn't look too good. Just looking at him. And his eyes look a little red. He's not being himself."

"Yeah," said Paige. "I mean that's not how he is."

"Yep," replied Ms. Roxanne. "He's an energetic guy, so this stuff, yeah . . ."

They asked Sam again if he wanted to eat. He nodded. While he was sitting down, but not really eating, his mom took his temperature. Her face darkened as she watched the number climb.

"Yeah, and I gave him Motrin earlier. Okay ninety-nine degrees, not so good. Especially with Motrin, which probably brought it down." Paige sighed. "Well, I didn't want to go home. I know they're not gonna be happy about it."

"Well, what are you supposed to do?" Ms. Lisa said.

"Right."

Paige left to talk to an administrator. Then she returned and said, "Okay, we can go home. Do you wanna go home, Sam?"

He nodded slowly. "Casey, I'm going home."

"That's okay," I said. "That's good. Go home and rest."

Paige felt unable to simply call Sam and herself out of being at Sunshine Head Start for a sick day. She had pressures from two sides: she needed her callout from work to be seen as warranted, and she also needed Sam's absence to be noted as a sick day. To accomplish this, she spent her time and energy bringing Sam into school, putting his sickness on display. She was strategic in having her coworkers—Ms. Roxanne and Ms. Lisa—affirm his sickness so that they would support her staying home.

In general, Paige felt that her job was not supportive of her as a single, poor, working mother, which was ironic given that it was a child care center. Another example of lackluster support occurred when the center closed for professional development days. Paige did not have backup child care or family help. Paying a babysitter for the day would cost more than her daily wages at Sunshine Head Start. Yet the preschool required her to be there and would not let her bring Sam along.

Ultimately, Paige's motherhood was under scrutiny. For all the supports and ease that working at her son's school provided, the fact that the preschool was a Head Start school meant that the school administrators had a wide view of her family life.

Paige's and Isaac's mom's experiences in these two incidents show the disposition toward scrutinizing families for out-of-the-ordinary events. Whether it was a midweek absence or a domestic violence incident, when family disruptions happened, the conversations around them were fractured among teachers, children, and families.

Restricted Celebrations

Head Start had more formal policies about celebrations. Just like the attendance policy, which aimed to promote positive school experiences but sometimes created friction, the celebration policy had purportedly positive aims of being broadly supportive to families. At Head Start, policies around holidays were like those at public schools, where schools are not supposed to make one religiously based holiday supreme. Head Start wanted the teachers to check with each family before celebrating a single holiday.

This policy would be slightly onerous at any school. But in the segregated context of Sunshine Head Start, where a third of the children were often recently enrolled, teachers did not always know families well. The holiday policy caused upset among teachers and some families.

During Work Time, Julian pointed at Ms. Roxanne's shirt and shouted, "Halloween!"

Ms. Roxanne laughed. Her shirt was white with faint outlines of pumpkins and ghosts.

"Well, he said it," Ms. Roxanne remarked. "We can't do jack-o-lanterns at school, but they didn't say anything about shirts. We can cut pumpkins because it's science—you know, the seeds and the different sizes. But we can't cut into their sides and do faces or designs, because then it's a jack-o-lantern. Well, we could, but we'd have to get permission from all the parents. In the past there's been a Jehovah's Witness family, and they don't do anything, not even birthdays."

Ms. Roxanne and the other teachers told me that they enjoyed celebrating holidays. According to Ms. Roxanne, the center had previously celebrated holidays quite freely. But recently the school had begun to enforce federal regulations, and now teachers had to get permission from all the parents in advance of each holiday. From Ms. Roxanne's perspective, this was yet another task to add to her very full workload.

Some parents were unhappy with the holiday policy change. On a May morning, we were eating plain Cheerios with bananas for breakfast. Briana entered, holding a sleeping Shawn on her shoulder. A few people called out, "Hi Shawn!" While she signed him in, Briana talked in low tones to Ms. Roxanne. Then she gently nudged Shawn awake and placed him on the floor. Her voice was now audible to the room at large. "Yeah, what happened to Mother's Day stuff?" she said. "I look forward to those things. I save them." She shifted her stance to address the other teachers who were serving breakfast. "I mean he's at daycare anyway. He's gonna scribble, so can't you just put Mother's Day on it?"

Ms. Roxanne said, "Yeah, well, now we're not supposed to do that for holidays. Especially Christmas."

Briana shook her head as she walked toward the door. She stopped near the door, placed a hand on her hip, and said, "Okay, but who wouldn't want their three-year-old to give them something for Mother's Day?"

There was a heavy silence, and then Ms. Roxanne replied, "Well, I'm sorry. I can ask them about it, but . . ."

Briana expelled a harsh sigh and exited. After she closed the door, Shawn went to the door and kicked it, about ten times, scowling.

We ate in silence for about a minute. Ms. Roxanne frowned while checking off the meal count on the clipboard. "I'm getting it from all sides lately," she said, her voice shaking a little. "I guess I can't do anything right. Show me where in my job description it says my job is to make Mother's Day presents? I'm not an arts and crafts leader! I mean, I'll do those if they help with one of the [educational] objectives, but. Sorry your Mother's Day wasn't perfect. That's the least of my worries right now."

To the extent that parents saw teachers as part of their village, it made sense that they would expect collaboration for holidays. Shawn's mom was raising three kids. Her two older kids had attended Sunshine Head Start and had brought home crafts for Mother's Day that she cherished. She had come to expect the teachers to lead Shawn in creating a Mother's Day item for her. Given that Shawn was only three, he would be unlikely to create a gift for his mom without assistance from someone older. But from the teachers' point of view, other time demands were more important than holiday crafts, especially given that doing such crafts might require extra paperwork.

In some cases, the Sunshine Head Start teachers creatively attempted to acknowledge holidays while avoiding conflicts with family preferences and paperwork. To acknowledge Halloween, the Sunshine Head Start teachers decided to have a pajama party. "That way, the kids get to dress in some kind of way, but it's not full Halloween," Ms. Roxanne reasoned. "It's hard because some of them have older siblings, and they get to dress up for school, so the parents just assume that the little kids are supposed to, also. I bet you a few kids will still come in costume."

Ms. Paige said she was excited because she was going to wear her sweats.

Ms. Roxanne chimed in, "Yeah, I don't really have nice or fun pajamas, so I went out last night and bought some Packers ones."

Ms. Paige quipped, "Well, actually, I don't wear anything to sleep, but I figured you guys wouldn't wanna see that."

We all laughed.

To make the pajama party happen, the teachers told families about it at pick-up for the preceding three days and sent home a little paper reminder.

In communities, celebrations highlight social connections between people. When celebrations take place at school, they make it clear how families are connected and how, collectively, teachers, families, and kids work together to create special moments. They can also provide a chance for extended face-to-face conversations among families and teachers. But with the intervention of requirements around holidays, Sunshine Head Start did not do class parties. Instead, celebrations seemed to only cause distance between families and Sunshine Head Start.

Mandated Space Sharing

To connect with families outside the complexities of holiday celebrations, Sunshine Head Start required three home visits per year. A home visit occurs when the family meets with a teacher and social worker at a location outside of the school. The teacher talks with the child and family about family life and child development.

Though home visits are pitched as being collaborative and providing greater connections between school and home, ultimately families had to agree to participate in home visits as a condition of enrolling in Head Start. Home visits were not completely optional. The teachers said some kids delighted in having their teacher at home—they showed the teachers their toys and their bedrooms. In this way, home visits gave teachers more information about family's lives. From Sunshine Head Start's point of view, ideally all three home visits would actually happen in the families' homes. However, the family social worker at Sunshine Head Start told me that most parents did home visits at their house and then requested that the subsequent two visits be elsewhere, like at the park near the preschool. This shows that many Sunshine Head Start families did not feel that home visits warranted the potential inconvenience of having a teacher in their home.

Having early childhood professionals in one's home could be interpreted by some families as inviting further scrutiny into their home lives. As sociologist Kelley Fong documents, poor mothers use selective visibility in their interactions with institutional agents like teachers whom they know to be mandated reporters of neglect or abuse.[9] For some families, long marginalized by various social systems, each decision to further engage with school personnel could result in them learning information about family challenges that could be used to scrutinize or control the family.

Finally, Sunshine Head Start offered an optional form of family engagement. They invited families to monthly special events called "Family Fun Nights." These were held around 5:30 p.m., after most families would have picked up their children. Family Fun Nights invited children and their families to school. The school social worker, and sometimes the teachers, planned these events. They were optional for families. Frank, the school cook beloved by teachers and families alike, made dinner for the attendees. One time a fire truck came, and the kids could go on it. Another time, the social worker planned a carnival-type event with games and activities set out on the playground.

Sometimes Family Fun Night was a parent education session. For one event, a child behavior specialist visited. The next day, Ms. Roxanne said that it was a good time. "The parents were asking questions like, 'Why is it so hard at bedtime?' It was really nice because we were all like talking and laughing and relating to each other," she reflected. Sometimes, the planned Family Fun Nights were a "miss," like when they made play dough and sent it home. Later, some of the parents complained that their kids got it stuck in the carpet, leading to a difficult clean-up job. For families that rented apartments, this kind of damage could create problems with the return of their security deposit.

Family Fun Nights stood out as a truly optional form of family engagement. They varied in their aims—some were for genuine family entertainment, while others aimed to educate and improve parents. Families did not pay to attend or help with organizing Family Fun Nights. The school social worker organized the events with Sunshine Head Start's families in mind—knowing that all of them were poor and likely did not have money to spare for extra items.

The mandated home visits were a potential policy of scrutiny, and families' typical response to them showed a sense of distance rather than closeness. Family Fun Nights were closer to optional family engagement, though they sometimes were based on the assumption that families needed to improve, rather than that families could show up as they were to enjoy time with teachers and their children.

Open Talk about Family Disruptions at Great Beginnings

In contrast to Sunshine Head Start, which was enmeshed in policies of scrutiny and had families experiencing stigmatized disruptions, Great Beginnings operated privately and had families less likely to experience stigmatized disruptions. In terms of policy, so long as Great Beginnings met licensing and accreditation requirements, the school staff had latitude to engage with families. Families' affluence even dulled the effect of the most important blanket policy requirement that Great Beginnings and Sunshine Head Start shared—mandatory reporting. In Wisconsin, teachers are required to report any evidence of child abuse or neglect. Yet Great Beginnings' class-advantaged families avoided many of the stressors that make such abuse and neglect more likely.[10] Though the same mandated reporter policy existed, it was less likely to be activated in this context than in a preschool enrolling poor families. Further, Great Beginnings' white families did not have intergenerational histories of government-endorsed scrutiny, and so the risk of teachers asking a question that families would interpret as prying was lower. Accordingly, I did not hear about fears of "trouble" if teachers asked the wrong questions.

Absent teachers' concerns of "trouble," Great Beginnings had more open information flows about family disruptions. When I observed in February, I was constantly looking out for mentions of family stressors. What I heard mentioned was travel—either for family vacation, or a parent traveling for work.

Just as the Sunshine Head Start kids had drawn on family happenings in their pretend play, Great Beginnings kids did the same.

One morning during Free Choice Time, Sarah and Esther were sent to the Dramatic Play Center.

Sarah and Esther determined together that they would each be mothers with a baby. Sarah explained to me, "One baby is named Baby Genius, and one is named Rainbow."

"I'm late for work and my friends are worried," Sarah said.

Esther did not answer; she continued making breakfast. Then Esther picked up a plastic phone and said, "Ring ring, ring ring." She looked at Sarah pointedly. "That's your phone I'm calling."

"Where's my phone?" Sarah began searching for another plastic phone.

Esther didn't help Sarah but continued talking into her phone. "This is the teacher. I'm at my teacher seat eating lunch. The kids are doing good today."

"Okay thanks," said Sarah, finally opting to just talk into her hand. "I'm at work."

"Okay, bye," Esther said.

Sarah put a book (*The Day the Crayons Quit*) on her lap. She placed both hands on it like it was a laptop and mimed typing. "I'm working," she announced.

Esther began bustling about the play kitchen. "Hey, how about we were going on vacation? And we had to pack because we were going on vacation?"

Sarah agreed to this plan, so the girls packed a tote bag and left for their vacation.

Family moments were fodder for pretend play. At Sunshine Head Start, the family moments I saw enter pretend play were sometimes poverty-induced challenges. At Great Beginnings, the family moments were affluence-induced opportunities, like going on vacation. What is important is that—at least when it came to enacting these scenarios in pretend play—the children at both schools were unbothered by the events. Children did enact urgency, frustration, and stress. But the Sunshine Head Start kids did not include pretend crying or actions that would denote their enactments of jail or lacking money for the bus as especially terrible.

At Great Beginnings, teachers felt that parents traveling was key information they needed to have. Talking about how they engaged with families, Ms. Erica remarked, "Communication is key for both ways. [Parents] can communicate with us, and we have to communicate. In the morning, especially, it is nice to know when someone's mom or dad is on vacation. Or out of town. Last year we had a family who didn't tell us when the other one was out of town for business and then, their child got sick and it is like, 'Who are we supposed to call?'" Ms. Erica was so accustomed to knowing about family travel that this one incident of missing information stood out in her mind as an inconvenience.

Observing open conversations about family disruptions was illuminating for me—because when teachers, parents, and children had a similar base of information, the teachers acted on this information with tailored, explicit support. These open conversations were helped along by the fact that the family events in question were less stigmatized—they were the irregularities of upper-middle-class family life.

Usually, a parent trip was a mere point of conversation among children, parents, and teachers. But sometimes kids were upset about their parent's absence during their day at school. Lucy's dad dropped her off on a Monday morning. He told the teachers that his wife had just left for a work trip. After her dad left for work, Lucy shuffled sullenly to the Dramatic Play area and started throwing toys at the ground. A teacher told her, calmly, that she would have to pick them up. At this, Lucy started to cry. For the next fifteen minutes, Lucy cried, while repeating "I want my mommy" at intervals. The teacher hugged her, and then she calmed down.

Lucy participated in Group Time, breakfast, and Free Choice Time without mentioning her mom. But then, during Outside Time, she began repeating that she wanted her mommy. Lucy spent a lot of this time sitting or standing next to Ms. Erica, whom she had a special bond with. Eventually, while the class lined up to return inside, Ms. Erica said, "What if, when we go inside, we look on the map to see where mommy is? Maybe we can look and see if she's close to any of the structures in our class [architecture] book. Would you like that?"

"Yes, I would like that," Lucy said.

Because Lucy's family disruption was known to the teachers and openly discussed by Lucy, her dad, and the teachers, the teachers were able to provide customized support to Lucy as she dealt with negative feelings about the disruption. In addition to hugs and comfort, Ms. Erica went a step further by using the book she had created about world architecture to turn Lucy's sad moment into a one-on-one learning experience. That kind of intervention was possible because Lucy was explicit about what was making her sad, and further, the teachers were aware of why Lucy's mom was gone and felt comfortable talking openly about it with Lucy and her parents. They did not express the fear of "getting in trouble" as the Sunshine Head Start teachers might have.

Lucy's hard morning differed from most of the instances of kids crying and throwing toys at Sunshine Head Start in that the teachers knew the cause of her behavior. While the Sunshine Head Start teachers could also hug and comfort children who were acting out, they typically did not have open conversations about family stressors that might have caused the behavior. Even when they did have information, as with Jasmine's parents' domestic dispute, they did not talk about it openly with the children. When the Great Beginnings teachers provided one-on-one attention to help Lucy process her feelings, they sent a message to Lucy and the Great Beginnings children that it was okay to talk about negative feelings about family events while at school. They also communicated that—to an extent—teachers could provide one-to-one attention to help process these feelings.

In the same week that Lucy's mom traveled, travel came up several other times. Carter talked about his family's upcoming vacation in Florida. Grayson mentioned that both his parents were going on a work trip, and so his grandparents were going to stay with him. On Wednesday, during drop-off, one of the teachers shared with two different parents that she was soon going on a cruise in Mexico. Both times, the parents told her that they had been to Mexico, too. The parents offered travel tips and stories.

While she was supervising kids on the playground, Ms. Paula and I discussed parent travel. "It is really common," she said, "especially if a parent works at one of the tech companies. A lot of them will switch. So Owen's mom was just gone on business, which means his dad will probably go soon. So, you know, then they're in a single-parent situation, at least for a bit."

I remarked that it seemed like all the kids had two parents involved in their life. "Yeah," she responded. "They all do."

"How many of them are divorced?" I asked.

She said that this year there was only one child with divorced parents—Charlie.

At Great Beginnings, teachers counted on having general information about each family, and particularly the comings and goings of parents. They were aided by the relative homogeneity among their families—all children had two parents involved throughout the year. This differed from Sunshine Head Start, where family structures were more diverse, and for some families, shifted every few months, as when a single parent got a new romantic partner who began to help with the kids. What drew teachers' curiosity at Great Beginnings was knowing when a parent went out of town. Even in my one month at Great Beginnings, I found it hard to keep track of whose parents were gone, where they went, and why. But the teachers knew their students' families better than I did and were accustomed to getting and remembering this information about family disruptions.

Unrestricted Celebrations

At Great Beginnings, both celebrations and chances to share space were focused on offering what I would call amenities to families. As a private school, Great Beginnings decided on its own how to acknowledge celebrations. The teachers were not under the program-specific mandate to get parent permission before holidays. They were also not concerned about asking parents to spend time and money to support school events. Absent arduous paperwork and with the added resource of being able to ask for parent donations, Great Beginnings had two parties a year for Halloween and Valentine's Day, at the school, during most parents' working hours. Parents brought the food and signed up to contribute food and decorations.

Because I observed in February, I was able to attend the Valentine's Day party. Parents were invited to attend. I asked Ms. Paula how the school told parents about the party. She said they had emailed them three weeks in advance. "The families are very busy," she said. "They need lots of notice."

While the class was on the playground for Outside Time, a staff member rearranged all the tables in the classroom to create one long table covered with a white paper tablecloth and confetti hearts. In the cleared space where the tables had been, they hung a piñata.

Parents started to arrive. The kids were looking through the tall glass windows to watch for when a parent showed up. When they noticed one, they announced it to their classmates: "Ruby, your mom is here!" In total, two-thirds of the children had a parent attend. The parents formed a circle around the kids and used their cell phones to snap photos when their child hit the piñata.

Then the kids sat at the long table with their parents to decorate cupcakes and drink bottled water—these supplies had been donated by parents. The kids had previously made Valentine's Day boxes at home with their parents. After that, the children sat with their parents to read their valentines. The teachers and I sat with the children who did not have a parent come. The party lasted less than an hour. Later that day, when the parents had left, the teachers had each child stand in front of the class and thank their classmates for bringing valentines for the party.

Notice the difference in how special occasions were institutionalized at each preschool. Great Beginnings was able to host holiday celebrations with ease, though they chose more secular holidays—Valentine's Day and Halloween, instead of Christmas, for example. But these might be events to which Jehovah's Witness families would object. Great Beginnings did not mention to me whether they had considered this possibility. Presumably they knew enough about their students' families to be aware of religious diversity. Great Beginnings further invited families to bring things and hosted the events during parents' workday, assuming that this would not be an imposition for most of the parents, who had salaried, flexible jobs.

Optional Space Sharing

In addition to the holiday parties, Great Beginnings sometimes hosted a Parents' Night Out, where the parents could drop their kids at the school, for an extra fee, so that parents could enjoy a date night. This practice, which happens at some other middle-class and affluent preschools, functions as an amenity for families. It was an extra offering, predicated on several things: parents having money to spend on leisure activities for their date; parents being accustomed to hiring a paid, unrelated babysitter for a date night, as opposed to having kin watch their children; and teachers' earnings being low enough to make the extra pay from Parents' Night Out enticing. Though Sunshine Head Start teachers would likely also appreciate extra pay if allowed to babysit, it was against Head Start policy for teachers to babysit children. The average rate for babysitting was twelve dollars per hour for one child, something beyond the means of most Head Start families, who themselves worked minimum wage jobs for $7.25 per hour.

Finally, Great Beginnings did not have home visits. The only reason why a Great Beginnings teacher or staff member would come to a family's home would be if the family invited them there. This seemed to mostly happen because the family had asked a teacher to babysit their child while they were away on a date night or for work-related travel.

Though the other three Great Beginnings teachers had babysat earlier in their teaching careers, Ms. Erica, in her twenties, was the youngest teacher and did the most babysitting at the time of my observations. She had babysat in high school, before working at Great Beginnings. I asked her if her roster of families had increased since she started working at the preschool.

"Oh, without a doubt, yes. Without a doubt, because the parents here know that they are getting good quality care for babysitters. Almost all of my families are through Great Beginnings. Actively, right now, I babysit like eleven different families."

"Do you babysit for extra money, or to see the kids, or both?" I asked.

"Usually, it is for extra money, I am not going to lie," Ms. Erica replied. "I love, though, one family that I am babysitting on Friday. They are like my children. I love them very much. I have their Christmas present in my car. I have had it for months. It is like a second family, kind of."

Ms. Erica had taught the family's older son when he was four and would eventually teach his younger brother when he became old enough for her classroom. Though she met almost all her babysitting clients through the preschool, most of them were not in her classroom—they were sometimes younger children in other classes.

When Ms. Erica worked as a paid babysitter, she was there to work for the family, not to work with them, as a home visitor would hope to do. The terms of engagement for a paid babysitting job and for a home visit differ. Paid babysitters enter the home as an employee and, in some cases, a pseudo-family member. Babysitters move throughout the home and have wide-ranging access to the home without the parents present. While babysitting, the teachers might glean details about the kids' lives that would increase familiarity. Home visitors defer to the family more as a guest and would not help themselves to food in the fridge, for example. Home visitors also enter the home as relative outsiders armed with child development knowledge, potentially creating a different power dynamic. Ultimately, being able to choose to hire teachers as babysitters functioned as an amenity for Great Beginnings families. Hiring babysitters was optional, was meant to enhance families' lives, and was done on families' terms.

The Consequences of Communication in Segregated Villages

Family disruptions—from business trips to incarceration—are patterned by class and race. While affluent and poor parents alike experience substance abuse and domestic violence, the rates of each of these things are higher for poor families. Other family disruptions are deeply racialized, such as eviction and family separation by child protective services.[11]

Affluent children might get shielded from challenging family disruptions. On the one hand, their parents were less likely to deal with eviction, hunger, and other pressing challenges. Their parents face stressors, too, but may have had more resources to discuss and to some extent resolve these stressors without telling their kids about them. The exception would be visible changes that are unavoidably communicated to children—miscarriages, moves, and divorce. At, Great Beginnings, the children participated openly in some conversations about less stigmatized family challenges. Teachers could validate the children's information about family events as worthy of conversation, and as normal, legible family stressors. The Great Beginnings teachers were able to do this, in part, because of their small class size and stable enrollment, two factors that allowed them to develop more familiarity with children and families.

Some poor children are highly exposed to and aware of family disruptions. This happens, in part, because the challenges and time required for poor parents to get their needs met can result in some children experiencing "adultification," wherein poor children have adult-like responsibilities and knowledge.[12] For example, young kids often have to accompany their parents on visits to welfare offices and other social services, which makes them more aware of the details of family hardship.[13] Yet at Sunshine Head Start, teachers treated children as though they were in a separate sphere. Even when children brought up family disruptions, teachers did not see these as bids for direct conversation. Teachers' fear of "trouble" led them to avoid talking directly to children and families, and instead to talk about family disruptions among themselves. The implication of this was that poor kids of color did not learn to openly discuss family events with teachers. This unrecognized cognitive labor that poor children of color do—determining which family moments could be discussed with teachers and which could not—may have entrenched a sense of distance between home and school.[14]

In the United States, many working parents partner with child care providers to be day-to-day members of their proverbial village in raising children. By focusing on how families and preschools come together, we can see how intimate and supportive these villages are. The two preschools approached family engagement with their segregated groups of families differently. But both fell short. Great Beginnings offered family engagement as optional amenities geared toward joy or easing families' stress. But this presumed that children were getting needs met at home and reinforced a sense of teachers being there to serve parents' needs, rather than being full partners in raising children. Sunshine Head Start layered on requirements and mandates intended to prevent any gaps in getting children's needs met. But this left a sense of distance for some families.

Briana articulated the distance she kept from the Sunshine Head Start teachers, despite having sent her kids there for nearly a decade. As we sat in a spare room at the preschool for our interview, I asked her, "Do you feel like the teachers are kind of on your side, and support you, or do you feel like it's more of a distance?"

"About what?"

"About everything, like do you feel like they understand your life . . . ?"

"I don't know, I'm not that open and friendly with my life, so. People that need to know, they know. They usually know, they know I don't ever go to the Family Fun Nights, they know I don't like a lot of paperwork. Then like they had to come to the house [for home visits]. You know I'm used to Roxanne and the social worker coming to the house. So I'm just not really open, and friendly like that."

For all the mandated forms of engagement Sunshine Head Start implemented, Briana kept her distance, choosing to divulge only what was necessary for her to stay on good terms with the preschool. Sunshine Head Start had been part of her village for ten years, and with the recent death of her mom, was now a key support for her youngest son, Shawn. Yet the teachers were not people to whom she wanted to confide either the stress or the joy of her long-awaited Disneyworld vacation.

BURNED OUT

Teaching amid Trauma

After eight years as a lead teacher at Sunshine Head Start, Roxanne had moved on to a different preschool. A few months into her new job, she met me at Starbucks for an interview. "I stayed for the kids," she told me. "Everything is new to them, every day is new, so it's just so cool. So like when kids discover something new it is the most amazing thing, like 'look what I found!' But you don't know, every day is going to be different, some days are hard, like with jumping off tables, cussing. . . . I knew with most of the kids that it was coming from the stress in their life." She paused and began to cry. "Yeah, and I'm not judging the parents at all, because believe me, that was one thing I learned too, those parents are under huge amounts of stress, and they're doing the best that they can."

Roxanne, a white woman with brown hair and a calming smile, was in her thirties during my observations. She went to college to become a special education elementary school teacher. She was first hired to be a substitute teacher for the city's Head Start programs, including Sunshine Head Start. Eventually she was given her own classroom. Reflecting on the administrators who hired her, she said that they were "amazing, they just totally got what early childhood is about." Roxanne felt then, and still feels, that the most important part of early childhood is nurturing children's social and emotional skills. She grew to love helping the kids process their feelings. The children doted on her, often shouting her name when they saw her coming into the classroom. In the mornings, there were usually several children sitting on her lap or pulling her hand to show her something.

But parts of the job weighed on her. The hours were heavy, as was the paperwork: "It's a forty-hour job, but you could be there until six, seven, eight, nine at night, just depending on what paperwork was due." And the pay was lower than she would like. It was enough to live on, but not enough for anything extra. She worked holidays at a clothing store for extra income. Ultimately, the stress of working with families facing enormous challenges, whose children, in turn, acted out at school, added to her sense that she needed a change.

Head Start is lauded for its relatively high pay and benefits, extensive training and teacher support, and family engagement. And yet, these programmatic aspects were insufficient to buffer Sunshine Head Start teachers from the stress arising from student behaviors—which traced to poverty-related stressors and racial trauma. In contrast, Great Beginnings had fewer program-level supports, yet the teachers there had fewer children per year needing special help. Absent the stress of dealing with challenging behaviors, these teachers enjoyed more positive one-on-one moments with children.

The segregation of poor and rich children clusters poverty-related trauma in one classroom, and affluence-related expectations for amenities in another classroom. These divergent job demands translated into unequal levels of stress. The Sunshine Head Start teachers experienced high stress and burnout, and in some cases, held negative views of their students. The Great Beginnings teachers experienced shorter-term stress and held glowing views of their students.

Race and class segregation creates work experiences for teachers that are both different and unequal. While the differences the teachers experienced reflect an unequal society, they add strains on teachers that can reproduce inequality in three ways: by fostering negative views of poor children of color; by making teachers feel stressed, which can negatively impact child development; and by leading to teacher turnover, which gives poor children of color less experienced teachers. Segregated classrooms created distinctive work environments, which, in turn, impacted the way children experienced their teachers— either as stressed and busy, or as calm and available.

Starting Preschool Teaching in Segregated Contexts

Preschool classrooms usually have two or more teachers. Lead teachers manage the curriculum and classroom routine. Lead teachers are required to have a bachelor's degree and experience in education. Associate teachers support lead teachers and must have completed early childhood coursework. Sunshine Head Start also employed some teacher aides, who were in the process of taking early childhood courses. Both schools also employed floating teachers, who helped classrooms to cover for teachers' breaks or days off.

Women's pathways into preschool teaching bifurcated along two paths: either straight from college and into teaching, or a more winding path from service jobs into teaching. The lead teachers, Roxanne and Kim, as well as Erica, the Great Beginnings assistant, took the first path. They went to college to become elementary teachers but found through side jobs that they loved working with slightly younger children. The assistant teachers at Sunshine Head Start took the second path: they worked various service jobs before settling into working with children.

Kim, a white woman in her thirties, was the lead teacher at Great Beginnings. Kim was assertive and confident with adults, but you quickly saw her softer side emerge when she interacted with young children. Kim loved travel and told me about memorable past trips and upcoming adventures she had planned. She followed a similar pathway as Roxanne into teaching. Both Kim and Roxanne worked throughout their schooling to pay the bills: they worked at cheese stores, fast food restaurants, and clothing stores. They also babysat for families. Kim worked full-time as a floating teacher during college. When she graduated, she became a permanent teacher with her own classroom.

Erica, a white woman in her early twenties, was Kim's associate teacher. Erica had seemingly boundless energy and a positive attitude. Erica and Kim separately told me that they really enjoyed working together. They shared lesson planning so that Erica could progress toward eventually becoming a lead teacher. Though Erica was not the lead teacher, she was on a similar pathway as that of the lead teachers and hoped to be a lead teacher when a spot opened at Great Beginnings. During high school, Erica worked part-time as a teacher aide in a toddler room at Great Beginnings. She went to college intending to teach preschool, working as a float teacher at Great Beginnings the whole time. She was hired as the associate teacher immediately after finishing college.

The Sunshine Head Start associate teachers graduated high school and then took a longer path into preschool teaching. Julie, who was in her fifties, was a white woman with red hair that she usually wore in a ponytail with styled, teased bangs. She described her style with the children as "old-school." Julie loved the hugs and cuddles the children gave her, but she was also comfortable saying no, firmly, when she felt it was needed. She was the teacher I most often heard express frustration with the kids. For example, she was running Circle Time on a day when the kids were rowdy. Her brow furrowed, she said to the class, "You're being irritating. Keep your voices off and turn your listening ears on or we'll keep sitting here." Ms. Julie's style contrasted with the softer style of some teachers, who might say no to kids but would often explain their reasoning to children. After high school, Julie was a bartender for a decade. She then tried an office job for a few years, but found she wasn't good with office work. After a short time of working at a cosmetics store in a mall, she moved into a job at a different child care center for kids aged two to age ten. Speaking about this first child care job, she told me, "It kind of just fell in my lap, so a friend of mine told me about it, and I went over there and talked to the lady, and she basically hired me on the spot." Julie worked there for five years. Then that child care center closed, and Julie applied to work at Sunshine Head Start. By the time of my field work, Julie had been working at Sunshine Head Start for twelve years.

Lisa, a white woman in her early thirties, had worked at a convenience store, then at a pizza place, then as a home health aide. Lisa loved a good joke and was often the teacher to find artistic activities on social media that she would introduce to the children. She first came to Sunshine Head Start as a cook. After three years of being a cook, she became a teacher aide, and then an associate teacher. She liked teaching the children independence and social skills. She said her dream job was to run a child care center out of her home, so she could control her own hours and curriculum. Lisa's path into teaching represents the openness envisioned for teacher aide roles and associate teachers at Head Start—that through these roles, people could rise to the role of lead teacher.[1]

All teachers told me that they loved the job because of the kids. Kim said, "I'm really truly enjoying working with this age group. Like you always have your little hiccups here and there but overall, I mean I absolutely love coming in and getting like a bazillion hugs and kisses." Four-year-olds can be cuddly, inquisitive, and excited—traits their teachers enjoyed.

The teachers also felt that the preschool years were an important time to hone the children's social and emotional skills. Despite parents and media often focusing on early reading and math, early childhood professionals prioritize being able to regulate one's emotions and interact positively with peers and teachers. They see these skills as foundational for being ready for kindergarten. The teachers universally agreed with this sentiment, and they found it extremely rewarding when the children improved their social and emotional skills. Thinking of a boy who had struggled to connect to his classmates, Julie recounted, "One day, one of the little girls tripped and fell, and he just ran over to her, and said, 'Are you okay? Can I help you feel better?' You know, exactly what we've been asking them to do, and then he does it! It's like wow, he actually did it.'"

In spite of the passion and skill required to teach young children, accepting the job of a preschool teacher meant accepting low wages. In Wisconsin, preschool teachers' average annual wage was about thirty thousand dollars per year in 2019, half of what elementary school teachers earned.[2] The Sunshine Head Start teachers told me they enjoyed the health care and other benefits that came with a county job. But still, the pay was a challenge. All of the teachers had either worked a second job while teaching, or had juggled continuing education with teaching, out of financial necessity. The Sunshine Head Start teachers worked service jobs. Roxanne had her seasonal retail job. Julie had worked the one Sunshine Head Start job for many years but had recently picked up a second job. On top of her full-time work at the preschool, she worked about twenty hours a week—evenings and weekends—as a restaurant hostess. Lisa worked the least outside of her work at Sunshine Head Start, but she was still taking her early childhood classes after work. She occasionally babysat and pursued network marketing sales.

Megan, a school-district-funded substitute, had taken the job at Sunshine Head Start in part because it was one of the best-paying jobs she had found as a preschool teacher. She had been cleaning houses one day a week on top of her teaching work but had stopped doing that after she and her husband had a baby. She was waiting nervously to hear about a potential raise from Head Start. She reflected, "I mean people love to work with kids. Educators, they go into this job because they love kids, but then you get into education, and you realize I cannot live on this amount of money. I can't afford child care for my own child, yet I'm here taking care of other people's kids." Instead of using a child care center, Megan paid her mom "much less than daycare" to watch her baby while she worked at Sunshine Head Start. Despite the low pay, Megan enjoyed the job. She intended to stay for ten years, so that the government would forgive her student loan debt. After that, she was considering becoming a curriculum coach for preschool teachers.

Though Great Beginnings was a private preschool, the wages were still low, in line with pay in the early childhood field. Instead of working second jobs in the service industry, teachers babysat for Great Beginnings families and others. Kim had babysat more often when she was younger and had needed money to pay off her student loans. Erica, her assistant teacher, worked full-time at Great Beginnings but also babysat five to seven days per week. Some of the Great Beginnings parents hired her to provide early-morning, evening, and overnight care while they were on business trips. She also babysat for parents' date nights.

Sunshine Head Start teachers were not allowed to babysit for families. Even if it were allowed, the average pay for in-home babysitting was twelve dollars per hour per child in Madison. This cost was out of reach for poor families, as the Wisconsin minimum wage was $7.25 an hour. That the Great Beginnings families were able to pay for private babysitting, on top of the $1,248 a month they paid in school tuition, was a testament to their financial means. Though both sets of teachers faced low pay, the Great Beginnings teachers' ability to earn a higher wage, potentially with no taxes taken out, through connections at their preschool gave them a financial advantage. Date-night babysitting also provided opportunities to be paid while sitting down, for example, when kids are asleep. This contrasts with many service jobs, where there is surveillance over one's work and where resting while "on the clock" is frowned upon.[3] Teachers started their careers in similar ways and with similar low wages, yet, a few years into their work, important differences emerged in pathways to additional income through babysitting.

In addition to opportunities for side jobs, a major early difference in experience was that Sunshine Head Start teachers faced enormous extra stresses related to social and emotional well-being among their students. Megan, the Sunshine Head Start substitute teacher, was especially able to articulate the difference, because she had previously worked at Great Beginnings. At Great Beginnings there had usually been one challenging child per year, who perhaps had sensory issues, or who was in the process of being diagnosed with attention deficit disorder.[4] But these children were individuals who stood out from the class as a whole. At Sunshine Head Start, Megan explained, "We'll have one class where there's like seven to eight kids that have some real challenging behaviors." Accordingly, she noted, "It's a really tough job, it's intense, much more intense than I ever experienced at my old Great Beginnings job, and here we're short-staffed on top of it."

At Sunshine Head Start, the children who struggled to manage their behavior and emotions were typically experiencing family transitions and trauma such as parental incarceration or eviction. These family events happened year-round. Sometimes children's behaviors acutely affected teachers when children injured them during outbursts. A child stomped on Lisa's foot so hard that her toe broke. She had to work in a walking boot for several weeks after. Teachers had been spat on, hit, kicked, and bitten over the course of their careers.

Enrollment shifts added to workload, too. At Sunshine Head Start, about twelve to fourteen children were stably enrolled, while the other three spots were occupied by children who rotated in and out. This shifting enrollment added extra paperwork for teachers and also required adjustment from the whole class to incorporate newcomers. For example, one January, three new children started in the same week, causing small hiccups as everyone adjusted. Teachers spent time helping the new children adjust. Shayla peed her pants almost daily for the first few weeks. The teachers discussed this at nap time, trying to figure out if Shayla was nervous in the new environment or if something else was going on. The traumatic nature of childhood poverty in the United States can affect children's behavior in the classroom.[5] When a classroom is segregated such that most or all children are poor, the chances of multiple children needing extra teacher support increase vastly.

In contrast, at Great Beginnings, the teachers had one child out of twelve who needed extra attention and sometimes behaved aggressively, especially during nap time. But they said that he had improved since the start of the school year in August, so that by the time I observed in February, he participated easily in classroom activities. Enrollment was stable. At Great Beginnings, it was uncommon for children to leave the classroom and thus open spots for newcomers. In February, when I observed, the class roster had been the same since August. When a classroom segregates all affluent children, poverty trauma is completely removed. Children's behavior became a defining feature of the work environment for teachers.

Social and Emotional Learning at Sunshine Head Start

Sunshine Head Start was a lively place. There were up to seventeen children and three teachers. Kids laughed, played in large groups, and talked to teachers. But the classroom always had multiple children dealing with poverty-related traumas. Sometimes these children behaved in aggressive, challenging ways. This occupied the teachers' time, because ensuring that the kids were safe was fundamental. It meant, in a sense, that the teachers were occupied dealing with pressing social and emotional skills, like how to channel anger and disappointment without hurting other people. They were stuck on social and emotional learning.

Teachers struggled with the challenging behaviors themselves, but also with the fact that kids' behavior felt unpredictable. Describing the children, Lisa said, "They're different every day, you never have the same thing every day when you walk in. You don't know what they're going to say to you, how their nights were, when was their last meal. You don't know where they even slept last night. One day one child can be as happy as can be, the next day they're coming in all sad, and all angry, you don't know why." Lisa was describing her experiences with children's behavior changing day to day. According to what I observed, her description depicts about a third of the class—children whose parents were separating, whose families were experiencing housing instability, or whose families were struggling to keep the lights on. The instability, made more likely by poverty in the United States, appeared to affect some of these children's behavior through negative emotions and either aggressive or withdrawn behavior. For example, I observed children say they were angry, kick the wall, jump off tables, throw things at their peers, or refuse to play for half a day.

One day after nap time, the class was sitting down to do puzzles. Isaac told me, "I'm going to have a bad day. Bad days are for hitting and taking."

"Who told you that?" I asked.

"No one, I just thought it up," he said. "I'm just going to sit here and do puzzles and never get up." He had worn SpongeBob pajamas that were a bit short on him and didn't reach his Spiderman rain boots. He had been wearing a Spiderman pajama shirt, but it got wet at a table activity, and so he had to wear a Packers sweater and was disappointed by this. He asked to put the Spiderman one back on but was told no by the teachers, because it was too wet.

Children acting out drew more of teachers' attention. Teachers would pair up with them, coaching them to be gentler with peers, to participate in Circle Time, and to use kind language. Unlike these children who struggled, however, the majority of the children had families who were poor but stable.

In light of challenging behavior that felt unpredictable, teachers often speculated as to why the behaviors occurred. Julie said this was her biggest challenge at work: "Why is someone this little, this angry in the first place? That's the hardest, is understanding why their behaviors are the way they are. I mean, why does one child jump, and hit, and whatever he can do to hurt somebody, but then the next child is mellow, and sweet as can be, and hugs, and snuggles? It's just very frustrating to understand that." Most of the time, the teachers were just guessing and making generic assumptions that the kid might have "been through a major trauma."

Even though only a proportion of the class behaved in unpredictable, challenging ways, the teachers often calibrated their supervision around managing these children. In practical terms, the difficult behaviors of some children meant that the teachers spent much of their day responding to repeated problem incidents. Megan experienced this on the playground one day. The class was out on the playground. Julian and

Hannah began arguing, and Julian shoved a wooden crate onto Hannah's face. They were both crying. Megan jogged over to them. Each child told Megan what happened and then Hannah left to play elsewhere. Megan continued talking with Julian; Julian was sobbing and flailing his arms. Then he kicked Megan. She told him he needed to "take a break." She led him to the ledge along the bike path and they sat there talking for a few minutes.

While they were talking things out, two children in the sandbox started yelling at each other. Megan left Julian to go address the issue in the sandbox. While she was in the sandbox, Julian got up, still wailing, and started tossing tricycles around the bike path. Megan called for help. Rebecca and Lisa came over together and coaxed Julian to go inside.

Megan responded to back-to-back behavior issues, yet was still unable to see all the children through their difficult emotions. When teachers were pulled to respond to these conflicts, they missed out on chances to comment on children's activities or to simply play with children. In our interview, Megan said, "That's the sad part, just all your attention, and all your energy is focused on managing that behavior, and all the other children that are doing what they're supposed to do and are there to learn and to have fun, don't get any of that [attention]." Children's behavior also meant that some teachers, especially the assistant teachers, spent much of their time oriented toward problems and stopping negative behavior.

Challenging behaviors sometimes led teachers to change their plans. One morning, I sat at the activity tables next to Roxanne while she remarked on pictures that the children were drawing. Instead of having the children draw a picture of whatever they wanted, as she had originally planned, Roxanne had the children draw a picture about how they could be safe in the classroom. She told me, "It was crazy this morning, my friends were hitting, and kicking, and stepping on each other's feet. I hate to do this; this was supposed to be a fun activity." Roxanne shifted her lesson plan from an activity that emphasized choice and creativity to an activity that emphasized safety. In these moments, the whole class missed out on an open-ended activity. But Roxanne also missed out on realizing play-based lesson plans she had been excited about.

According to the Sunshine Head Start teachers, challenging behavior made their job hard and behavior oriented. Roxanne said, "It's a hard job, like I told you, I mean when you've got kids jumping off the shelves, and you're getting flipped off . . ." The Sunshine Head Start teachers were used to these behaviors as routine challenges.

In Roxanne's view, the paperwork requirements made her main goal of helping children develop socially and emotionally even harder. As the lead teacher, every day Roxanne had to count attendance at the start of the day and before and after transitions outside the classroom. She had to count who ate breakfast, lunch, and snack. She had to write notes documenting children's development, amounting to about fifty notes for each of the seventeen children, entered at three points during the school year. She had to organize home visits and then reflect on them. She had to write progress reports for Madison's four-year-old kindergarten program. She had to write weekly lesson plans. She had to write newsletters for families. She often commented that this paperwork stressed her out: "There's so much paperwork, and it's like I don't need to be doing paperwork, I need to be in that room with them. I know what I'm doing, you know? I know what's developmentally appropriate."

Roxanne found the paperwork taxing, both because she disliked the task itself and because she saw it as pulling her out of the classroom, where she could do the kind of instruction and interaction that she found most important. By implication, the paperwork that pulled her out of the classroom also strained the assistant teachers, who were left behind to take charge of coaching children through conflicts and deescalating challenging behaviors. Overall, the poverty-related trauma that children experienced affected their behavior, and the government's interest in tracking and evaluating the results of Head Start funding for poor children added extreme strains to the workload of Head Start teachers.

Viewing Children as "Work"

At Sunshine Head Start, teachers' descriptions of the class as a group reflected the challenging context in which they worked. When describing the classroom generally, the teachers sometimes described it as chaotic, crazy, or overwhelming.

When I walked into the classroom, Lisa looked up from setting art supplies on the tables. Her face was red and blotchy, and she looked upset. "Just so you know," she said, "it's chaotic today."

"Oh yeah?" I responded. Our conversation ended there.

On a different morning, I entered and saw Rebecca in the Quiet Area with Cameron. She was holding up a beanbag while Cameron kicked at it and scowled.

"Hi," Rebecca said. "Where were you yesterday? We missed you."

"Hi," Julie added. "And welcome to Bedlam," she said with a laugh.

Teachers often commented that the classroom was loud, crazy, or busy. These pronouncements came even on days with typical teacher-student ratios.

Shifting attendance added to the unpredictability. It also meant that teachers were used to not having a full class. Because it was common for at least one child to be absent, the teachers noticed when the classroom was at full capacity. A full list meant a more challenging day ahead. One afternoon, as we were leaving the multipurpose playroom to return to the classroom, Roxanne commented, "Okay, I got the count [of the children] today. Whew. Full list." The adults exchanged dark looks.

The teachers' sense was that each child's attendance added to their work, and so, conversely, any child's absence meant a slight break. This was also apparent to me when teachers characterized low-attendance days as easy.

When I got to the classroom, there were only seven children sitting around the Circle Rug.

"Good morning," Camila, a teacher aide, said. "Hey, do you see these low numbers [low attendance]?" She was smiling.

Julie also greeted me cheerfully. Later that day, she mentioned that that day had been a nice end to a really stressful week. The teachers described days with lower attendance as less stressful and days with the full list as a little overwhelming.

Teachers felt the absence of certain children as even more of a relief. Cameron had been kicking people and jumping on shelves for weeks. But then one week, Cameron was absent for a few days. On his first day back, we were seated at breakfast. Cameron was very talkative while he ate. I said to the room at large, "I missed Cameron; it's been a few days."

Julie replied from her table, "Yeah, k-i-n-d-a, m-a-y-b-e."

I didn't understand what she was trying to spell out, so I said, "What? Sorry, I can't spell."

"Kinda sorta maybe."

"Yep," I said. "It's so much livelier when he's here."

"Yeah, but quiet is nice too . . . ," Julie said.

Children like Cameron created extra demands on teachers' time and attention, two things that were hard to come by in their preschool classroom. Teachers seemed to slightly dread these children's attendance, and, conversely, experienced their absence as a relief.

Teachers' ambivalent appraisals of children were also apparent when teachers reflected on their work during interviews. When Sunshine Head Start teachers described the kids, they were often unable to mention positive aspects of their job without adding a corollary statement about the challenges of kids' behavior. When I asked Julie what her favorite part of the job was, she replied, "The kids. Just how different they are, and how sweet and snugly they can be *when they're not acting up* [emphasis added]." Julie's description, even in a comment on the best parts of the job, was decidedly ambivalent.

Her view of the class became formalized when she renamed the class. I was sitting at an activity table, dumping glitter on glue. We were decorating a giant sheet of paper that the kids had painted the day before. Julie was spelling out "The Wildcats" with glue. She told me that was our new class name.

I asked her who came up with the name.

"I did," she replied. "We were brainstorming a new name, and since we're always running around, I figured 'Wildcats.' I wanted 'Busy Bees,' but that was taken."

Julie's choice for a class name was illustrative of how she thought of the kids—as wild and busy. References to bad behavior peppered most of teachers' comments about children. While interviewing Roxanne, I asked her to elaborate on her goals for the children's development. She highlighted social and emotional skills and gave this example: "You can respectfully decline to play with so and so in the Block Area. You may not pummel the crap out of them. You can say, 'Hey, I don't want to play with you,' and that's okay."

The Sunshine Head Start teachers had complex views of the children whom they worked with. At Sunshine Head Start, teachers' appraisals of children were infused with references to misbehavior. Sunshine Head Start teachers' views of the children as a group became either ambivalent or negative. Though the class included quiet children, children who complied with all classroom rules, and children who rarely required special attention, these children were invisible in teachers' descriptions of the class as consisting of poor children with stressful home lives and challenging behaviors. On the one hand, the teachers' focus on these kids in their group descriptions is understandable. As evident in the moment with Ms. Megan on the playground, much of teachers' day was spent addressing behavior issues, keeping challenging behavior front of mind. However, teachers' characterizations extended to the whole group of children. This negative outlook can affect teachers' ability to bond with children and continue to support them.[6]

Job Stress and Turnover

The behavioral needs of the children and the noise of play at Sunshine Head Start sometimes became overwhelming. Roxanne was a competitive runner and worked out several times a week to help manage her stress. But this was not always enough. One morning, Roxanne and I chatted about how she had been tired recently. When I asked if there was a particular reason why, she explained, "I've been coming a little earlier. 'Cause otherwise when I get here, everyone is here, and it's kind of overwhelming. So, I've been trying to come in earlier when there's fewer kids. I can kind of get comfortable, set things up." To adapt to chaotic classroom conditions, Roxanne had chosen to extend her workday. But still, her stress turned to burnout, and then to turnover for the preschool: Roxanne found a new position as a lead teacher in a private school. Her new preschool had a curriculum, too, but it had much less paperwork because it was not Head Start funded. The parents there were from diverse cultural backgrounds and had different family circumstances, which would offer a change of pace.

After Roxanne left, Sunshine Head Start hired Kayla, a young blonde woman with large brown eyes. She had worked at an affluent preschool while finishing her bachelor's degree. We sat down for an interview in the multipurpose room at the school, and she told me, "I've been on the verge of quitting like a hundred times, like every day I walk out like 'why do I work here?' But then I start thinking about it, and I think about the kids, and the relationships that I've made, and it makes it worth it." Kayla was four months in when we sat down for an interview, and she told me immediately that she still cried in her car after work most days. She was working about sixty hours a week, spending nights and weekends on paperwork and lesson plans.

She also found the physicality of the job intense. She said this was the hardest aspect of the job. She explained,

> The other day a kid just bit me, and I had a huge bruise. I was so surprised, I didn't even know what to do, so he bit me for like a good ten seconds before I was like, "Get off me," because I didn't want to hurt him, but he was . . . ouch. Then one of the big things we have right now are the kids climbing on the furniture. And before we were kind of ignoring it, but then I talked to my director. We're only supposed to ask them verbally to get down. If they don't after two seconds, then we're supposed to help them down. Most of what happens is like they will hit you, or like push you, and then they'll just get right back up. Which is not funny, but it's *kind of* funny, because you know exactly what they're going to do. Then some of the littler ones will grab my glasses and throw them—they're a hundred dollars.

Considering her intense hours, daily stress to the point of crying, and the physical challenges, Kayla was already planning to look for a job as second-grade teacher in the local school district the following school year. The Sunshine Head Start teachers were passionate about the early childhood years and about helping children. But they came up against big challenges and did not see Sunshine Head Start as a dream position that would define their careers. Teacher turnover affects the work environment for the teachers left behind and breaks a significant relationship between teachers and children.[7] Turnover is a challenge for any preschool, but if teacher turnover becomes concentrated among children in poverty, it can reinforce race and class inequality.

Beyond Social and Emotional Learning and Being a "Lifer" at Great Beginnings

Great Beginnings had a relatively calmer classroom environment. The teachers also emphasized social and emotional learning, but they felt that, a few months into the school year, the kids had internalized these skills. This meant that the teachers could spend time on enriching lesson plans. It also allowed them to speak positively about their students as a group.

When I observed in February, the children sometimes spoke loudly or ran around the classroom. This behavior was met with admonishment from teachers. But on a typical morning, the children played in groups of two or three. Children often chose to quietly read a book alone, even when assigned to the Block Area or the House Area. Accordingly, I heard few characterizations of the classroom as overwhelming or busy. At Great Beginnings, the teachers spoke in unequivocally glowing terms about the children as a group. When I asked Erica what she enjoyed about her job, she responded, "Everything. The people, the kids, the freedom to do what they want, the freedom to teach them what I want. I love the moment when they are able to do something that they weren't able to do. You can celebrate the little victories with them. You see them grow." Teachers had optimistic views of children. When I asked Kim to expound on her developmental goals for children, she mentioned social skills, just like Roxanne. However, her description centered positive behavioral goals, rather than behaviors to eliminate. She said, "We really want to make sure that kids are able to start a conversation or interact, engage, and to play with other people."

When Great Beginnings teachers did mention challenging behavior, it was in reference to particular children, rather than the kids as a group. Kim explained, "[It's] part of the job, but after a time that can be extremely wearing when it's tantrum after tantrum after tantrum. . . . Sometimes it can be a challenge, especially when you have a one-teacher ratio. It's hard to be able to do those particular things with the child when you don't have somebody to help with all of the other children." Like the Sunshine Head Start teachers, Kim considered challenging behavior to be a hard part of the job. But to meet the needs of one child with challenging behavior, Ms. Kim asked her center director for more staff. Her request was granted. After that, she told me she felt equipped to teach the class the way she wanted to.

At both schools, teachers' views of children echoed the work they did with the children. At Sunshine Head Start, the teachers spent a great deal of their time coaching children through conflicts and responding to challenging behaviors; their view of the children reflected these challenges. At Great Beginnings, teachers spent most of their time reading to children and supporting their play-based curriculum; their view of the children was more optimistic. They also enjoyed being able to follow the children's academic interests. One morning in the teachers' lounge, Erica showed me a large, laminated book she was making for the class. She said the kids were really interested in buildings and maps. So, she had made a book about these topics. She noted, "It's really nice to be able to focus on things they're interested in instead of just socioemotional all the time." Absent the work of having multiple challenging children to deal with, the Great Beginnings teachers made elaborate lesson plans focused on children's interests.

In the context of their classroom, where behaviors, enrollment, and attendance were more stable, the Great Beginnings teachers had the time and attention to devote to students. They also did not label their students as a group in negative ways. Overall, Great Beginnings teachers viewed their students positively. They were teaching a group of socioeconomically advantaged, and mostly white, children. As white students, these children held positions and identities presumed to be normal.[8] The end effect was that Great Beginnings children had the benefit of teachers who highlighted the best of their behavior and focused on their learning. The teachers individuated the children—not just in their descriptions of children's behavior but in their teaching.

Great Beginnings teachers had much less paperwork do. However, they excelled in offering parents constant communication. I thought this might be stressful to teachers, but they did not describe it as such. The teachers sent newsletters weekly that described lesson plans and included photos. Ms. Paula was distinctly proud of the newsletters and the events that the school offered. One day while the class was napping, she brought her laptop over to me to show me the latest newsletter she was working on. She also showed me the newsletters that had gone out every month since September. Each newsletter addressed a theme for the month, and explained, in detail, how each play center had been changed to match the theme. For example, for February the teachers were focusing on the Arctic. They had put cotton in the Block Area and added arctic play animals to the Sensory Table. The newsletters also detailed the field trip or enrichment activity each month. They did a library visit, an apple farm visit, a magic show, and a fire truck visit. At Great Beginnings, parents and administrators expected this "paperwork," but the preschool's funding did not hang in the balance. They also did not have many of the tracking systems present at Head Start, like food tracking and extensive developmental notes.

In contrast to the Sunshine Head Start lead teachers who either left or planned to leave, Great Beginnings teachers were extremely satisfied, not just with the job of teaching preschoolers but with doing it at Great Beginnings. Jessica, a teacher in a different Great Beginnings classroom, told me, "We have a lot of people in other centers come to observe or walk around our center a lot. I think it is because we have high standards. And we are nationally accredited, but we also don't have tons of turnover. We have had years where people have moved or had kids and stayed home. But, once you are here, you are a 'lifer.'" Kim told me that she had no plans to leave. When I asked Erica, the Great Beginnings assistant teacher, if she had a dream job, she said, "This is it! People ask, 'Are you a Great Beginnings for-lifer?' I might be. I don't think I am going to be an associate [teacher] with Kim forever. Though, she has warned me that I need to be. When a lead position opens up at Great Beginnings, depending on the age, I might apply for it."

The Great Beginnings teachers loved both their job and their center. They cited the benefits, the curricular freedom that was absent arduous paperwork, and the chance to see all the kids grow and learn over the course of the year. Their workplace narrative of people being "lifers" shows how satisfied teachers were with their jobs and stands in stark contrast to the burnout of teachers at Sunshine Head Start. As a result, teachers new to Great Beginnings encounter a highly experienced cadre of teachers to aid in their professional development. And the white, middle-class children who attend Great Beginnings generally count on continuity in their teachers, adding predictability to lives that are already afforded more stability because of their families' financial resources.

Segregated Preschools Are Unequal Work Environments for Teachers

The Sunshine Head Start classroom environment included unpredictable enrollment, attendance, and behavior. This unpredictability related to experiences like eviction, foster care, and chronic stress, experiences that disproportionately affect families in poverty and families of color.[9] The unpredictability affected teachers' workday, and in turn may be a reason why other researchers find that teachers' interactions with children are often less warm and enriching in majority-poor preschools.[10] The Sunshine Head Start I studied had favorable classroom indicators on paper—the ratio and class size were low (and lower still on days when children were absent), the materials in the classroom were plentiful, and the teachers were experienced and well trained. And yet, teachers still felt that the classroom environment was overwhelming. The stress of poverty permeated the classroom in the form of unpredictable enrollment and behavior, and it impacted teachers' work experiences.

Not all preschools serving majority-poor students were Head Start programs like the Sunshine Head Start was. While unpredictable behavior is more likely in any majority-poor preschool, Head Start programs include high standards and interventions. Each intervention can require teachers to do paperwork documenting what they did. The activities and paperwork are intended to support higher-quality classrooms. But this paperwork adds to teachers' stress.[11] Roxanne experienced this paperwork as an impediment to allowing her to spend time coaching children on classroom behavior. Her absence may have added to the workload of the assistant teachers who remained behind in the classroom.

In contrast, at Great Beginnings, children's family lives translated into predictable enrollment, attendance, and behavior. Teachers took attendance for granted and rarely commented on it. Great Beginnings teachers identified that challenging behavior could be a hard part of the job. However, the children who were challenging stood out as individuals, allowing teachers to maintain a rosy outlook on the children in general. These teachers planned to stay at the school long-term, and many of them were already almost a decade into their careers at the same school. This meant that the Great Beginnings children and families could further count on stability in their teachers.

Teachers' experience of the classroom shaped the way they talked about the kids. For example, Sunshine Head Start teachers used words like "chaotic," "overwhelming," and "Bedlam," terms that match a culture of poverty discourse that characterizes poor people's lives as chaotic.[12] This has consequences both for the specific children who misbehaved and also for the other children who followed class rules but were characterized negatively. The whole class was referred to as the "Wildcats."

Teachers' work experiences are important because in addition to affecting the teachers, they affect students. Some research suggests that teachers' stress impacts children much in the same way that parents' stress results in harsher parenting and in children acting out.[13] In one study, teachers reporting more workplace stress because of demands like "many responsibilities, little time, and many interruptions" related to a higher sense of conflict with children.[14] If we hope for young children to have calm, available teachers, and if we hope for teachers to be workers with manageable, positive workplaces, then concentrating poor children within classrooms may interfere with these ideals. So long as poverty in the United States remains punishing, stressful, and interlaced with unpredictable access to housing, food, and social support, preschool segregation may undermine efforts to support poor children and their teachers.[15] Racism interweaves with the punishing nature of poverty in the United States. Black, Hispanic, and Indigenous families experience more contact with the police, a higher likelihood of being incarcerated, higher rates of eviction, and higher rates of poverty due to structural and institutional racism.[16]

Segregation thus concentrates the effects of structural racism and punishing poverty in some classrooms. On the other hand, segregation enables affluent students and teachers to learn and work within spaces where the problems of American poverty and racism are merely abstract.

Roxanne left Sunshine Head Start—and her segregated classroom with poor students of color—for a job at a preschool that served a group of racially mixed, middle-income students in an act of self-preservation. She cried many days before leaving, and many days after. Yet she felt that she needed a lower-stress work environment if she were to continue to teach preschoolers. It turned out that at her new school, the families had more resources and the children's behavior was accordingly easier to manage.

After talking to Roxanne for more than an hour at Starbucks for our interview, I asked how things at her new job compared to Sunshine Head Start. She said it was very different: "The behaviors aren't quite as big when it comes to anger, or aggression. I don't hear cussing. I can't tell you the last . . . like I haven't seen any tables fly. I have seen chairs flipped over, and I've seen climbing on shelves, but it's like once in a couple weeks. I mean it's not every day, multiple times a day."

"Do you think they're just less stressed in general?" I asked.

"It's funny because [my new coteacher] keeps saying to me, 'It's similar, kids are still kids.' And I'm like, I mean yes, they are kids still, you'll still see certain kids who are seeking more attention and stuff, but they're not doing it in aggressive manners. But like I said, I mean they're all, most of the kids are living right in the community. So they have steady housing. I mean they bring their own lunches, so they do have access to at least lunch. No one seems to be worried about starving. I'm struggling with not being as connected with our families. I'm getting there. We have conferences coming up next week, and I'm excited to kind of get to talk to parents more, but a lot of the parents don't stay and talk with us a whole lot."

"So how long do you think you'll be at your new school?

She replied with a small smile. "I hope a long time. I like it a lot. I love that I get to teach, I mean it's just amazing. My [new] boss is like, 'I trust you; I don't need to see your lesson plan; I don't need to come in your room. I know that you're the best, I know that you know what you're doing.' So I see myself there for a long time, but hopefully they'll keep me."

CONCLUSION

Looking Forward

At the end of May, Sunshine Head Start had the children who were going off to kindergarten in the fall switch to a summer class to prepare for kindergarten. This meant that many children were in their final days in Ms. Roxanne's class.

Isaac and I were sitting next to his nap-time mat.

"Don't you want to get a book?"

"I'm waiting for Ms. Rebecca's books," he said.

"Well, we could probably read a whole book in the meantime. Or do you just wanna talk?"

"Let's talk. What do you like to have for your lunch?"

"Ham sandwiches?" I said playfully.

He was smiling broadly and had a silly look on his face. "I like grilled cheese, and soup with it."

"I'm gonna miss you," I said. I was feeling sad. I didn't think he heard me, because he kept talking about lunch, the tomato soup that he liked.

Then he said, "Where are you going, you're not coming back?"

"No, I am coming back, but you are going off to kindergarten."

"Yeah," he said. "You're not coming to that? You have to stay here because the other kids like you?"

"Yes. Plus, I'm not turning five, so I don't go to kindergarten."

"Oh," he said. "I'm gonna miss you too. But people are coming with me. Julian is coming, and Michael to my class."

"Are you and Julian gonna play together? Are you friends again?"

"Yeah, we will be friends in the new class. Or we might not play for a while until we can forgive each other, then we will be friends again."

Isaac, who had bright eyes and a talkative nature, had been on-and-off best friends with Julian for two years. Sometimes Isaac led their pretend play too much, bossing Julian when he wasn't in the mood for it. They had been in a prolonged fight a few weeks earlier, placing their young friendship in jeopardy. Both boys had a lot happening at home: Julian's mom was back from jail; and Isaac's mom was having a difficult, unplanned pregnancy. But I had not seen the boys talk much about these family happenings lately. For now, Isaac was looking to the future, a major transition for him from preschool to kindergarten. He seemed as confident about his move to kindergarten as he was in his long-term friendship with Julian.

Sunshine Head Start did a lot to mark the transition to kindergarten. Their biggest event of the year was the end-of-the-year celebration, which kids alternated between calling "the party" and "the graduation." It was held at the school from 5:30 p.m. to 7:30 p.m. The teachers and kids had been practicing their performances for a few weeks. On the night of graduation, families first milled around in their kids' classrooms. Most kids had several family members present. Isaac's grandma, mom, and baby sister came. Julian's mom came, along with his two siblings and his mom's boyfriend, Adrian, whom Julian had lately been calling "dad." Dustin's mom came and brought her four older sons. The two teenagers mostly sat to the side with surly expressions, and the two elementary schoolers played with classroom toys.

Then we had dinner. Frank made food and set it out, buffet-style, on a long table in the hallway. Families made plates and came back to the classroom to eat, sitting in little chairs at the tables and joking about how they didn't fit.

Then we all moved to the multipurpose room. Though only about thirty children were graduating, and the graduating children were not occupying seats, all fifty or so of the seats were taken by moms, dads, grandmas, uncles, and baby cousins. The teachers and I stood in the hallway to offer more seats to families. But still, some adults had to stand along the back wall, and teenagers sat cross-legged on the floor.

Our class performed first. The kids sang two songs that they had sung in Circle Time all year long. Then the other preschool class performed. Their class stood in V-formation, and each child had an instrument—maracas, tambourines, and hand-held drums. The children sang a song about a spaceman while their teacher played acoustic guitar. For a second song, they danced to the song "Forever Young." Each boy paired with a girl, and the teachers danced with one another. At the end of the song, all the boys knelt and offered a rose to their girl partners. Many in the audience sighed fondly. The third song was a popular pop song that had an accompanying dance. Our class and some of the older siblings spontaneously joined the dance.

After the performances, the school social worker screened a slide-show with pictures of the kids playing at preschool, set to music. When their child came on the screen, the child's family cheered and grinned. I overheard one parent remark to another, "It's nice to see what they do here all day. I feel like we never get pictures." The event ended with children coming up, one by one, and getting a graduation certificate from the director of the preschool.

Families' support for their child's education and joy at this transition was clear. The next step was an assumption, rather than a choice. All the kids who were age-eligible for kindergarten would be moving from Head Start to elementary school.

* * *

At Great Beginnings, parents were already starting to think ahead to kindergarten in February. Ms. Erica explained,

A lot of parents now are wondering what to do for next year. This is the make-or-break time, because in our class, they can go on to the other classroom or they can go to kindergarten. It is the parents' choice. We have some kids that are going to go to the other class and we have some kids who are going to kindergarten. And for one kid who is going on to kindergarten, they don't know where they want to put her. Because they don't like the school district that they are in, but they aren't super-religious, so they don't want to go to a Catholic school. It is trying to come up with resources and different things like, "This is an open enrollment school, you could go here." When that happens, I say, "Let me see if I can find stuff for you." Then, I talk to Ms. Kim and we come up with something together. Then, we send it to the parents.

In Wisconsin, kids are eligible for kindergarten if they have turned five by September 1. The Great Beginnings class for older four-year-olds had some kids with September and October birthdays who had just missed the cutoff and would be nearly six by the time they started kindergarten. But it also had children with spring and summer birthdays who were already eligible for kindergarten but whose parents decided their child would benefit from entering kindergarten at an older age. This practice is called redshirting. Researchers have found that male, white, and upper-income children are much more likely to be redshirted than their peers.[1] When Great Beginnings offers a class largely for this purpose, they provide institutional support for white, upper-class families to tailor their schooling plans for their children's maximum advantage.

Such a curated approach to planning a child's entrance to kindergarten is more common among families that have options because of class advantages. At one Sunshine Head Start Family Fun Night, I attempted small talk with Isaac's mom. It was March, and I knew he would be off to kindergarten in the fall. "Do you know what school he'll go to for kindergarten?" I asked her. She shrugged and kept eating. In general, the idea of "choosing" a kindergarten was not discussed at Sunshine Head Start. Even more foreign was the idea of having a child delay kindergarten when they were age-eligible to go. Head Start would not pay for an additional year, and so keeping a child out of kindergarten would come at the family's expense.

And so, after two substantially different preschool experiences, all of the Head Start children and many of the Great Beginnings children would be going on to kindergarten. Some Great Beginnings children would continue to private schools—including Catholic schools and small independent schools for "gifted and talented" children. The children from both schools shared the experience of having had previous group education, knowing how to interact with teachers, and experiencing other key elements of kindergarten preparation. Yet each group of children would have experienced different implicit lessons about what it means to be a member of a school classroom, what to expect from their teachers, and how to manage their time, their bodies, and their property in a large group setting. These inequalities may only widen as children progress through elementary schools.[2]

Segregation and the Four Ways of Talking about Preschool

When we center segregation as an operating force in preschool children's experiences, it becomes clear how family circumstances crystallize in different, unequal ways within a classroom. This affects the feeling of classrooms: from how teachers and children spend their time to scripts for pretend play to access to toys to conversations between parents and teachers. Segregation clarifies the four discourses about preschool described in the book's introduction.

First, let us return to the idea of preschools as places where *teachers are key educators*, almost mirroring the role of intensive motherhood that some children get at home. The early childhood field trains teachers to be child development experts, and preschool lead teachers nationally are largely white women with college educations.[3] At Sunshine Head Start and at Great Beginnings, the lead teachers were indeed college-educated, white women with similar views on early childhood. Positioning teachers as the primary drivers of children's development makes teacher attention into a precious commodity. Yet segregation made it so that Sunshine Head Start teachers had to stretch their attention much further than the Great Beginnings teachers—despite the schools having identical teacher-to-student ratios on paper. These similar, and excellent, ratios are encouraging because they are a lever that policy makers could pull to try to improve preschool. Yet the low ratios were insufficient to change the fundamental fact of one classroom having high family needs from racialized trauma and poverty and one classroom having none of these needs. In this way, segregation was more powerful than attempts to tweak the classroom environment by making more teacher attention available to each child.

The second discourse, with centuries-long roots, is the idea that *preschool is compensatory* for children from poor families. This discourse has classist and racist assumptions baked into it. The rhetoric of poor families as fundamentally flawed intersects with views of Black, Hispanic, and Indigenous families as flawed.[4] And even in contemporary times, when we fuel the *preschool as compensatory* discourse, it can have racist results—results that reinforce racial inequalities. Even though today it may be less common for policy makers to explicitly describe families of color as broken, the discourse of poor families as broken often comes to a similar result, because people of color make up a disproportionate share of poor families.[5]

But the *preschool as compensatory* discourse is a problem for another reason, too: it leads us to focus on children's individual family "shortcomings" and thus on delivering resources to these individual children. When some preschools group marginalized children together, it makes resource delivery more efficient. We can group children from poor families and deliver things like nutritious food, tooth brushing, reading, and an overall "enriching environment." I view this method of grouping children more critically. It is segregation by social class, which often creates racial segregation because structural racism has made it so that families of color are more likely to be poor. In my observations, class segregation was indeed efficient in providing "compensatory" resources to poor children. Yet there were unintended consequences that mattered for poor children when they were segregated within classrooms, from strains on their teachers to turnover among classmates. Affluent children, too, are harmed by segregation—they can develop an outsized sense of entitlement to adult attention, become unprepared for changing classroom conditions, and learn about economic need as an abstract problem rather than an embedded aspect of daily life.

A further way that segregation amplifies preschool discourses is by enhancing how preschools provide services. Poverty gave the Sunshine Head Start families some financial experiences in common. For example, they did not have spare money for enrichment activities, date nights, and to fund class parties. These circumstances shaped the activities and enrichments that the preschool offered to families. But while I try to highlight the variation among these families—for example, some families moved and were evicted a lot, others lived in the same apartment for years—this variation was not as salient for programming purposes. The Sunshine Head Start teachers had one set of practices for the whole class, and these practices often centered the poorest children. Recall teachers' choices to forbid personal objects and to avoid open conversations with families for fear of seeming to pry.

Meanwhile, affluent schools like Great Beginnings approached service provisions with a concentrated version of the *preschool as supplement* discourse. Rather than spending time on tooth brushing and offering classes on parenting, the school organized field trips and offered to babysit children so parents could go on date nights. They had an amenities-focused approach. These preschools provide extras oriented toward pleasing children and families, rather than focusing on providing basics that are assumed to be lacking at home. In short, segregating children in classrooms accentuates the presumed differences among the groups of children, and only fuels these two classed, racialized discourses about preschool.

There are at least two antidotes to these amplified discourses about preschools' connections to families. One is to recognize that all families—including poor families and families of color—enrich their children and have strengths. Preschools can be great partners in child development for all families. But when we envision preschools as partners in child development, we need to think of preschools as fundamentally group learning environments—which means that segregation by race and class are important features of classrooms. Integrating classrooms could be a way to bring families' diverse strengths into one setting, while balancing out different needs that families from affluent and poor families might have. A more balanced approach might be to the benefit of all families. Some affluent parents might have things to learn about parenting or need help getting their children's teeth brushed. Some poor parents may want their child to experience Show-and-Tell and may not need social worker support to meet needs. Class-integrated programs might encourage classroom-level rules that integrate not just the children but different kinds of family realities.

A second, powerful antidote is to think of children as belonging to families, rather than as individuals who just happen to be in families. That would require us to not be easily satisfied that poor children are getting resources delivered via school. A truly family-centered approach to enriching children would focus on ameliorating poverty, so that families have the financial resources and emotional bandwidth to meet their child's needs at home. This would give preschools an easier, joyous job in partnering with families, rather than the heavy burden of being social service provisioners who must compensate for harsh, antifamily policies in the United States at large.

Finally, the fourth way of talking about preschools is as *sites of unequal socialization*. The dominant idea here is that children learn about race, class, and gender systems and their place within those systems when they attend preschool. Centering segregation is critical here, because we can see how approaches to race, class, and gender end up clustering in different kinds of programs. Other scholars have worked in this vein. Sociologist Heidi Gansen attended to the class and race compositions in classrooms as she analyzed messages about gender and sexuality that children grapple with in preschool. Researchers Nelson and Schutz selected two majority-white but class-segregated classrooms and observed how the organization of the day and talk between teachers and children resulted in unequal socialization about school environments. Naming the segregation at play here is important. It clarifies that clustering children by social class also clusters and concentrates the effects of the messaging that classroom environments send to children. In the cases of Sunshine Head Start and Great Beginnings, if we imagine a world where the classrooms were mixed by social class, this would sometimes change the conditions under which teachers make classroom rules. Things like Show-and-Tell—easy to implement when you can be sure your students' families are not facing material hardship—would cause more friction in a mixed-income environment. In other cases, teachers might organize time in a similar way. Perhaps if Great Beginnings had a classroom where only two-thirds of children were affluent, they would keep their tight management of free play time and seek to direct children to activities that facilitated well-roundedness. But instead of a group of mostly white and all middle-class children being influenced by this play-time organization, there would be some lower-income children of color who would be influenced as well. As we continue to investigate how preschools function as early institutions where children have raced, classed, and gendered experiences, my findings further suggest that researchers should attend to the background features of classrooms that shape what is possible. Factors like class size, teacher-to-student ratio, and segregation matter for broad socialization of children within preschools.[6]

The Puzzle of Segregation and Expanding Preschool Access

We are in an exciting moment where preschool is a key conversation point among policy makers. One top idea is to create "universal preschool" for four-year-olds. Often cities and states that roll out universal preschool will do so with special supports and prioritization in mind for four-year-olds in poverty. This is done because of substantial evidence that preschool is especially beneficial to boosting the pre-kindergarten skills of children from poor families.[7] Universal preschool efforts are expansions of the early childhood system that we have—which is a largely segregated system. Segregation seems to rarely be a factor in the way places plan their universal preschool rollout. But it can be. We need to ensure that all kids have access to preschool, ensure that preschool is affordable, and ensure that preschools are inclusive.

The first thought many have for expanding preschool is to add preschool classrooms onto elementary schools. Elementary schools are an attractive option for several reasons. They are a known institution to parents. Public schools are inherently seen as providing an education, in contrast to child care centers, which are sometimes derogatorily called "daycares" and incorrectly presumed to be providing basic health and safety but not education. Public schools also offer jobs with higher pay scales and better benefits for teachers than many private preschools, which are often women-owned small businesses.

But elementary schools adding on preschool classrooms can have down sides. Public school buildings are pitched more toward the older children within them and are built to manage large groups of children through activities. This can mean, for example, that four-year-olds spend a great deal of time walking the halls from their classroom to the cafeteria, and from their classroom to the playground. At public schools, preschool teachers' main supervisors are school principals, who now have children aged four to age eleven under their purview, and who may not understand the approach of early educators.

For many families, sending their four-year-old to a public elementary school is not especially convenient. For example, if you have two kids, age four and age two, you may prefer to have them together in the same building. But public schools do not accommodate infants and toddlers. The hours can be inconvenient too. Most schools consider a full day to be about 6.5 hours—from 8:30 a.m. to 3:00 p.m. Parents who have an eight-hour workday, plus a mandatory lunch break and a commute, need more care for their child than that. Yet when elementary schools do offer "wraparound care," children might be required to be five or six to attend. These challenges box out certain families: single parents with limited kin support and dual-working parents with nine-to-five jobs, in particular. Preschool classrooms in elementary schools work well for other families—and not only for families that have stay-at-home parents or can afford nannies. Poor and working-class families are diverse and may have kin support or opposite work schedules that mean the limited hours are ideal for them.

Public schools have a role to play in preschool expansion, but letting public schools be first in line has major equity risks. A critical step toward a less segregated preschool expansion is to create what is called a "mixed-delivery system," where public schools, child care centers, and in-home child care providers are all financially supported to teach preschoolers.[8]

Preschool classrooms already operate in privately run child care centers that can be included in universal preschool. These private centers vary in class and race composition and should be part of the mixed-delivery system so as to allow for greater diversity of classes, including middle-income families and families who work full-time. These centers, as well as in-home child care centers, more often can educate infants and toddlers and provide age-appropriate, wraparound care from 7:30 a.m. to 5:30 p.m. Some centers orient to serving low-income families. These centers accept child care subsidies, are skilled at the burdensome paperwork that accompanies such subsidies, and may serve a higher proportion of families of color, depending on the racial demographics of their wider city. On the other hand, some private centers are vehicles for intractable segregation among the white and wealthy—for example, some private schools charge high fees and do not accept child care subsidy programs, essentially ensuring that they are inaccessible to poor families. Because of existing racial gaps in wealth and income, these schools are accessible to only small percentages of Black, Hispanic, and Indigenous families.

Finally, home-based child care centers are important to include because they are more segregated than center-based child care.[9] Blocking them out of expanded preschool access leaves some children in highly segregated programs. However, some of these home-based child care centers, alongside some larger child care centers, intentionally gather children of color to provide culturally affirming care. For example, there are preschools designed to foster Black excellence and positive identity development. There are home-based child care centers that have Spanish-speaking teachers and provide a closer home-school connection for Spanish-speaking families. These programs increase the degree of segregation in a system overall but do so for reasons that may counter racial inequality. Including these potential "counterspaces" in a state-funded universal preschool system could have extremely positive effects on reducing racial inequalities in society more broadly.[10]

Mixed-delivery models have the potential to broaden access to preschool. But mixed-delivery models do not inherently lead to affordable programs. After the critical first step of designing a program inclusive of these types in an expanding system, the next step is true affordability. Child care subsidies can help make child care affordable. Families qualify for a child care subsidy based on their income. Once a family is approved for funding, they search for a program that takes their subsidy and that fits their needs. This is a challenging, time-consuming search, as programs are not required to accept subsidies at all, so families may call a dozen places to hear that only two of them will accept their subsidies. We need strong policies that incentivize more child care providers to accept state subsidies.

Increasing class integration might reduce racial segregation somewhat, but it would not do so fully. Racial segregation is a reality made by humans for the purpose of fostering inequality so that white people could have more resources at the expense of people of color. Just as racial inequalities were constructed in race-conscious ways, countering these strong social realities requires some race-conscious policies. For preschool, one step is assisting majority-white preschools in becoming more inclusive and culturally responsive to children of color, and in having antiracist policies that ensure that children of color are valued fully. Given documented implicit bias among preschool teachers, as well as tendencies to suspend and expel Black four-year-olds at higher rates than their white peers, it is critical to improve the majority-white preschools into which some families of color will integrate.[11]

Another approach to racial inclusivity is to explicitly support early childhood teachers and directors of color. Teachers of color make up a large portion of the early childhood field, but often work in centers with low resources and low wages. Teachers of color are overrepresented in classrooms in assistant or aide roles, rather than in lead teacher roles. Further, despite high rates of teachers of color in the field, center directors are largely white.[12] These disparities reflect broader racial inequalities that filter through to the requirements of starting and running a center. To run a child care center, you need education and qualifications—these cost money and time. Many child care centers operate as small businesses—requiring directors to manage personnel, building operations, accounting, and taxes, alongside the core work of supporting child development. We know that women of color have less wealth to draw on and invest into maintaining a business, and so it is unsurprising that women of color are underrepresented among child care center directors.[13] The current lack of support for women of color in the early childhood field is insidious given that women of color cared for and educated previous generations of young children. For those with the knowledge and interest, we can support them in being at the center of policies for preschool and child care expansion.

This book is about preschool. But it is about much more than that. It is about broad social problems of punishing the poor, treating families like private islands that must solve all their own problems, and directing money to Head Start with more enthusiasm than directing money straight to families that work full-time but are nonetheless living in poverty. Elevating preschool as an antipoverty policy presumes that we can be successful by channeling resources through school institutions, rather than directly to families. Yet my observations show that this is unsuccessful in segregated contexts—especially because what children experience at home and outside of school comes into the classroom.

In the United States, we ask for preschool to do something that we don't ask of any other institutional experience. Through one fantastically enriching year, the hope is that poor kids will be equipped to succeed in navigating underfunded, unequal institutions as they progress through the rest of their lives. Public discourse is normalizing pouring more into the fourth year of a child's life than into their first, second, or third years of life.

If we want to understand why race and class inequalities are so intractable in general, we must look to the beginning. Preschool should be one key piece in a puzzle of supports that interlock to foster children's dignity and growth. Yet one of our most darling, bipartisan-supported, antipoverty policies—preschool—is delivered in segregated contexts, and with some unintentional but nonetheless unequal results. The problem of segregated preschools is low on the agenda, even for advocates and policy makers who care deeply about preschool expansion. Many conversations are focused on pressing issues like the fact that many families live in child care deserts; that preschool is unaffordable for many families; and that preschool teachers are shamefully underpaid for the important work that they do. Since preschool is not yet available to all, the fact that the preschools that families can access are segregated seems like a problem to tackle later. But today's preschool children deserve integrated, equitable classrooms where they can learn and grow.

ACKNOWLEDGMENTS

The research and writing for this book spanned nine years. In that time I moved two states, held three different full-time jobs, had three babies, and made countless friends.

My family deserves so much of my gratitude. I thank my grandmother for caring for me for nearly a decade and for helping me catch up in school. She took me to the library, attended my parent-teacher conferences, and always told me that I had to go to college and that I could get a PhD if that was my dream. I thank my mom for always giving me the best of what she had to give and for loving me always. My brother Julian has been my sweet, optimistic supporter—first when I was scared and lonely at college, and later when I would call to complain about the challenges of this project. My sibling Shalia has been my cheerleader. I am grateful to the emotional support Shalia provided, for the rejuvenating trips back home in California and later in New York, and for the long phone calls and check-ins.

I met my husband, Darian, as I finished field work and began writing. He has given me unconditional love, pep talks, and free time to write. I am thankful to have a partner who supports my work and who shares the mental, emotional, and physical loads of family life fairly. Our three children—Amari, Rashad, and Naya—were born between finishing field work and the publication of this book. They taught me so much about early childhood and gave me the motivation to go on. I could not have written this book without our sprawling village of child care centers and schools that have been partners in raising our children: the UW-Madison Child Development Lab, Stepping Stones Montessori, 1080 Learning Center, and Greenlee Elementary School.

I had a large chosen family that helped me thrive during this research. Itanza Lawrence kept me going with weekly phone conversations for the last few years. She read my fellowship applications, listened to me cry about rejected manuscripts, and generally kept me sane. Katie Fallon has been there since the first days of my research. She was the most fantastic combination of best friend, coach, confidante, and colleague. Martha Goodge was a dear friend and roommate. She listened to many late-night complaints in our kitchen about the challenges of ethnography and helped me understand teachers' points of view. I will forever be in her debt. Towards the end of my field work, Jamie Hawkins became my trusted confidante and an immense source of support in juggling motherhood and work.

I am indebted to Mustafa Emirbayer, Myra Marx Ferree, Linn Posey-Maddox, and Robert Nix for their guidance on pushing my ideas through from early drafts to clear arguments. Alice Goffman was the earliest supporter of this project. She brought her insight and enthusiasm to every piece of writing I brought her. I credit her for teaching me how to do ethnography well and for helping me persist through two years of field work.

I benefited from outstanding undergraduate research assistance. Thank you to Michelle Koffa, Adeena Guyton, Anastasiya Apalkova, and Susan Back, each of whom is intimately familiar with my field notes and did an excellent job coding them with me.

Funding was critical to this project. I am grateful for support from the National Science Foundation, the Ford Foundation, the Wisconsin Collective for Ethnographic Research, and the Institute for Citizens and Scholars.

In the final stretches of writing, I benefited enormously from conversations with my colleagues at the University of Denver, and especially from my writing group with Hava Gordon, Jared Del Rosso, and Lisa Martinez. I also shared drafts with what I called my assistant professor writing crew: Jennifer Bouek, Christina Cross, Kelley Fong, Hope Harvey, and Anna Rhodes. In 2021, Maia Cucchiara, Karin Martin, and Stefanie Mollborn participated in a book workshop. They read an early manuscript draft and gave detailed, much-appreciated feedback. My friends Daanika Gordon and katrina quisumbing king stuck with me through the very end, reading drafts, talking through arguments, and cheering me on. Ilene Kalish was an ideal editor, supportive of my vision for the book but also pushy where I needed her to be. Emily Wright did a fantastic job copyediting the manuscript.

Finally, this work would not have been possible without the teachers, families, and children who let me into their lives. Thank you to both Sunshine Head Start and Great Beginnings for putting up with me in their spaces for such a long time. Special thanks to Paige and Sam, who gave me many rides, were a second family to me in Wisconsin, and shaped my views on family engagement at Head Start. Field work was joyful because of the kids who let me join in on space expeditions and in thrilling encounters with witches, and because of the teachers who let me navigate the classroom in my own way. Though I fear that my research did little to improve things for the children and teachers navigating tough situations at the time of my field work, I hope that this book will bring depth and real people to conversations about what preschool should be like in the United States.

APPENDIX

Research Methods

I started this project with a major guiding notion: that even four-year-old children have a sense of their own experiences and of inequality. My hope was to learn about their developing views of their racial identities and of racial inequality. I was captivated by the work of sociologist Debra Van Ausdale, who, in the 1990s, had observed a preschool with a multicultural curriculum. Her article and book with Joe Feagin laid out a sociological analysis of how children used race and racism in interactions at school. I read her work in 2012. Her observations were nearly twenty years old, and in that time, color-blind racial discourse had spread. I yearned to return to a Head Start to better understand questions that arose from previously working at a Head Start preschool. I found a center that had a racially diverse group of students and assumed that it would be an ideal context in which to observe how children develop racial understandings.

Origins of the Study: Sunshine Head Start

In August 2013, I called a local Head Start and asked if I could come do a research project there. I arranged a time to meet with the center director, Max. We had an extended conversation about sociology, early childhood, and what Head Start was like. Max gave me a tour of the building and then we discussed where I should do my observations.

Max said that there were two classrooms for four-year-olds. He decided to have me in Ms. Roxanne's classroom because it had a "good group of children" and a teacher who was very experienced.

I visited Ms. Roxanne's classroom over the course of the next two years, going on days or at times that my schedule allowed. During the school year, I visited two–three times per week, for a few hours at a time. In the summers, I went four days a week, for five to six hours at a time.

As discussed in chapter 4, Paige and I developed a close relationship after she saw me waiting at the bus stop about a half-mile from the preschool. She pulled over and offered me a ride home. When she learned that I bused to the preschool for my visits, she offered to give me a ride whenever she could. Paige worked as a teacher aide at Sunshine Head Start, and her son, Sam, attended. Through these rides to school, Paige and I became close. We began to hang out outside of the preschool, too—I joined her and her children for weekend outings, dinners, and trick-or-treating. We often discussed my research. Paige's family was the only one I spent time with outside the classroom.

To my great surprise, my elaborate plan to highlight race in children's play and conversation was a bust. I rarely heard children mention race or racial categories. The teachers were largely unaware of children's cultural backgrounds. So instead, I let the children be my guide for how to focus my observations. At first, my field notes focused on ordinary things (I wrote at least ten pages of field notes about hand washing, children being counted by teachers, and other mundane things). But within a month, my field notes focused on moments that children imbued with extra emotion or discussion. My field work focused on quests to sneak personal objects into school, the complex task of getting pretend play going, children tracking other people's families at drop-off and pick-up, several months of children cursing at school, and more.

The "Least Adult" Approach in Practice

Before starting field work, I planned to do the "least adult approach."[1] The least adult approach means minimizing your inherent authority and knowledge as an adult. Previous ethnographers who have used this method noted that children spoke to them differently, and that children did not alter their behavior in their presence.[2] I told the teachers that I did not want to discipline the children, and they agreed to this. Instead, I "closely followed children's ways, initially observing and imitating their words, actions, and responses, and gradually getting my line of action into theirs."[3]

In trying to implement the least adult approach, I experienced early tensions with teachers, who at first saw me as an all-purpose extra set of hands. For example, in my first week, Ms. Lisa asked me to lead a table activity with the other teachers. I agreed half-heartedly. I ended up doing a bad job, and the teachers joked that I was not cut out to be a teacher. I rebuffed future requests to do tasks that only teachers did, like reading a book to the whole class at Circle Time, by restating that I wanted to spend my time with the children.

In the end, I settled on doing small helping tasks, remixing the approach Nancy Mandell used.[4] She did not do things like tie shoes or read books to children, claiming that these were "teacher tasks." I felt that not doing these things would be deceptively downplaying my cognitive and fine motor skills. Plus, I had observed that children helped peers with tasks that they were able to do. I saw no harm in doing some things that children asked of me.

The advantages of the least adult approach became clear a few months into my Head Start field work. Children began to gossip, curse, and snatch toys in front of me. They would sometimes glance furtively at a teacher while they did this, to see if they were going to get in trouble. But most of the children began to take for granted that *I* was not going to scold them or tell on them. Sometimes the children would argue about something and look to me for guidance, and I would suggest they ask a teacher. In many ways, the role I settled into in the classroom reminded me of my childhood self—I was overly helpful, obsessed with reading, and wary of rule breaking but sometimes still complicit in it.

Despite using the least adult approach, my adultness still critically affected my role in the space. For example, the teachers saw my accounts as inherently credible, in contrast to the children's. I was asked to confirm which child was playing with a toy first, if a child was actually cleaning up, or if a child had in fact gone to the bathroom. These are things that teachers rarely asked of children, and if they did ask children, they never trusted a child's response as wholeheartedly as they did mine.

Being a least adult also created awkward moments between the teachers and me. For example, I often tried to participate in pretend play and jokes as children did. This sometimes involved breaking the rules—I had to play a witch, a zombie, or a policeman, thereby colluding in violent play. I had to answer a child's question of "guess what?" allowing them to say "chicken butt" (a phrase the teachers disliked) and burst into giggles.

Often the children and I successfully avoided the teachers' punishments. But when teachers noticed us breaking a rule, they seemed irritated with me in particular. One day during Work Time, I told Isaac (truthfully) that I was tired and I wanted to take a nap.

"You could take a nap," he said, "but we will wake you up." Then he and two other boys started ordering me to take a nap. They chased me to different classroom areas, and I lay down in each area and would pretend to sleep until they played instruments right in my ear. We all laughed. We repeated this sequence a few times, moving through the House Area, the Block Area, and then settling in the Quiet Area.

At this point, Ms. Julie said, "Come on, only one friend in the Quiet Area! Go!"

The children scrambled off. Ms. Julie shot me an irritated look. I felt awkward and as though I was annoying Ms. Julie. I waited about half a minute and then left the Quiet Area. In immersing myself in children's activities, as in this case, I sometimes undermined teachers' rules.

It took time for me to settle in at Head Start. I felt extremely uncomfortable at first. I wanted to behave similarly to children, but there are limits there. For example, at nap time, the children take off their shoes, lie on blue mats, and go to sleep. Teachers sit at the tables, eat lunch, and stare at their phones. Teachers' behavior was much more appealing to me, but I was wary of "siding" with them, and of missing out on what was going on with the children. In this case, I developed a routine of sitting next to children at the start of nap time, just as teachers did. But I remained there for all of nap time so I could observe and overhear things from kids who were not actually asleep. My guiding principle was to participate in children's activities, up to the point of it being socially awkward or creepy.

The children at Sunshine Head Start took several months to adjust to my unfamiliar role. At first, they asked me often if I was someone's mom, or perhaps a teacher. Eventually, most of them called me just "Casey," much in the same way Bill Corsaro was treated in his landmark preschool ethnography.[5]

With the teachers, I talked about personal stuff, kept them updated on the shifting focus of my research, and asked for their opinions on things, from the children's choices in friends to the validity of state licensing visits. There were moments when they seemed uncomfortable being observed, or with what I would write in my notes. As seen in the preceding chapters, especially chapter 4, I included some examples of behavior they might find unflattering. But overall, I was a sympathetic observer to teachers at Sunshine Head Start. They were accepting of my presence, insisted that it was helpful to have me around, and were encouraging about my studies.

Adding a Comparative Case: Great Beginnings

My ethnographic training was heavily shaped by Alice Goffman, who in turn was shaped by some of her mentors, including Mitchell Duneier and Elijah Anderson. Alice implored me to continue my field work for more than three years and sometimes assumed that I would do so. She was right that there is much to learn and understand, even in the social space of one classroom. Yet I found myself becoming bored at Sunshine Head Start. In the first year, I observed a group of kids who were three and four. At the end of that year, the four-year-olds graduated and went to kindergarten. The kids who had been three were now the oldest in the class. Their looming graduation felt like a nice time to wrap up my field work.

On a practical note, I found myself going to the preschool less and less or going and having a great time but taking few field notes. One of Alice's truisms began echoing in my head, something like, "If you do field work but don't write up the field notes, you are just hanging out." So I planned to begin another phase of the study that would include a series of overnight visits at children's homes.

I had to abandon this plan for two reasons. First, I had planned to use grant money to pay families—both as an incentive to participate in the study and to recognize the costs of having me as a "boarder" for most of a month. However, the university required that I ask families for documentation and fill out an I-9 to receive the incentive. I consulted with Paige about this, and we agreed that it would be hard to recruit families with this structure. Head Start families are eligible for wraparound child care and, often, other social programs based on income eligibility. Having one month when they earned six hundred extra dollars of reported income might cause complications for them that might make the opportunity less attractive. Second, I became pregnant and I did not want to deal with the physical symptoms of the pregnancy while doing overnight visits.

I thus decided to do a short comparative case instead. I was originally attracted to the idea of the study being only about low-income Head Start families of color and asking questions about the basic process of socialization. I felt compelled by Alford Young Jr.'s charge that sociologists should use poor people and people of color as informants on general aspects of social life (in my case, as people experiencing socialization).[6]

However, I also wondered what important aspects of the classed nature of growing up at preschool were invisible to me because I had only observed Head Start preschools. I knew that one of the Head Start teachers, Ms. Megan, had worked at Great Beginnings, a highly rated preschool in the city. She had often remarked how different the two schools were for her as a teacher.

She connected me with the site director of Great Beginnings. We arranged for me to observe in the classroom daily for one month. This preschool was on the opposite side of town from my home and Head Start. I had a friend who worked near Great Beginnings, and she offered me a ride to the preschool. This structured my field work so that I arrived at 7:15 a.m. and left at 4:00 p.m. I visited for one month, during February 2016.

From Immersive Ethnography to Focused Ethnography

At Head Start, my goal was to do an immersive field work project—one premised on understanding local meanings and beliefs and representing them accurately.[7] I wanted to get to know a group of children and teachers and come to understand the dynamics of the social world in the preschool classroom.

After two years of field work in one classroom, I felt knowledgeable about the workings of the preschool. The rituals and taken-for-granted assumptions about how a preschool classroom operates were things I generally understood. For example, my early field notes include long reflections on the amount of hand washing preschoolers are asked to do, on teachers' "obsession" with counting the number of children in their care, and on the ways that teachers symbolically distance themselves from children. These things continued to be true during my field work, but I devoted less time to understanding and documenting them.

In contrast to Head Start, where my goal was to get to know the children, the teachers, and the classroom as well as possible, my approach at Great Beginnings was to observe specific features of social life and to compare them to Head Start. Working on the premise of "alerity" as a warrant for focused ethnography, my goal was to further develop my working theories about preschool social life in areas like children's access to objects, children's logics of pretend play, and teachers' control of children's behavior.[8] I wanted to know if the theories I had proposed held up in other field sites. My visits were targeted and took place over a short period of time.

At Sunshine Head Start, I settled into a role in the classroom that felt comfortable to me. Great Beginnings was a different story. As a nationally accredited private school, Great Beginnings was somewhat used to hosting student teachers and other observers. But neither of these roles matched what I wanted to do. Student teachers, well, teach. They take an active role in classroom affairs and are mentored by the lead teachers. The other typical observers that Great Beginnings (and Sunshine Head Start) hosted were people there to assess quality and safety. These observers come with a checklist on one day for a few hours. They avoid participating in the classroom. They are present explicitly to judge classroom practices.

Between my focused ethnography approach—where I had a list of themes I was looking for—and my two years of experience doing field work, I barely took notes in front of the teachers. If I heard a conversation I knew I would want near-verbatim notes for, I jotted down notes on a piece of scrap construction paper. I then went to the staff break room for lunch and expanded the notes via the Notes app on my cell phone.

Two weeks into my field work, the teachers essentially intervened. I received an email from the school director, asking me how my project was going and whether she and the teachers could see a copy of my notes. Initially, I interpreted this as a normal case of interest and concern. It is hard to be someone's object of study. I do believe that people in a research study are entitled to know what is being said about them. But then, I spoke to each teacher one on one. One of the four teachers admitted that they had been discussing whether I was taking notes at all. The director's email was less about wanting to double-check the content and more a matter of oversight because they thought I wasn't doing my job. I also was in a back break room and overheard the teachers talk about me, saying, "What is she even doing here?"

These encounters left me very upset. I am of two minds about them. On the one hand, I have empathy for the teachers and their experience of being observed and perhaps even judged by an outside observer. I know this happens in all kinds of field sites. I had not had the chance to update them on my research at that point. But I also had not exactly planned on doing so. When my field work started, I had them sign consent forms and explained my project. At that point, I told them about the themes of the project and what I was looking for. In comparison to the slow evolution of the project while at Sunshine Head Start, I thought I had been extremely specific with the Great Beginnings teachers about what I was looking for.

On the other hand, it felt like a racial microaggression. I was one of two Black adults in the building, and their assumption that I wasn't doing my job offended me. I did my best to repair the situation by talking with each teacher and further explaining the project and how I approach ethnography. I still felt distant from the teachers after that moment. As I described in chapter 2, the Great Beginnings teachers' stance was to direct me around the room somewhat like a child or brand-new teacher aide.

Attempting focused ethnography while enacting the least adult approach was challenging, too. Only some of the children seemed to view me as a least adult by the end of my month at Great Beginnings. Many of them still referred to me as "teacher" and were asking me to do teacher tasks when I left.

Data Analysis

I used a combination of focused coding and interpretative analysis to code both field notes and transcripts. I used the software program MAXQDA. I began coding my field notes during field work, using descriptive codes to capture key themes.[9] After completing field work, I worked with four undergraduate research assistants to inductively code the full field notes. Research assistants suggested codes as they read the field notes. We then created a final code sheet and did one last coding of the field notes.

The coding helped me to sift through the five hundred pages of field notes I had amassed, and to easily double-check that I had not missed instances relevant to my claims about the data. However, my analysis of the snippets of data evolved and changed over the many years I worked on the project.

Finally, after I had written a draft of the book, I wrote out the argument of each chapter. I then read, page by page, through all the field notes and interviews to scrutinize my arguments and look for contradicting evidence. This practice enriched chapter 4 the most and resulted in my expanding each chapter with further examples.

Limitations

I had to make constant decisions about where to be within the classroom. These decisions involved trade-offs, especially during free play periods when children were spread out across the different centers in the classroom. I often chose to go to the House Area or the Block Area at Head Start. These tended to have the biggest groups of children and were least likely to be supervised by a teacher. I felt that I would see more of children's peer culture there. Hanging out there meant I soon started playing with the same children over and over. Some of them referred to me as their friend. For months at a time, I would mostly play with these children, which meant I missed out on happenings in the rest of the classroom. I tried to use more structured times of the day, like meal times, lining up to go outside, and sitting in Circle Time, to observe what was happening with a greater number of children.

I often avoided the activity tables. These were on the other side of the classroom, and teachers tended to run tabletop activities there. Because of their location, sitting at the activity tables made it easier to watch dynamics in the whole classroom. However, I avoided them because I sometimes felt uncomfortable using the least adult approach and trying to let children lead when the teachers were close by. It was also hard to closely observe children's pretend play on the other side of the classroom.

At Great Beginnings, the teachers more often dictated where I went. I sensed that they saw me as a resource to enrich the children. They would send me to areas to pair up with certain children and refer children to me if they wanted someone to read them a book. I was also sent between Side 1 and Side 2 depending on which classroom the teachers thought needed more "help" that day. This hindered my success in using the least adult approach, with teachers continually marking me as a special helper and authority figure. However, Great Beginnings was quieter than Head Start, and so I could often overhear what children in other parts of the room were saying no matter where I was. Overall, my data represents some children better than others and represents children much more than teachers.

NOTES

Introduction

1 All names of people and of the two schools are pseudonyms. In this book, I have decided to include simple descriptions of children's features rather than to racially categorize them. I would have opted for racial categorizations, but in both preschools, children rarely verbalized a racial identity. Also, the teachers rarely discussed racial identity directly, and when I asked, teachers were often unaware of families' heritages, beyond basic categories like "Africa" or "Latin America." The teachers all identified their race as white, either in our interviews or over the course of my observations.

2 Kids Count Data Center 2018.

3 This is the recommendation of the National Association for the Education of Young Children (NAEYC).

4 This is a practice called "redshirting," and some parents use it to make sure their children are maximally positioned for academics and athletics by being slightly older than the peers in their grade.

5 I view race and class as always intersecting. The racial composition of my field sites—where nearly all the poor children were children of color and nearly all the affluent children were white—misses many race-class intersections of interest. It also means I cannot analyze potential racial discrimination from teachers. But it does not mean that racism was not operating in classroom life. For example, racism explains how these groups of children ended up in these classrooms, and also the higher poverty rates among Black, Hispanic, and Indigenous children. I encourage readers curious about racial discrimination in preschool classrooms to read Gansen (2021).

6 Kids Count Data Center 2018.

7 Race to Equity Team 2013.

8 Greenberg and Monarrez 2019.

9 Modern early childhood advocates discourage distinguishing between "care" and "education," citing that these two activities are not separate endeavors. I agree. In this chapter, I discuss historical developments in contexts where groups of children come together, sometimes under the official aim of "care" and sometimes under the official aim of "education." I combine the two because the reality of children's and caregivers' experiences is that a mix occurred—a matron might wipe a child's nose and also sing them a rhyming song, for example. I also intermix "preschool" and "child care." Preschools are a form of child care.

10 Constitution and Bylaws 1828; Steinfels 1973; Tank 1980.

11 Tank 1980: 26.

12 Tank 1980: 22.

13 Beatty 1995: 22; Mintz 2004; Tank 1980.

14 Cahan 1994: 14. Mothers' pensions were another program that fluctuated in popularity.

15 Rose 1999: 30.

16 Rose 1999:16, 36.

17 Rose 1999: 36.

18 Du Bois 1898; Rose 1999: 30–38.

19 Rose 1999: 57.

20 Beer 1957.

21 Cahan 1994; Rose 1999.

22 Cahan 1994: 29.

23 Steinfels 1973: 65.

24 Steinfels 1973: 66.

25 Allen 2017.

26 Allen 2017; Beatty 1995.

27 Allen 2017: 133.

28 Allen 2017: 134.

29 Allen 2017: 134.

30 Cahan 1994: 31; Rose 1999: 121.

31 Rose 1999: 115.

32 Rose 1999: 120.

33 Cahan 1994: 37.

34 Rose 1999: 145–46.

35 Cahan 1994: 41.

36 Cahan 1994.

37 Cahan 1994.

38 Tank 1980: 381.

39 Cahan 1994: 194.

40 Tank 1980: 375.
41 Cahan 1994: 43.
42 Cahan 1994: 43.
43 Cahan 1994: 46.
44 Cahan 1994.
45 Cahan 1994.
46 Patterson 2000: 279.
47 Lewis 1966.
48 In 1965, Daniel Patrick Moynihan, then the assistant secretary of labor, wrote a report for President Johnson centered on the issue of Black unemployment. Officially entitled *The Negro Family: The Case for National Action*, the report is known as "the Moynihan Report."
49 Moynihan 1965: 3–4.
50 Liebow 1967.
51 Liebow 1967: 23.
52 Patterson 2000.
53 Lewis 1966.
54 Moynihan 1965: 4.
55 Bloom 1965.
56 Recommendations for a Head Start Program 1965.
57 Wisconsin Historical Society Archives 1968.
58 Recommendations for a Head Start Program 1965.
59 Recommendations for a Head Start Program 1965.
60 Gillette 2010.
61 Vinofskis 2005: 75.
62 Vinofskis 2005: 78.
63 Gillette 2010: 263.
64 Vinofskis 2005: 15.
65 Gillette 2010: 271.
66 Rose 1999: 125.
67 National Center for Education Statistics 2019b.
68 National Center for Education Statistics 2019b.
69 Child Trends Data Bank 2016.
70 Fram and Kim 2012.
71 Reid et al. 2015.
72 Barnett 2008; Magnuson, Ruhm, and Waldfogel 2007.
73 Downey and Condron 2016.
74 Hays 1996.
75 Macdonald 2010: 8.
76 Bianchi 2000; Coontz 1992.
77 Ishizuka 2019; Manning 2019.
78 Dow 2019; Manning 2019; Rangel and Shoji 2021.
79 Calarco 2018.

80   Despite the air of objective universalism that dominated earlier decades of developmental psychology, children's needs are always shaped by cultural and societal context.

81   Nelson and Schutz 2007.

82   Affluent and white families tend to have fewer children, and are more likely to live far from extended family (Livingston 2015).

83   Nelson and Schutz 2007; Streib 2011.

84   Van Ausdale and Feagin 2001.

85   Gansen 2017; Martin 1998.

86   While the children also had experiences that were deeply gendered, I focus less on gender in this book. I encourage readers to consult work by sociologists Heidi Gansen (2019) and Karin Martin (1998) on this topic.

Chapter 1. "Is That How We Behave?"

1   Wisconsin Department of Children and Families 2020.

2   National Association for the Education of Young Children 2009.

3   Sapolsky 2005.

4   Routines can have a stabilizing effect.

5   Gerstel and Clawson 2015; Haskins, Amorim, and Mingo 2018.

6   Hagerman 2018.

7   Engel et al. 2021; Pianta et al. 2005.

8   Head Start 2020.

9   Harvey 2022.

10   See Thorne (1993) about elementary school playground dynamics on this same point.

11   Four children at Sunshine Head Start were native Spanish speakers: Alicia, Luz, Jasmine, and Gabe. They were learning to speak English. These four children defaulted to playing with one another and to speaking Spanish or a mix of Spanish and English among themselves. None of the teachers spoke Spanish. After six years of instruction in Spanish and a term of study abroad in Ecuador, I had some Spanish skills, mostly in listening and reading. But I knew Spanish well enough that I was the only adult able to really talk with these four children in Spanish.

12   Sunshine Head Start used PALS-PreK and the Creative Curriculum for Preschool.

13   Engel et al. 2021; Pianta et al. 2005.

Chapter 2. Play Time

1   National Association for the Education of Young Children 2009.

2   Lareau 2011; Manning 2019.

3   Rafalow 2018.

4 Anyon 1980; Golann 2015; Rafalow 2018.

5 See chapter 4 in Corsaro 2003.

6 Ms. Megan had previously worked at Great Beginnings, which might explain why her approach to play is similar to that of Great Beginnings teachers. However, I also observed Ms. Roxanne make similar overtures in the few times I saw teachers get involved with peaceful play at Sunshine Head Start.

7 See Lareau 2011. It is also reminiscent of Nelson and Schutz's (2007) findings in a mixed-age child care center.

8 This process mimicked the gendered chase-retreat dynamic that Barrie Thorne (1993) observed among elementary schoolers in the 1980s.

9 In this way, the teachers accept gendered terms for the way boys and girls can use space. For more on preschools as sites that produce gender difference, see Martin 1998.

10 Ms. Erica is doing Second Step, a socio-emotional curriculum for preschool.

11 Calarco 2011; Lareau 2011; Streib 2011.

12 Developmental psychologists might notice a common divergence in children's behaviors. Some children respond to trauma with "externalizing behaviors" like hitting and aggression. Others respond with "internalizing behaviors," becoming detached, shy, or despondent.

13 Rios 2011.

14 While this book details teacher involvement in pretend play, an important chance for children to exercise autonomy, others have written about classed patterns in the way teachers and children talk to one another (see Nelson and Schutz 2007 and Streib 2011).

15 Calarco 2018.

16 See, for example, Rafalow 2020.

Chapter 3. Toys in Cubbies

1 See Stockstill (2021) for a discussion of the distinctions between children's access to personal property and their access to classroom property.

2 Pugh (2009) also notes that at the high-poverty after-school program she observed, staff did not involve themselves in children's discussions of property. This meant that children created their own economies of dignity.

3 Other boys of color developed the same behaviors—including Julian's best friend, Isaac.

4 Wisconsin State Legislature n.d.

5 Ferguson 2001.

6 Ferguson (2001) found that teachers and school staff viewed Black elementary school boys as criminal; this shaped the way they disciplined kids. Gilliam and colleagues (2016) conducted an experiment with preschool teachers asking them to look out for misbehavior while watching a video of preschool children playing.

The teachers spent more time looking at Black boys than at the other children, noticing slight misbehaviors as a result.

7 Pugh 2009.

8 I did not observe these instances of kids having the same toy resulting in exclusion (for example, kids teasing the children who did not have that toy).

9 I do not know whether the other four-year-olds at Great Beginnings or Sunshine Head Start received an allowance, but this was the only time I heard allowance mentioned in my two years of observations.

10 Goddard 2018.

11 Goddard 2018.

12 Lareau 2011.

13 See, for example, school uniform policies, or consider the ability to personalize one's clothing or trinkets at work (National Center for Education Statistics 2019a).

14 Calarco 2018; Lareau 2011.

Chapter 4. Don't Talk about Disneyworld

1 Shrider et al. 2020.

2 Farley and Squires 2005.

3 Shrider et al. 2020.

4 See Desmond et al. (2013) on Black mothers and eviction; see Fong (2019) on mothers of color and Child Protective Services surveillance.

5 Fong 2023.

6 I experienced the unease of wondering how kids at the preschool would recount our interactions at home. One time, Isaac and I discussed his elaborate plan to steal a van, drive to Walmart, and get ourselves some superhero movies. It was imaginative yarn spinning. Yet I wondered the whole time what would happen if he went home and told his mom something like "Casey and I are going to steal a van and go to Walmart," especially since his mom knew that "Casey" was a twenty-five-year-old woman.

7 Fong 2019.

8 US Department of Health and Human Services 2016: 17.

9 Fong 2019.

10 Sedlak et al. 2010.

11 Bureau of Justice Statistics 2014.

12 Burton 2007.

13 Watkins-Hayes 2009.

14 See, for example, Jennifer Randles (2021) on the cognitive labor that poor mothers do to meet family needs.

Chapter 5. Burned Out

1 Styfco and Zigler 2010.
2 Bureau of Labor Statistics 2021.
3 Payne 2018.
4 At Great Beginnings, challenging child behavior seemed to be medicalized, as is common with affluent families. See Conrad 1992.
5 Dodge, Pettit, and Bates 1994.
6 Whitaker, Dearth-Wesley, and Gooze 2015: 66.
7 Cassidy et al. 2011.
8 Frankenberg 2001.
9 Desmond et al. 2013; Jiang, Ekono, and Skinner 2014; Linver, Brooks-Gunn, and Kohen 2002.
10 Pianta, Hamre, and Nguyen 2020.
11 Bullough, Hall-Kenyon, and MacKay 2012.
12 Ladson-Billings 2017.
13 Linver, Brooks-Gunn, and Kohen 2002.
14 Whitaker, Dearth-Wesley, and Gooze 2015.
15 Edin, Tach, and Sykes 2015; USDA 2021.
16 Desmond et al. 2013; Reskin 2012.

Conclusion

1 Bassok and Reardon 2013.
2 Calarco 2018; Golann 2015.
3 Bureau of Labor Statistics 2021.
4 Quadagno 1994.
5 Shrider et al. 2020.
6 Gansen 2021; Nelson and Schutz 2007.
7 Magnuson et al. 2004; Magnuson, Ruhm, and Waldfogel 2007.
8 Hunt Institute 2022.
9 Greenberg and Monarrez 2019.
10 Keels 2020.
11 Zinsser 2022.
12 Ulrich, Hamm, and Herzfeldt-Kamprath 2016.
13 Bureau of Labor Statistics 2021.

Appendix

1 Van Ausdale and Feagin 2001; Mandell 1988.
2 Mandell 1988.

3 Mandell 1988: 439.
4 Mandell 1988.
5 Corsaro 2003.
6 Young 2008.
7 Higginbottom, Pillay, and Boadu 2013.
8 Higginbottom, Pillay, and Boadu 2013; Knoblauch 2005.
9 Miles, Huberman, and Saldaña 2014.

REFERENCES

Allen, Ann Taylor. 2017. *The Transatlantic Kindergarten: Education and Women's Movements in Germany and the United States*. New York: Oxford University Press.

Anyon, Jean. 1980. "Social Class and the Hidden Curriculum of Work." *Journal of Education* 162(1):67–92.

Barnett, Steven W. 2008. *Preschool Education and Its Lasting Effects: Research and Policy Implications*. Boulder, CO: Education and the Public Interest Center & Education Policy Research Unit. http://epicpolicy.org.

Bassok, Daphna, and Sean F. Reardon. 2013. "'Academic Redshirting' in Kindergarten: Prevalence, Patterns, and Implications." *Educational Evaluation and Policy Analysis* 35(3):283–97.

Beatty, Barbara. 1995. *Preschool Education in America: The Culture of Young Children from the Colonial Era to the Present*. New Haven, CT: Yale University Press.

Beer, Ethel S. 1957. *Working Mothers and the Day Nursery*. New York: Whiteside and Morrow.

Bianchi, Suzanne M. 2000. "Maternal Employment and Time with Children: Dramatic Change or Surprising Continuity?" *Demography* 37(4):401–14.

Bloom, Benjamin S. 1965. *Stability and Change in Human Characteristics*. New York: Wiley.

Bullough, Robert V., Kendra M. Hall-Kenyon, and Kathryn Lake MacKay. 2012. "Head Start Teacher Well-Being: Implications for Policy and Practice." *Early Childhood Education Journal* 40(6):323–31.

Bureau of Justice Statistics. 2014. "Household Poverty and Nonfatal Violent Victimization, 2008–2012." https://bjs.ojp.gov.

Bureau of Labor Statistics. 2021. "Geographic Profile for Preschool Teachers, Except Special Education." www.bls.gov.

Burton, Linda. 2007. "Childhood Adultification in Economically Disadvantaged Families: A Conceptual Model." *Family Relations* 56(4):329–45.

Cahan, Emily D. 1994. *Past Caring: A History of U.S. Preschool Care and Education for the Poor, 1820–1965*. New York: National Center for Children in Poverty, Columbia University.

Calarco, Jessica McCrory. 2011. "'I Need Help!': Social Class and Children's Help-Seeking in Elementary School." *American Sociological Review* 76(6):862–82.

———. 2018. *Negotiating Opportunities: How the Middle Class Secures Advantages in School*. New York: Oxford University Press.

Cassidy, Deborah J., Joanna K. Lower, Victoria L. Kintner-Duffy, Archana V. Hegde, and Jonghee Shim. 2011. "The Day-to-Day Reality of Teacher Turnover in Preschool Classrooms: An Analysis of Classroom Context and Teacher, Director, and Parent Perspectives." *Journal of Research in Childhood Education* 25(1):1–23.

Child Trends Data Bank. 2016. *Children, Birth through 4, with Employed Mothers: Percentages by Primary Type of Care Arrangement: 1977–2011*. www.childtrends.org.

Conrad, Peter. 1992. "Medicalization and Social Control." *Annual Review of Sociology* 18:209–41.

Constitution and Bylaws of the Infant School Society of Boston. 1828. Boston: T.R. Marvin.

Coontz, Stephanie. 1992. *The Way We Never Were: American Families and the Nostalgia Trap*. New York: Basic Books.

Corsaro, William A. 2003. *We're Friends, Right? Inside Kids' Culture*. Washington, DC: Joseph Henry Press.

Desmond, Matthew, Weihua An, Richelle Winkler, and Thomas Ferriss. 2013. "Evicting Children." *Social Forces* 92(1):303–27.

Dodge, Kenneth A., Gregory S. Pettit, and John E. Bates. 1994. "Socialization Mediators of the Relation between Socioeconomic Status and Child Conduct Problems." *Child Development* 65(2):649–65.

Dow, Dawn Marie. 2019. *Mothering While Black: Boundaries and Burdens of Middle-Class Parenthood*. Berkeley: University of California Press.

Downey, Douglas B., and Dennis J. Condron. 2016. "Fifty Years since the Coleman Report: Rethinking the Relationship between Schools and Inequality." *Sociology of Education* 89(3):207–20.

Du Bois, W. E. B. 1898. *The Philadelphia Negro: A Social Study*. Philadelphia: University of Pennsylvania Press.

Durst, Anne. 2005. "'Of Women, by Women, and for Women': The Day Nursery Movement in the Progressive-Era United States." *Journal of Social History* 39(1):141–59.

Edin, Kathryn, Laura Tach, and Jennifer Sykes, eds. 2015. *It's Not Like I'm Poor: How Working Families Make Ends Meet in a Post-Welfare World*. Oakland: University of California Press.

Engel, Mimi, Robin Jacob, Amy Claessens, and Anna Erickson. 2021. "Kindergarten in a Large Urban District." *Educational Researcher* 50(6):401–15.

Farley, John E., and Gregory D. Squires. 2005. "Fences and Neighbors: Segregation in 21st-Century America." *Contexts* 4(1):33–39.

Ferguson, Ann Arnett. 2001. *Bad Boys: Public Schools in the Making of Black Masculinity*. Ann Arbor: University of Michigan Press.

Fong, Kelley. 2019. "Concealment and Constraint: Child Protective Services' Fears and Poor Mothers' Institutional Engagement." *Social Forces* 97(4):1785–1809.

———. 2023. *Investigating Families: Motherhood in the Shadow of Child Protective Services*. Princeton, NJ: Princeton University Press.

Fram, Maryah Stella, and Jinseok Kim. 2012. "Segregated from the Start: Peer Context in Center-Based Child Care." *Children and Schools* 34(2):71–82.

Frankenberg, Ruth. 2001. "The Mirage of an Unmarked Whiteness." Pp. 72–96 in *The Making and Unmaking of Whiteness*, edited by E. Klinenberg, I. J. Nexica, and M. Wray. Durham, NC: Duke University Press.

Gansen, Heidi M. 2017. "Reproducing (and Disrupting) Heteronormativity: Gendered Sexual Socialization in Preschool Classrooms." *Sociology of Education* 90(3):255–72.

———. 2019. "Push-Ups versus Clean-Up: Preschool Teachers' Gendered Beliefs, Expectations for Behavior, and Disciplinary Practices." *Sex Roles* 80(7–8): 393–408.

———. 2021. "Disciplining Difference(s): Reproducing Inequalities through Disciplinary Interactions in Preschool." *Social Problems* 68(3):740–60.

Gerstel, Naomi, and Dan Clawson. 2015. "Normal Unpredictability and the Chaos in Our Lives." *Contexts* 14(4):64–66.

Gillette, Michael L. 2010. *Launching the War on Poverty: An Oral History*. Oxford: Oxford University Press.

Gilliam, Walter S., Angela N. Maupin, and Maria Accavitti. 2016. "Do Early Educators' Implicit Biases Regarding Sex and Race Relate to Behavior Expectations and Recommendations of Preschool Expulsions and Suspensions?" New Haven, CT: Yale University, Child Study Center.

Goddard, Colleen. 2018. "The Significance of Transitional Objects in an Early Childhood Classroom for Children and Teachers." *Dimensions of Early Childhood* 46(1):6–9.

Golann, Joanne W. 2015. "The Paradox of Success at a No-Excuses School." *Sociology of Education* 88(2):103–19.

Greenberg, Erica, and Tomas Monarrez. 2019. "Segregated from the Start: Comparing Segregation in Early Childhood and K–12 Education." Washington, DC: Urban Institute.

Hagerman, Margaret A. 2018. *White Kids: Growing Up with Privilege in a Racially Divided America*. New York: NYU Press.

Harvey, Peter Francis. 2022. "'Make Sure You Look Someone in the Eye': Socialization and Classed Comportment in Two Elementary Schools." *American Journal of Sociology* 127(5):1417–59.

Haskins, Anna R., Mariana Amorim, and Meaghan Mingo. 2018. "Parental Incarceration and Child Outcomes: Those at Risk, Evidence of Impacts, Methodological Insights, and Areas of Future Work." *Sociology Compass* 12(3):1–14.

Hays, Sharon. 1996. *The Cultural Contradictions of Motherhood*. New Haven, CT: Yale University Press.

Head Start. 2020. "Head Start Program Performance Standards Related to Oral Health." https://eclkc.ohs.acf.hhs.gov/.

———. N.d. "1302.16 Attendance." In "Head Start Program Performance Standards." Retrieved September 12, 2022. https://eclkc.ohs.acf.hhs.gov.

Higginbottom, Gina M., J. J. Pillay, and N. Y. Boadu. 2013. "Guidance on Performing Focused Ethnographies with an Emphasis on Healthcare Research." *Qualitative Report* 18(9):1–16.

Hunt Institute. 2022. *Strong Foundations: Promoting Diverse and Inclusive Preschool Settings*. Cary, NC: Hunt Institute.

Ishizuka, Patrick. 2019. "Social Class, Gender, and Contemporary Parenting Standards in the United States: Evidence from a National Survey Experiment." *Social Forces* 98(1):31–58.

Jiang, Yang, Mercedes Ekono, and Curtis Skinner. 2014. *Basic Facts about Low-Income Children: Children under 18 Years, 2014*. New York: National Center for Children in Poverty.

Keels, Micere. 2020. *Campus Counterspaces: Black and Latinx Students' Search for Community at Historically White Universities*. Ithaca, NY: Cornell University Press.

Kids Count Data Center. 2018. "YoungStar Child Care Quality Rating for Providers." Retrieved January 19, 2018. https://datacenter.kidscount.org.

Knoblauch, Hubert. 2005. "Focused Ethnography." *Forum: Qualitative Social Research* 6(3).

Ladson-Billings, Gloria. 2017. "'Makes Me Wanna Holler': Refuting the 'Culture of Poverty' Discourse in Urban Schooling." *Annals of the American Academy of Political and Social Science* 673(1):80–90.

Lareau, Annette. 2011. *Unequal Childhoods: Class, Race, and Family Life*. 2nd ed. Berkeley: University of California Press.

Lewis, Oscar. 1966. *La Vida: A Puerto Rican Family in the Culture of Poverty; San Juan and New York*. New York: Random House.

Liebow, Elliot. 1967. *Tally's Corner: A Study of Negro Streetcorner Men*. Boston: Little, Brown.

Linver, Miriam R., Jeanne Brooks-Gunn, and Dafna E. Kohen. 2002. "Family Processes as Pathways from Income to Young Children's Development." *Developmental Psychology* 38(5):719–34.

Livingston, Gretchen. 2015. "Childlessness Falls, Family Size Grows among Highly Educated Women." Washington, DC: Pew Research Center.

Macdonald, Cameron Lynne. 2010. *Shadow Mothers: Nannies, au Pairs, and the Micropolitics of Mothering*. Berkeley: University of California Press.

Magnuson, Katherine A., Marcia K. Meyers, Christopher J. Ruhm, and Jane Waldfogel. 2004. "Inequality in Preschool Education and School Readiness." *American Educational Research Journal* 41(1):115–57.

Magnuson, Katherine A., Christopher Ruhm, and Jane Waldfogel. 2007. "Does Prekindergarten Improve School Preparation and Performance?" *Economics of Education Review* 26(1):33–51.

Mandell, Nancy. 1988. "The Least-Adult Role in Studying Children." *Journal of Contemporary Ethnography* 16(4):433–67.

Manning, Alex. 2019. "The Age of Concerted Cultivation: A Racial Analysis of Parental Repertoires and Childhood Activities." *Du Bois Review* 16(1):5–35.

Martin, Karin A. 1998. "Becoming a Gendered Body: Practices of Preschools." *American Sociological Review* 63(4):494–511.

Miles, Matthew B., A. Michael Huberman, and Johnny Saldaña. 2014. *Qualitative Data Analysis: A Methods Sourcebook*. 2nd ed. Newbury Park, CA: Sage Publications.

Mintz, Steven. 2004. *Huck's Raft: A History of American Childhood*. Cambridge, MA: Belknap Press of Harvard University Press.

Moynihan, Daniel Patrick. 1965. *The Negro Family: The Case for National Action*. Washington, DC: US Department of Labor.

National Association for the Education of Young Children. 2009. "Position Statement: Developmentally Appropriate Practice in Early Childhood Programs Serving Children from Birth through Age 8."

National Center for Education Statistics. 2018. "State Education Practices, Table 5.3: Types of State and District Requirements for Kindergarten Entrance and Attendance, Waivers and Exemptions for Kindergarten Entrance, by State: 2018." https://nces.ed.gov/.

———. 2019a. "Fast Facts: School Uniforms." https://nces.ed.gov/.

———. 2019b. Annual Reports: "Enrollment Rates of Young Children." https://nces.ed.gov/.

Nelson, Margaret K., and Rebecca Schutz. 2007. "Day Care Differences and the Reproduction of Social Class." *Journal of Contemporary Ethnography* 36(3):281–317.

Nursery for the Children of Poor Women. 1854. Constitution, By-Laws, and Regulations of the Nursery for the Children of Poor Women in the City of New York. New York: Billin and Brothers Printers.

Patterson, James T. 2000. *America's Struggle against Poverty in the Twentieth Century*. Cambridge, MA: Harvard University Press.

Payne, Julianne. 2018. "Manufacturing Masculinity: Exploring Gender and Workplace Surveillance." *Work and Occupations* 45(3):346–83.

Pew Research Center. 2015. "Parenting in America: Outlook, Worries, Aspirations Are Strongly Linked to Financial Situation." Washington, DC: Pew Research Center.

Pianta, Robert C., Bridget K. Hamre, and Tutrang Nguyen. 2020. "Measuring and Improving Quality in Early Care and Education." *Early Childhood Research Quarterly* 51:285–87.

Pianta, Robert, Carollee Howes, Margaret Burchinal, Donna Bryant, Richard Clifford, Diane Early, and Oscar Barbarin. 2005. "Features of Pre-Kindergarten Programs, Classrooms, and Teachers: Do They Predict Observed Classroom Quality and Child–Teacher Interactions?" *Applied Developmental Science* 9(3):144–59.

Pugh, Allison. 2009. *Longing and Belonging: Parents, Children, and Consumer Culture.* Berkeley: University of California Press.

Quadagno, Jill S. 1994. *The Color of Welfare: How Racism Undermined the War on Poverty.* Oxford: Oxford University Press.

Race to Equity Team. 2013. *Race to Equity: A Baseline Report on the State of Racial Disparities in Dane County.* Madison: Wisconsin Council on Children and Families.

Rafalow, Matthew H. 2018. "Disciplining Play: Digital Youth Culture as Capital at School." *American Journal of Sociology* 123(5):1416–52.

———. 2020. *Digital Divisions: How Schools Create Inequality in the Tech Era.* Chicago: University of Chicago Press.

Randles, Jennifer. 2021. "'Willing to Do Anything for My Kids': Inventive Mothering, Diapers, and the Inequalities of Carework." *American Sociological Review* 86(1):35–59.

Rangel, David, and Megan N. Shoji. 2021. "Social Class and Parenting in Mexican American Families." *Sociological Perspectives* 64(4):587–610.

Recommendations for a Head Start Program by a Panel of Experts. 1965, February 19. Washington, DC: US Department of Health, Education, and Welfare. Wilbur J. Cohen Papers. Wisconsin Historical Society.

Reid, Jeanne L., Sharon Lynn Kagan, Michael Hilton, and Halley Potter. 2015. *A Better Start: Why Classroom Diversity Matters in Early Education.* Washington, DC: Poverty & Race Research Action Council.

Reskin, Barbara. 2012. "The Race Discrimination System." *Annual Review of Sociology* 38:17–35.

Rios, Victor M. 2011. *Punished: Policing the Lives of Black and Latino Boys.* New York: NYU Press.

Rose, Elizabeth R. 1999. *A Mother's Job: The History of Day Care, 1890–1960.* New York: Oxford University Press.

Sapolsky, Robert. 2005. "Sick of Poverty." *Scientific American* 29(6):93–99.

Sedlak, Andrea J., Jane Mettenburg, Monica Basena, Ian Petta, Karla McPherson, Angela Greene, and Spencer Li. 2010. "Fourth National Incidence Study of Child Abuse and Neglect (NIS–4): Report to Congress, Executive Summary." Washington, DC: US Department of Health and Human Services, Administration for Children and Families.

Shrider, Emily A., Melissa Kollar, Frances Chen, and Jessica Semega. 2020. "Income and Poverty in the United States: 2020; Current Population Reports." Washington, DC: US Government Publishing Office.

Stearns, Peter N. 2003. *Anxious Parents: A History of Modern Childrearing in America.* New York: NYU Press.

Steinfels, Margaret O'Brien. 1973. *Who's Minding the Children? The History and Politics of Day Care in America.* New York: Simon & Schuster.

Stockstill, Casey. 2021. "The 'Stuff' of Class: How Property Rules in Preschool Reproduce Class Inequality." *Social Problems* 70(4):1–21.

Streib, Jessi. 2011. "Class Reproduction by Four Year Olds." *Qualitative Sociology* 34(2):337–52.

Styfco, Sally J., and Edward Zigler. 2010. *The Hidden History of Head Start.* New York: Oxford University Press.

Tank, Robert Melvin. 1980. "Young Children, Families, and Society in America since the 1820s: The Evolution of Health, Education, and Child Care Programs for Preschool Children." PhD thesis, Department of History, University of Michigan.

Thorne, Barrie. 1993. *Gender Play: Girls and Boys in School.* New Brunswick, NJ: Rutgers University Press.

Ullrich, Rebecca, Katie Hamm, and Rachel Herzfeldt-Kamprath. 2016. *Underpaid and Unequal: Racial Wage Disparities in the Early Childhood Workforce.* Washington, DC: Center for American Progress.

USDA. 2021. "Key Statistics and Graphics: Food Security Status of U.S. Households in 2021." Economic Research Service, US Department of Agriculture. Retrieved March 15, 2022. https://www.ers.usda.gov.

US Department of Health and Human Services. 2016. "Head Start Program Performance Standards." 45 CFR Chapter XIII, September.

Van Ausdale, Debra, and Joe R. Feagin. 2001. *The First R: How Children Learn Race and Racism.* Washington, DC: Rowman & Littlefield.

Vinofskis, Maris A. 2005. *The Birth of Head Start: Preschool Education Policies in the Kennedy and Johnson Administrations.* Chicago: University of Chicago Press.

Watkins-Hayes, Celeste. 2009. *The New Welfare Bureaucrats: Entanglements of Race, Class, and Policy Reform.* Chicago: University of Chicago Press.

Whitaker, Robert C., Tracy Dearth-Wesley, and Rachel A. Gooze. 2015. "Workplace Stress and the Quality of Teacher-Children Relationships in Head Start." *Early Childhood Research Quarterly* 30:57–69.

Wisconsin Department of Children and Families. 2020. "DCF 25. Licensing Rules for Group Child Care Centers and Child Care Programs Established or Contracted for by School Boards." https://dcf.wisconsin.gov.

Wisconsin Historical Society Archives. 1968. Wilbur J. Cohen Papers, Box 112, Folder 2. November 12, 1968. Memo, re: Head Start, from Jule M. Sugarman, Associate Chief of Children's Bureau.

Wisconsin State Legislature. N.d. "Statutes, Chapter 941, Crimes against Public Health and Safety: 941.299 Restrictions on the Use of Laser Pointers." https://docs.legis.wisconsin.gov.

Woolley, Helen T. 1926. "The Real Function of the Nursery School." *Child Study* 3:6–10.

Young, Alford. 2008. "White Ethnographers on the Experiences of African American Men: Then and Now." Pp. 179–202 in *White Logic, White Methods*, edited by T. Zuberi and E. Bonilla-Silva. Washington, DC: Rowman & Littlefield.

Zinsser, Katherine M. 2022. *No Longer Welcome: The Epidemic of Expulsion from Early Childhood Education*. New York: Oxford University Press.

INDEX

Abbott, Grace, 14

absences: Head Start required explanation for, 119–22; at Sunshine Head Start, 46, 147–48

academic skills, preschool improvement in, 22

adult authority: affluent, white children behavior endorsement by, 79; Great Beginnings' deeper relationship with, 84

adultification, of children, 134

affluent and white families: adult authority endorsement of child behavior in, 79; behavior medicalization of, 83, 191n4; children shielded from family disruptions in, 134; extended family and, 188n82; fewer children of, 188n82; kindergarten and nursery school for, 7; Pugh on symbolic deprivation of, 100

Anderson, Elijah, 179

assimilation, 9

associate teachers, 138–39

attendance: Great Beginnings celebrations and parent, 131–32; Great Beginnings constant, 46; increase in 1970s and 1980s, 21; Sunshine Head Start absences in, 46, 147–48

autonomy: compromise of creative, 73–74; Great Beginnings, less play and, 58, 62; increased peer conflict and, 70–71; through open-ended play, 61; physical harm at Sunshine Head Start and, 69–70; poor children upward mobility impaired by, 63; from pretend play, 70, 189n14; segregation and, 62

autonomy over play: by children of color, 84–85; paradox in preschool, 84–86; at Sunshine Head Start, 58, 62, 84

babysitters: Great Beginnings teachers as paid, 133–34, 141–42; Sunshine Head Start, restrictions on teachers as, 141

Beer, Ethel, 10

behaviors, 189n6; affluent and white family adult authority endorsement of, 79; affluent family medicalization for, 83, 191n4; Circle Time correction of, 58; Great Beginnings, classmate correction of, 40; management of, 37–38, 143–44; safe, 39, 43, 66–67, 70, 95, 143, 146; teacher stress from, 137; from trauma, 7, 27, 142, 143–44, 189n12

Black children: higher poverty rate of, 6, 185n5; kindergarten, lack of funding for, 12; Sunshine Head Start, segregation of, 6; viewed as criminals in elementary school, 189n6

Black family: assimilation inability of, 9; concerted cultivation and, 24; Moynihan Report on weakness of, 16–17

Bloom, Benjamin, 17

body management, Sunshine Head Start Circle Time and, 36–40

Boston Infant School, 7–8

Cahan, Emily, 14

Calarco, Jessica, 24

celebrations, at Great Beginnings: Halloween and Valentine's Day parties, 131–32; parent attendance at, 131–32; parent email notifications of, 131; of personal property, 87, 101–3, 107; unrestricted, 131–32

celebrations, at Sunshine Head Start: Halloween restrictions, 123, 124–25; holiday policy on parent permission for, 122–23; restricted, 122–25

Center Time indoor free play, at Sunshine Head Start, 42–46

chase-retreat dynamic, on gender, 71–74, 189n8

child abuse and neglect, mandated reporting for, 115

child care: federal government funding of, 13–14; government WWII support of, 15; preschool as form of, 7, 186n9;

as private choice, 22, 114, 166. *See also* segregated child care

Child Protective Services (CPS), x, 190n4; family separation from, 134; mandated reporting to, 115

children: adultification of, 134; affluent and white families fewer, 188n82; class clustering of, 164; classroom property access for, 89, 107, 189n1; preparation for racism, 24; property discussion by, 189n2; segregation in lives of, 27–28; Sunshine Head Start conflict solving by, 85; teacher stress impact on, 155; viewed as work at Sunshine Head Start, 146–49. *See also* Black children; Hispanic children and family; Indigenous children; poor children; white, middle-class children

children of color: autonomy over play by, 84–85; creativity of, 63, 65, 67, 68, 78, 85; culturally affirming care for, 164, 167; family moments discussion by, 134; negative views of, 63, 137; personal property and, 88, 90, 94, 107–8; segregation of, 6, 22, 59, 84–85. *See also* Black children

Circle Time, at Sunshine Head Start: behavior management during, 37–38; body management learned through, 36–40; children physical activity during, 37–38, 41; classroom rules review, 39; daily routine recitation during, 38; group conversation and behavior correction during, 58; social learning during, 37–38

class: clustering children by, 164; Harvey on comportment by, 41; Head Start segregation by, 21; inequalities, ix, 7, 88, 108; kindergartens positive connotation of, 11–12; parenting differences by, 24; race intersection with, 185n5; racial inclusivity through integration of, 167 class parties, Sunshine Head Start lack of, 125, 162

classroom enrollment: Great Beginnings predictable, 134, 143, 152, 154; Sunshine Head Start unpredictable, 142, 153–54

classroom property, children access to, 89, 107, 189n1

classroom ratings. *See* quality ratings

class size: of 17 at Sunshine Head Start, 4, 39, 45, 143, 146; of 12 at Great Beginnings, 43, 45, 93

clothing, personalization of, 98, 190n13

coaching strategies, for conflict, 43–44

communication, in segregated villages, 134–35

concerted cultivation, 25; of Black and Hispanic family and, 24; Calarco on, 24; Lareau on, 23–24, 62; Manning on, 24, 62; of white, middle-class children, 24, 62

conflict: attention to, 145; autonomy and increased, 70–71; coaching strategies for, 43–44; gendered form of, 71–74; Great Beginnings fewer problem-solving opportunities in, 63; over personal property, 94–97; in play at Sunshine Head Start, 63; Sunshine Head Start management of, 85–87; timer system prevention of, 76; Work Time coaching strategies for, 43–44

Cooke, Robert, 18

Cooke Committee, 18, 19

Corsaro, Bill, 179

CPS. *See* Child Protective Services

creative autonomy, compromise of, 73–74

Creative Curriculum for Preschool, Sunshine Head Start use of, 188n12

creativity: of children of color, 63, 65, 67, 68, 78, 85; emphasis on choice and, 145; in pretend play, 70, 79; Sunshine Head Start lack of comment on, 66, 69

criminals, Black elementary children viewed as, 189n6

cultural deficiency, in poverty, 17

culturally affirming care, of children of color, 164, 167

culture of poverty: Cooke Committee and, 18; cyclical poverty in, 15–16, 154; Head Start and, 20; Lewis on, 16; racism implication in, 16–17

curricula: Creative Curriculum for Preschool, 188n12; lead teacher management of, 138; PALS-PreK, 188n12; play-based, 5, 30, 62, 152, 185n2; Second Step socio-emotional, 189n19; Van Ausdale on preschool multicultural, 175

cyclical poverty, in culture of poverty, 15–16, 154

data analysis, in study, 183

day nurseries: for assimilation of immigrant children, 9; Beer on early, 10; early shortcomings of, 10; expansion of, 10; Franklin Day Nursery, 8; for poor children, 7; racism and segregation of, 9–11; reduced support for, 11; working motherhood and, 8–9

dental hygiene, 114; Head Start dentist visits and mandatory toothbrushing for, 35. *See also* toothbrushing

Deutsch, Martin, 20

discipline, 177; gendered, 88; self-, 18

Disneyworld: Great Beginnings and, 112, 113; Sunshine Head Start and, 110–12, 113, 135

divorce, 3, 130

domestic revolution, 8

domestic violence, 31, 113, 117, 130, 134

Duneier, Mitchell, 179

early childhood education: Bloom on, 17; enrollment in, 21; on learning through play, 61; NAEYC play-based curricula recommendations, 30, 185n3; racial segregation in, 21 elementary school: Black boys seen as criminal in, 189n6; playground dynamics at, 188n10; preschool expansion onto, 165–66

emotional skills: Sunshine Head Start on, 38, 143, 148; teacher pride in improvement of, 140. *See also* socio-emotional skills

enrollment: in early childhood education, 21; Great Beginnings stability in, 143; Sunshine Head Start shifts in, 4–5, 142; turnover in, 27, 31, 163. *See also* classroom enrollment

ethnography, study from immersive to focused, 180–82

eviction, x, 31, 84, 90, 134, 142

extended family, of affluent and white family, 188n82

externalizing behaviors, trauma response of, 27, 189n12

family: children of color discussion of, 134; Great Beginnings travel information of, 128–30; Sunshine Head Start support of, 5. *See also* affluent and white families; Black family; Hispanic children and family

family disruptions: affluent and white families shielding children from, 134; class and race impact on, 134; of divorce, 3, 130; of domestic violence, 31, 113, 117, 130, 134; of eviction, x, 31, 84, 90, 134, 142; with foster care, x, 29, 31, 153; gossip about, 115, 116, 118, 177; Great Beginnings open talk about, 127–31; Great Beginnings pretend play about, 127; homelessness, 31, 90, 100; housing instability, 113, 143; of incarceration, 11, 31, 91, 113, 116–17, 142; poor children exposure to, 134; of substance abuse, x, 134; Sunshine Head Start children pretend play about, 115–16; Sunshine Head Start, fractured talk about, 114–22

family-engagement practices: at Great Beginnings, 112–13; at Sunshine Head Start, 112–13, 135

Family Fun Nights, at Sunshine Head Start, 126, 135, 160

family-style eating, 35, 36, 48, 112

family surveillance, at Great Beginnings: divorce information, 130; family disruptions open talk, 118–19, 127–31; family travel information, 128–30; interventions for family disruptions, 129; optional space sharing, 132–34; unrestricted celebrations, 131–32

family surveillance, at Sunshine Head Start: family disruptions fractured talk, 114–22; Family Fun Nights, 126, 135, 160; incomplete information on family disruptions, 118–19; mandated home visits for, 125–26; mandated space sharing, 125–27; restricted celebrations, 122–25

Feagin, Joe, 175

Federal Emergency Relief Administration (FERA), 13–15

female-headed households, in poverty, 17

FERA. *See* Federal Emergency Relief Administration

Ferguson, Ann, 189n6

field trips: at Great Beginnings, 5, 6, 31, 57–58, 152, 163; at Sunshine Head Start, 4

fight, 2, 55, 94, 158. *See also* conflict

foster care, x, 29, 31, 153

Free Choice Time indoor play, at Great Beginnings, 45–46, 85

funding: Black kindergarten lack of, 12; for preschools, 13–14, 22

Gansen, Heidi, 164, 188n86

gender, 24, 27; chase-retreat dynamic, 71–74, 189n8; Gansen on, 164, 188n86; Martin on, 188n86; preschool as sites of broad socialization for conformity in, 26, 164

gendered access, to personal property at Sunshine Head Start, 98–100, 106
gendered discipline, 88
gendered form of conflict, 71–74
gentle touch practice, at Sunshine Head Start, 39, 64
Gilliam, Walter, 189n6
Goddard, Colleen, 107
Goffman, Alice, 179
gossip, about family disruptions, 115, 116, 118, 177
graduation: at Great Beginnings, 179; at Sunshine Head Start, 1, 158–59
Great Beginnings: adult authority deeper relationship at, 84; child behavior medicalization at, 191n4; class size of 12 at, 43, 45, 93; constant attendance at, 46; enrollment stability at, 143; family-engagement practices at, 112–13; family life surveillance indifference, 114; fewer conflict solving opportunities at, 63; few stigmatized disruptions at, 113, 114, 127; field trips at, 5, 6, 31, 57–58, 152, 163; frequent reading at, 40, 50, 58; graduation at, 179; holiday parties at, 132; home visits lack at, 132–33; less autonomy over play at, 58, 62; less mandated reporting from, 127; less paperwork at, 152; newsletters of, 6, 57, 152; one-on-time importance at, 82–83; open talk about family disruptions at, 127–31; paper poster routine at, 58; physical description of, 5; pick-up time formal parent communication, 57; play-based curriculum at, 62, 152; predictable classroom enrollment, 134, 143, 152, 154; pretend play about family disruptions at, 127; pretend play using adult techniques, 63; private operation of, 114; routine disruptions at, 31; routines at, 30; second outdoor time of, 56; segregation in, 6; Show-and-Tell of personal property, 89, 101–2, 106;

teachers as paid babysitters, 133–34, 141–42; teachers' positive view of children at, 152; toothbrushing absence at, 36; weekly email to parents by, 57; white, middle-class children at, 8, 74. *See also* Group Time; *specific activities*
group child care: Boston Infant School as first, 7–8; day nurseries for, 8–9; infant school movement and, 7–8
Group Time, at Great Beginnings: book reading during, 40; children as speakers and audience at, 41; children's room commanding opportunities, 41; children's stillness during, 41, 58; classmate behavior correction, 40

Hagerman, Margaret, 32
Halloween celebrations: at Great Beginnings, 131–32; Sunshine Head Start restrictions for, 123, 124–25
Harvey, Peter, 41
Head Start, vii; class segregation in, 21; cost of, 20; culture of poverty and, 20; family surveillance of worthiness by, 114; as life readiness program, 20; mandated health information in, 48; mandated home visits, 125–26; mandatory toothbrushing in, 35; minimum participation standards of, 114; origins of, 15–23; parents as substitute teachers and teacher aides, 20; required explanation for absences, 119–22; Shriver as head of, 19–20; whole-child approach of, 35, 48, 114. *See also* Sunshine Head Start
Head Start Planning Committee, on program ideal scale, 19
Hispanic children and family: concerted cultivation and, 24; higher poverty rate of, 6, 185n5
holiday parties: at Great Beginnings, 132; Sunshine Head Start restrictions on, 122–23. *See also* celebrations

home-based child care centers, 166–67

homelessness, 31, 90, 100

home visits, Head Start required: family disruptions information from, 125–26; mandated reporting concerns, 125

Hope Day Nursery for Black Children, 10

housing instability, 113, 143

immigration: day nurseries for assimilation from, 9; Johnson-Reed Act on quota-based, 11; Rose on working motherhood and, 9

incarceration, 11, 31, 91, 113, 116–17, 142

income-based subsidies, 22, 110, 111, 167

Indigenous children, higher poverty rate of, 6, 185n5

indoor play: Great Beginnings Free Choice Time, 45–46, 85; Sunshine Head Start Center Time, 42–46

inequalities: class, ix, 7, 88, 108; personal property rules by race and class, 88; property class and race, 108; racial, ix, 6–7, 88, 108; unintentional, through play, 62–63

infant schools, 8–9

Infant School Society, 8

instructional time, transitions and lack of, 58–59

intensive motherhood, 161; defined, 23; rise of, 23–25; teachers' interaction, mimicking of, 27

internalizing behaviors, trauma response of, 27, 189n12

intervention programs, of mindfulness, oral hygiene, literacy, 32

Jim Crow, 12

Johnson-Reed Act (1924), 11

Joseph, Frances, 12

kindergarten: for children of affluent and white families, 7; Great Beginnings transitions to, 159–60; lack

of funding for Black, 12; positive class-connotation of, 11–12; racial segregation of, 12; Sunshine Head Start transitions to, 157–58

laboratory school, 22

Lanham Act, 15

Lareau, Annette: on concerted cultivation, 23–24, 62; on control over time of children, 107

lead teachers, 139; bachelor degrees of, 138; curriculum and classroom routine management by, 138

learned helplessness, poverty and, 18

least adult approach, in study, 176–78

lesson planning, 38, 53, 58, 66–67, 138, 146

Lewis, Oscar, 16, 17

licensing, 22, 57, 179; Great Beginnings and, 127; open-ended play requirement, 61–62; preschool teacher requirements for, 23; state requirements, 30, 35

Liebow, Elliot, 17

life readiness program, Head Start as, 20

limitations, of study, 183–84

literacy, 32, 38

Macdonald, Cameron, 23

mandated home visits, at Sunshine Head Start, 125–26

mandated reporting: for child abuse and neglect, 115; Great Beginnings less, 127; home visits and concerns for, 125

mandated space sharing, at Sunshine Head Start, 125–27

Mandell, Nancy, 177

Manning, Alex, 24

Martin, Karin, 188n86

meals: family-style eating at, 35, 36, 48, 112; snack time and, 54, 146; at Sunshine Head Start, 33–35; teacher multitasking and, 32–36

medicalization, of child behavior benefits by affluent families, 83, 191n4

mindfulness, 32
mixed-delivery models, 166, 167
morning drop-off, teacher multitasking and, 32–36
mother's pensions movement, 11, 186n14
Moynihan, Daniel Patrick, 16–17, 187n48
Moynihan Report, 187n48; on Black family weakness, 16–17
multitasking, of teachers, 32–36, 84

NAEYC. See National Association for the Education of Young Children
nap time, at Great Beginnings: stuffed animal objects during, 53, 89, 101, 103; whispered conversation during, 53
nap time, at Sunshine Head Start: bathroom use before, 50; disruptions during, 52–53; sheets and blankets at, 50; special items brought at, 50–51; whispered conversation during, 51
National Association for the Education of Young Children (NAEYC), play-based curricula recommendations by, 30, 185n3
National Association of Colored Women, 12
National Federation of Day Nurseries, 10
negative views, of children of color, 63, 137
Neighborhood Centre Nursery School, 13
Nelson, Margaret, 25, 164
newsletters, 146; Great Beginnings, 6, 57, 152; Sunshine Head Start, 56
nursery school: Cahan on, 14; child development and education emphasis in, 13; for children of affluent and white families, 7; FERA program and, 14; middle-class mother use of, 13; Rockefeller Foundation importance for, 12; scientific research of, 13; socialization of children in, 13
nutrition, 10, 162

open-ended play: autonomy through, 61; licensing requirements for, 61–62
oral hygiene. See dental hygiene
outdoor times: as compensatory, 55; Great Beginnings second, 56; Sunshine Head Start requirement of two, 54
Outside Time: at Great Beginnings, 47; large group play during, 46; at Sunshine Head Start, 46–47

PALS-PreK, Sunshine Head Start use of, 188n12
paperwork: Great Beginnings less, 152; quality ratings supported by, 154; Sunshine Head Start large amount of, 56, 58, 137, 146; teacher stress from, 154. See also lesson planning
parenting: class differences in, 24; classes on, 163; cultural context of, 23; preschool as supplementary for, 26; stress and harsher, 155. See also concerted cultivation; intensive motherhood
parents: children information by teacher to, 53; Great Beginnings formal communication with, 57, 152; Great Beginnings weekly email to, 57; as Head Start substitute teachers and teacher aides, 20; Sunshine Head Start holiday policy for permission of, 122–23; Sunshine Head Start informal conversation with, 56
Parents Night Out, 6, 132
peer conflict. See conflict
Perkins, Frances, 14
personal property, 189n1; children of color and, 88, 90, 94, 107–8; classroom objects difference from, 89, 107; conflict over, 94–97; consequences of unequal access to, 106–9; race and class inequality rules for, 88; structural racism and poverty impact on, 88; of transitional objects, 106–7

personal property, Great Beginnings classroom rules for: books from home and, 101, 103–4; celebration of, 87, 101–3, 107; monthly toy and coat drive fundraisers of, 100–101; Show-and-Tell for, 89, 101–2, 106; stuffed animal objects during naptime and, 53, 89, 101, 103; support for, 103–6

personal property, Sunshine Head Start classroom rules for, 87, 96–97, 107; of children's clothing and outfit accessories, 98; cubbies as inaccessible, 92; cubby-or-pockets rule for, 91–95; gendered, racialized access to, 98–100, 106; storage in cubby at, 90

philanthropists, 8, 11

physical activity, at Circle Time, 37–38, 41

pick-up time: Great Beginning, formal communication with parents at, 57; Sunshine Head Start, informal conversations with parents at, 56

play: early childhood education on learning through, 61; unintentional inequalities through, 62–63

play, at Great Beginnings, 80; explicit negotiation on what and how to, 76–77; Free Choice Time label for, 75; scripting in, 77; staged play with multiple directors' approach for, 78; summary of, 79; teacher management of, 75, 78; teacher reprimands for inanimate objects and aggressive, 79; timer system and orchestrated, 75, 76

play, at Sunshine Head Start: child initiation and control of joining, 64–65; child management of, 85; children asking strategy for joining, 65; friends for comfort in, 71; improv team approach for, 78; lack of comment on creativity in, 66, 69; peer interactions for, 64–65, 85; summary of, 74; teacher reprimands for, 69, 79, 84; uncensored,

69; Work Time label for, 39, 43–44, 58–59, 64

play-based curricula, 5; at Great Beginnings, 62, 152; NAEYC recommendations for, 30, 185n2

play-based learning, Great Beginnings use of, 62, 152

playground, 4, 188n10

poor children: day nurseries for, 7; family disruptions exposure for, 134; upward mobility impaired autonomy for, 63

poverty: of Black, Hispanic, Indigenous children, 6, 185n5; Boston Infant School for families of, 7–8; cultural deficiency in, 17; deeper transition time and, 59; enrollment turnover from, 31; female-headed households in, 17; learned helplessness and, 18; Liebow on structural conditions for, 17; personal property impacted by, 88; preschool as antipoverty policy, 168; racialization of, 6; racism and, 155; structural racism and, 113, 155; Sunshine Head Start enrollment and, 4–5. *See also* culture of poverty; War on Poverty

preschool, 27; academic skills improvement from, 22; as antipoverty policy, 168; autonomy over play paradox in, 84–86; as child care form, 7, 186n9; on children belonging to families, 163–64; class and race segregation in, 6–7, 21; expansion onto elementary public school, 165–66; funding for, 13–14, 22; as group learning environment, 163; lead teachers at, 138; segregation and expansion of access to, 161, 165–69; star rating systems for, 22–23; teacher licensing requirements for, 23; teachers as key educators in, 25–26; Van Ausdale on multicultural curricula in, 175

preschool as compensatory, 161; racism and, 26; shortcomings of, 162

preschool as sites of broad socialization, 164; gender conformity and, 26; Van Ausdale study on children's racial attitudes, 27
preschool as supplement, 26, 163
pretend play: autonomy and, 70, 189n14; collaborative child-based system for, 64–67; creativity in, 70, 79; about family disruptions at Great Beginnings, 127; about family disruptions at Sunshine Head Start, 115–16; Great Beginnings, adult techniques for, 63; teacher-student games of, 42–43, 45
private centers, segregation and, 166
Progressive Era, 8, 9
Project Head Start, x; War on Poverty and, 15–16. See also Head Start
property: children customization of school through, 88–90, 107–8; children discussion of, 189n2; class and race inequality from, 108; white, middle-class children entitlement orientation, 108. See also personal property
public schools: opening between 1832 and 1838 of, 8; preschool expansion and, 165–66. See also elementary school
Pugh, Allison, 189n2; on symbolic deprivation, 100
punishment, 89, 99

quality ratings, 3, 7, 22; paperwork support for, 154
quality rating systems, 22–23; teacher emphasis in, 25–26; teacher-student ratios impact on, 25

racial inclusivity: through class integration increase, 167; through teachers and directors of color, 168
racial inequalities, ix, 88, 108; preschool segregation entrenchment of, 6–7
racialization: of poverty, 6; of working motherhood, 9

racial segregation, 9–11; in early childhood education, 21; in kindergarten, 12; in preschool, 6–7, 21
racism, 59; children preparation for, 24; culture of poverty implication of, 16–17; Hagerman on, 32; poverty and, 155; preschool as compensatory and, 26; racial discrimination and, 185n5; traumas from, 82. See also structural racism
Randles, Jennifer, 190n14
ratio. See teacher-student ratio
reading: Great Beginnings frequent, 40, 50, 58; Sunshine Head Start sporadic, 42, 48–50, 58
redshirting, 160, 185n4
research, scientific of nursery school, 13
Rios, Victor, 84
Rockefeller Foundation, for nursery schools, 12
Roosevelt, Franklin: FERA and, 13–14; Lanham Act and, 15
Rose, Elizabeth, 21
routine disruptions: at Great Beginnings, 31; in segregated child care, 59; at Sunshine Head Start, 31, 57–58; trauma and, 31. See also family disruptions
routines: Circle Time, daily recitation of, 38; differences in time use and, 32; at Great Beginnings, 30; stabilizing effect of, 31, 188n4; at Sunshine Head Start, 30

safe behaviors, Sunshine Head Start reinforcement of, 39, 43, 66–67, 70, 95, 143, 146
Schutz, Rebecca, 25, 164
Second Step socio-emotional preschool curriculum, 189n10
segregated child care: brief history of, 7–11; in day nurseries, 9–11; in kindergarten, 12; preschools and teacher unequal work environments at, 153–56; by race and class, 7; routine disruptions in, 59; teaching in, 138–43

segregation: autonomy and, 62; of children of color, 6, 22, 59, 84–85; children socialization experience connection with, 27; in lives of children, 27–28; as relational, 59; transitions and, 32; unintentional inequality through play, 62–63

Shayla, at Sunshine Head Start, 29–30

Show-and-Tell, 107; as adaptable among children with few personal possessions, 108; at Great Beginnings, 89, 101–2, 106

Shriver, Sargent, 19–20

skills: emotional, 38, 140, 143, 148; social, 37–38, 63, 67, 85, 139; socio-emotional, 38–39, 135–36

snack time, 54, 146

socialization of children: nursery schools on, 13; segregation connection with, 27

social skills, 139; Circle Time and, 37–38; creativity in children of color, 63, 65, 67, 68, 78, 85

socio-emotional learning: behavior management and, 143–44; Great Beginnings and, 150–53; Second Step preschool curriculum for, 189n10; Sunshine Head Start, 143–46; during Sunshine Head Start Circle Time, 37–38

socio-emotional skills: attention to, 38–39; development of, 135–36

space sharing: Great Beginnings optional, 132–34; Sunshine Head Start mandated, 125–27

Spanish language, viii–ix; home-based child care centers for, 167; at Sunshine Head Start, 64–65, 72, 81, 188n11

stabilizing effect, of routines, 31, 188n4

star rating systems, for preschools, 22–23

stigmatized disruptions: Great Beginnings few, 113, 114, 127; Sunshine Head Start frequent, 113, 114

stress: children impacted by teacher, 155; harsher parenting from, 155; single parent personal and financial, 110–12; Sunshine Head Start and job physicality, 150; of teachers, 137, 149, 150, 154, 155

structural racism: eviction as consequence of, 84; personal property impact from, 88; poverty and, 113, 155; Sunshine Head Start and, 85

study: data analysis in, 183; Great Beginnings comparative, 179–80; from immersive to focused ethnography in, 180–82; least adult approach in, 176–78; limitations of, 183–84; Sunshine Head Start origins of, 175–76

substance abuse, x, 134

Sugarman, Jule, 20

Sunshine Head Start: autonomy and physical harm at, 69–70; autonomy over play at, 58, 62, 84; Black segregation in, 6; children challenging behaviors at, 142; children problem solving through peer support at, 71, 85; children viewed as work at, 146–49; class size at, 4, 39, 45, 143, 146; conflict in play at, 63; conflict management at, 85–87; Creative Curriculum for Preschool use by, 188n12; on emotional skills, 38, 143, 148; enrollment and poverty line, 4–5; enrollment shifts at, 142; family-engagement practices at, 112–13, 135; Family Fun Nights at, 126, 135, 160; family support at, 5; field trips at, 4; fractured talk about family disruptions at, 114–22; frequent stigmatized disruptions at, 113, 114; graduation at, 1, 158–59; individual attention challenges at, 81–83; large amount of paperwork at, 56, 58, 137, 146; mandated forms of engagement at, 135; meals at, 33–35; newsletters of, 56; PALS-

PreK curriculum at, 188n12; personal property restrictions at, 87; physical description of, 3–4; pick-up time informal parent conversations, 56; pretend play about family disruptions at, 115–16; routine disruptions at, 31, 57–58; routines at, 30; safe behaviors reinforced by, 39, 43, 66–67, 70, 95, 143, 146; socio-emotional learning at, 37–38, 143–46; Spanish language at, 64–65, 72, 81, 188n11; sporadic reading at, 42, 48–50, 58; structural racism and, 85; study origins at, 175–76; teacher restrictions for babysitter role, 141; two required outdoor play periods at, 54; unpredictable classroom enrollment, 142, 153–54. *See also* Work Time; *specific activities*
symbolic deprivation, of affluent and white families, 100

teacher aides, 138, 139
teachers: associate, 138–39; of color, racial inclusivity through, 168; intensive motherhood mimicking by, 27; lead, 138–39; multitasking of, 32–36, 84; Nelson and Schutz on, 25; paths into becoming, 138–40; pay challenge for, 140; preschool licensing requirements of, 23; pride in emotional skills improvement, 140; quality rating systems emphasis on, 25–26; segregated preschools unequal work environments for, 153–56; stress of, 137, 149, 150, 154, 155; stress due to paperwork, 154; supervision styles and enrichment, 25; support expectations for white, middle-class children, 85; turnover of, 137, 149–50; work experience impact on children, 155
teachers as key educators, 25–26, 161
teacher-student games, of pretend play, 42–43, 45

teacher-student ratio: at Great Beginnings and Sunshine Head Start, 3; quality rating system impacted by, 25
teaching, at Great Beginnings: beyond socio-emotional learning, 150–53
teaching, at Sunshine Head Start: children viewed as work, 146–49; job stress and turnover, 149–50; socio-emotional learning, 37–38, 143–46
teaching in segregated contexts, 138–43
Thorne, Barrie, 189n8
timer system, for organizing play, 75, 76
toothbrushing: Great Beginnings absence of, 36; Head Start mandatory, 35
toys, 87–109, 190n8
transitional objects, developmental psychologists on, 106–7
transitions: disparities in, 32; Great Beginnings kindergarten, 159–60; lack of instructional time and, 58–59; poverty and deeper time for, 59; segregation and, 32; Sunshine Head Start kindergarten, 157–58
trauma, x; behaviors from, 7, 27, 142, 143–44, 189n12; from racism, 82; routine disruptions and, 31; teaching and, 136–56
turnover: enrollment, 27, 31, 163; teacher, 137, 149–50

universalism, 188n80
universal preschool (UPK), 28, 165, 166

Valentine's Day celebrations, at Great Beginnings, 131–32
Van Ausdale, Debra, 27; on preschool multicultural curricula, 175

War on Poverty, 18; Project Head Start and, 15–16; Shriver as head of, 19–20 white, middle-class children, 79; concerted cultivation and, 24, 62; cultural advantages of, 19; at Great Beginnings, 8, 74; property entitlement orientation, 108; teacher support expectations of, 85

white, middle-class mothers: employment increase in 1970s and 1980s of, 21; nursery school popularity, 13; Progressive Era and, 9

whole-child approach, of Head Start, 35, 48, 114

Women's Union Day Nursery, 10

working motherhood: day nurseries and, 8–9; increase in 1970s and 1980s, 21; Perkins' opposition to, 14; racialization of, 9; Rose on immigration and, 9; during WWII, 14–15

Work Time, at Sunshine Head Start: conflict coaching strategies during, 43–44; gentle touch practice before, 39, 64; Great Beginnings compared to, 58–59

World War II (WWII): child care government support during, 15; working motherhood during, 14–15

ABOUT THE AUTHOR

CASEY STOCKSTILL is Assistant Professor of Sociology at Dartmouth College. She received her PhD in Sociology from the University of Wisconsin–Madison in 2018. Her work has been recognized by the American Sociological Association and has been funded by the National Science Foundation, the Ford Foundation, and the Russell Sage Foundation.

CRITICAL PERSPECTIVES ON YOUTH SERIES

General Editors: Amy L. Best, Lorena Garcia, and Jessica K. Taft

Fast-Food Kids: French Fries, Lunch Lines, and Social Ties
Amy L. Best

White Kids: Growing Up with Privilege in a Racially Divided America
Margaret A. Hagerman

Growing Up Queer: Kids and the Remaking of LGBTQ Identity
Mary Robertson

*The Kids Are in Charge: Activism and Power in Peru's Movement
of Working Children*
Jessica K. Taft

Coming of Age in Iran: Poverty and the Struggle for Dignity
Manata Hashemi

The World Is Our Classroom: Extreme Parenting and the Rise of Worldschooling
Jennie Germann Molz

The Homeschool Choice: Parents and the Privatization of Education
Kate Henley Averett

Growing Up Latinx: Coming of Age in a Time of Contested Citizenship
Jesica Siham Fernández

Unaccompanied: The Plight of Immigrant Youth at the Border
Emily Ruehs-Navarro

The Sociology of Bullying: Power, Status, and Aggression Among Adolescents
Edited by Christopher Donoghue

Gender Replay: On Kids, Schools, and Feminism
Edited by Freeden Blume Oeur and C. J. Pascoe

False Starts: The Segregated Lives of Preschoolers
Casey Stockstill

Milton Keynes UK
Ingram Content Group UK Ltd.
UKHW011950111023
430421UK00004B/33/J